Missional Discipleship After Christendom

Formission
Rowheath Pavilion
Heath Road
Bournville
FORMISSION Birmingham B30 1HH

AFTER CHRISTENDOM *Series*

Series Preface: *After Christendom*

Christendom was an historical era, a geographical region, a political arrangement, a sacral culture, and an ideology. For many centuries Europeans have lived in a society that was nominally Christian. Church and state have been the pillars of a remarkable civilization that can be traced back to the decision of the emperor Constantine I early in the fourth century to replace paganism with Christianity as the imperial religion.

Christendom, a brilliant but brutal culture, flourished in the Middle Ages, fragmented in the Reformation of the sixteenth century, but persisted despite the onslaught of modernity. While exporting its values and practices to other parts of the world, however, it has been slowly declining during the past three centuries. In the twenty-first century Christendom is unravelling.

What will emerge from the demise of Christendom is not yet clear, but we can now describe much of Western culture as "post-Christendom."

> *Post-Christendom is the culture that emerges as the Christian faith loses coherence within a society that has been definitively shaped by the Christian story and as the institutions that have been developed to express Christian convictions decline in influence.*

This definition, proposed and unpacked in *Post-Christendom*, the first book in the After Christendom series, has gained widespread acceptance. *Post-Christendom* investigated the Christendom legacy and raised numerous issues that are explored in the rest of the series. The authors of this series, who write from within the Anabaptist tradition, see the current challenges facing the church not as the loss of a golden age but as opportunities to recover a more biblical and more Christian way of being God's people in God's world.

The series addresses a wide range of issues, including theology, social and political engagement, how we read Scripture, youth work, mission, worship, relationships, and the shape and ethos of the church after Christendom.

These books are not intended to be the last word on the subjects they address, but an invitation to discussion and further exploration. Additional material, including extracts from published books and information about future volumes, can be found at www.anabaptistnetwork.com/AfterChristendom.

Stuart Murray

The series includes the following titles:[1]

Stuart Murray,	*Post-Christendom*
Stuart Murray,	*Church after Christendom*
Jonathan Bartley,	*Faith and Politics after Christendom*
Jo and Nigel Pimlott,	*Youth Work after Christendom*
Alan and Eleanor Kreider,	*Worship and Mission after Christendom*
Lloyd Pietersen,	*Reading the Bible after Christendom*
Andrew Francis,	*Hospitality and Community after Christendom*
Fran Porter,	*Women and Men after Christendom*
Simon Perry,	*Atheism after Christendom*
Brian Haymes and Kyle Gingerich Hiebert,	*God after Christendom?*
Jeremy Thomson,	*Relationships and Emotions after Christendom*
Andrew Hardy and Dan Yarnell,	*Missional Discipleship after Christendom*
John Heathershaw,	*Security after Christendom* (forthcoming)
Joshua T. Searle,	*Theology after Christendom* (forthcoming)
Jeremy Thompson,	*Interpreting the Old Testament after Christendom* (forthcoming)
Lina Toth,	*Singleness and Marriage after Christendom* (forthcoming)

1. The series was published by Paternoster from 2004–15. Consequently, not all titles are currently available from Cascade Books.

Missional Discipleship After Christendom

Andrew Hardy

&

Dan Yarnell

 CASCADE *Books* • Eugene, Oregon

MISSIONAL DISCIPLESHIP AFTER CHRISTENDOM

After Christendom

Cascade Books
An Imprint of Wipf and Stock Publishers
199 W. 8th Ave., Suite 3
Eugene, OR 97401

www.wipfandstock.com

PAPERBACK ISBN: 978-1-5326-1893-2
HARDCOVER ISBN: 978-1-4982-4484-8
EBOOK ISBN: 978-1-4982-4483-1

Cataloguing-in-Publication data:

Names: Hardy, Andrew. | Yarnell, Dan.
Title: Missional discipleship after Christendom / Andrew Hardy and Dan Yarnell.
Description: Eugene, OR: Cascade Books, 2018 | Series: After Christendom |
    Includes bibliographical references and index.
Identifiers: ISBN 978-1-5326-1893-2 (paperback) | ISBN 978-1-4982-4484-8 (hard-
    cover) | ISBN 978-1-4982-4483-1 (ebook)
Subjects: LCSH: Discipling (Christianity) | Spiritual formation | Missions—Theory
    | Christianity—21st century | Missions
Classification: BV4520 H373 2018 (print) | BV4520 (ebook)

Manufactured in the U.S.A.   MARCH 9, 2018

Formission
Rowheath Pavilion
Heath Road
Bournville
FORMISSION Birmingham B30 1HH

We would like to dedicate this book to families, churches and leaders
who intentionally seek to shape those they care for
to become authentic followers of the Lord Jesus.

Contents

Introduction

> Postmodernists' replace . . . eternal truths with a story. But there
> is a profound difference between the two. For the postmodern-
> ists, there are many stories, but no overarching truth by which
> they can be assessed. They are simply stories. The church's af-
> firmation is that the story it tells, embodies, and enacts is the
> true story and that others are to be evaluated by reference to it.[1]

About This Book

Discipleship has always been important to the Christian faith because
of the need to shape the lives of believers to faithfully follow the Lord.
To some extent we may think of it as a formative process that is to be part
of a lifelong journey. We never stop following Christ as he beckons, "Come
follow me and I will make you fishers of men."[2] In this invitation there are
three things that we need to recognize.

First, Christ is always ahead of his people calling them to self-transcend their present horizon of life moving on to what comes next. We are a
people on a journey. We know this world is in need of renewal and complete
transformation. The church during Christendom was to some large extent
caught in a kind of time bubble, that caused the peoples of Western Europe
to largely consider themselves to be cultural Christians by birth but not

---

1. Newbigin, *Proper Confidence*.
2. Matt 4:18.

necessarily by conversion. Another issue was that people were converted but that is where it stopped, they were not as such challenged to develop and grow as disciples. For example, they may have claimed that they had said the sinner's prayer, but that is as far as their spiritual development seemed to go.

Christendom was by no means perfect, and warring Western Christian nations did not transform their politics, leaders, and people by the religion of Christendom. Christ beckoned from ahead and Western Christendom came to a cataclysmic end. Yet let us be circumspect here, Christ beckoned from ahead because Christendom was not the answer to the world's problems. Only Christ can bring the reign of God to full and final realization. Post-Christendom society unconsciously waits on the verge of what Christ is bringing into being next. We believe it requires the church to disciple a new generation who can participate with the Spirit of Christ in establishing his kingdom reign.

Second, it is Christ who "makes" each believer become all that they need to be, in order to live in an ongoing trust-based relationship with God. Discipleship has always been based on a divine deposit promised in the new covenant heart.[3] It is the real presence of Christ in each believer's innermost being who provides the energy, guidance and motivation that causes them to effectively follow him. It is also important for faith communities to provide an environment that stimulates the spiritual growth of each believer. In this case there is a need for Christian communities that hold people positively accountable for their Christian journey.

Third, Christ equips his followers to participate alongside his Spirit to make disciples of others. In Matthew 28:20 Christ promised to be spiritually present with his disciples. It is Christ who guides us to take part in the *missio Dei* to bring all who will to respond to the invitation to follow Jesus. Christ is present by his Spirit at work in the world today. There is a special charism for disciples that can be experienced by everyone of faith. It entails learning how to hear Christ's voice, so that we may discern all that he wants us to do in participation with him in his ongoing mission to reconcile the whole world to God. The *missio Dei* is also holistic in nature.[4] It does not just include preaching the gospel and personal salvation, it includes a whole range of involvement in society and ecological creation care in its scope. It also classically includes seeking for justice in a world full of injustice. In other words, it has a theology of liberation connected with it, because the

3. Ezek 36:26–27.

4. Holistic Mission Occasional Paper no. 33, produced by the Issue Group on this topic at the 2004 Forum for World Evangelization, hosted by the Lausanne Committee for World Evangelization in Pattaya, Thailand, September 29 to October 5, 2004.

in-breaking reign of God includes the restoration of unjust structures and systems in a fallen world, as well as the better care for creation.

During Christendom, mission was essentially the "West to the rest." It was not focused on the West. The Edinburgh World Mission Conference of 1910 was positive that most of its work of mission was accomplished among Western nations.[5] Radical decline in church attendance and loss of the influence of Christianity on public consciousness proved the opposite to the evaluation of the delegates at this conference. By the time of the 2010 Edinburgh World Mission Conference, the situation had reversed, with the rest coming to engage in mission in the West.[6] After Christendom,[7] Christianity is on the margins of society, no longer having a privileged place at the center of Western consciousness.

The world is on our doorsteps in the West today. The mission field is here. We live in a multicultural, pluralistic society. It is our claim that Christ calls all of his people to seek to bring the good news of the in-breaking reign of God to all of these peoples, as well as to reclaim secular society to come under the influence of the reign of God. In our view a new Christendom is not the answer to the needs of late modern people.

During Christendom, most believers did not consider in general that it was their role to disciple Westerners. It was assumed that everyone was at least theoretically and culturally a Christian. Having said this, the Wesley's preached the gospel of personal salvation. Their societies and schools shaped lay preachers and sought to equip lay members to take on roles of service and ministry and lifelong development. However, there was generally not an assumed need for ordinary lay believers to be disciple-makers in their own right. In our view, most believers today do not view themselves to be disciple-makers. Our use of the term "missional discipleship"[8] is deliberate. First of all, we use the word "missional"[9] to distinguish mission in the West from mission overseas, which has commonly been associated in popular imagination as the work of a specially called missionary caste.

Second, we use it to define every ordinary Christian to be a disciple-maker, suited to their gifts. We believe this is the call of Christ on every believer, to participate in God's mission, including the intentional discipling of others. It is not just disciple-making that is needed but it includes it. The gospel includes a social dimension to community work, as much as

5. Robinson, *Winning Hearts, Changing Minds.*

6. Kerr and Ross, *Edinburgh 2010.*

7. Murray, *Church After Christendom.*

8. Maddix and Akkerman, *Missional Discipleship.*

9. Van Gelder, *Missional Church in Context.*

communicating the gospel message. The Protestant ideology of the priesthood of all believers would seem to naturally imply the broader challenge of every follower becoming a kind of minister for Christ, sent to their neighborhoods and work places to make new disciples.

We argue that much more is needed than simple one-off training courses to develop disciples. Every believer is called to be a missional disciple in their everyday context, not as a duty, but simply because if they have a relationship with the Spirit of Christ, then their passions, beliefs, values and convictions will take on the fundamental motivation to bring others into a reconciled relationship with God.

Third, we suggest missional discipleship is Trinitarian, as God is a relational being in the person of the Godhead, and Christ continues that relationship with God's people through the Spirit. God, in his very nature, has always had humans in view as his creatures made to reflect his Triune image, who have been called to eternally participate in fellowship with God's self. In the God-man (Christ) all peoples are called to participate in God's eternal family, including his mission to reconcile them to become part of the family of God. In his very nature, God will never cease to be a Triune being of interrelationship with his people. Mission is an expression of this fundamental nature of the Trinity, therefore missional discipleship is intrinsic to God's plan to reconcile all things through Christ to become part of a family who follow a Triune God.

Section 1

Backgrounds to Discipleship

The After Christendom series has focused on what is coming next after a former Christendom period. Indeed, the series has also recognized that more than one version of Christendom may be said to have existed. The first version was that which was birthed in the time of Emperor Constantine, with the official acceptance of Christianity as the new religious faith of the empire. The second came in Europe among the tribes that followed the fall of the empire in the West. This section will focus on developments during Christendom which have been important precursors that will help to frame and inform discussion of discipleship after Christendom.

"Come, follow me"
—JESUS

"When Christ calls a man, he bids him come and die"
—DIETRICH BONHOEFFER

Chapter 1

Exploring Discipleship During Christendom

By Dan Yarnell

> I think it is fair to say that in the Western church, we have by
> and large lost the art of disciple making. We have done so partly
> because we have reduced it to the intellectual assimilation of
> ideas, partly because of the abiding impact of cultural Christi-
> anity embedded in the Christendom understanding of church,
> and partly because the phenomenon of consumerism in our
> own day pushes against a true following of Jesus.[1]

Discipleship has always demanded an informed response to the story
and experience of Jesus as an outworked expression within its various contexts and cultures over the centuries. As we begin to consider the
importance of missional discipleship, it is worth noting that discipleship
is not a new contemporary concern or issue. Each generation and expression of the faith has had to consider what it means to become a follower
of Jesus. At its best this has involved a strong consideration of the local
context where becoming and being a disciple finds authentic expression.
According to the author of Luke-Acts, this state of affairs was first encountered by the earliest Christians, as they had to prayerfully and intelligently consider what it meant for a Gentile to become a Christian. The
first church council in Jerusalem (Acts 15) therefore became a model of

---

1. Hirsch, *Forgotten Ways*, 104.

action-reflection approaches[2] that have been at the heart of missionary involvement across the centuries.

The advent of postmodernity, and thereby post-Christendom, has provided a new context for us to consider what and how discipleship can be expressed.

This challenge is especially so within the Western context, and hence the importance of this book. The strong Christian memory that once dominated the worldview of Western Europe enabled and perhaps encouraged a kind of subtle complacency, which meant that the Christian narrative was assumed to be the same as the cultural heritage of all Europeans, often being confused as one and the same. This inevitably meant a lack of consideration of what was authentic discipleship within a largely Christendom context of faith.[3] It would be this Western European version of the Christian narrative and its implications of discipleship that would be exported to other nations during the great missionary movements of the nineteenth and twentieth centuries.

An important way of engaging in this current challenge is to reflect on how followers of Jesus in different times of history and movements have sought to actively participate in the new life of the kingdom. The late missiologist David Bosch, following Hans Küng, identified six main Christian paradigms for an understanding of mission. Each of these paradigm shifts forced the Christian community to rethink and reengage itself in the *missio Dei*. Bosch's six paradigms are:

- The apocalyptic paradigm of primitive Christianity;
- The Hellenistic paradigm of the patristic period;
- The medieval Roman Catholic paradigm;
- The Reformation paradigm;
- The modern Enlightenment paradigm;
- The emerging ecumenical paradigm.

Bosch's contribution enables us to see this development and the affects and effects each of these paradigm shifts caused in the worldwide Christian community, which in each phase caused it to rethink and therefore

2. The model of action-reflection learning is often used in contemporary theological education and contemporary pastoral work, often making use of the pastoral cycle as an analytical tool. It tends to follow the experience-exploration-reflection-action approach to contextual ministry. See further Ballard and Pritchard, *Practical Theology*, 81–95.

3. Jenkins (2011), reminds us that for much of the formation of Christianity it was in fact the Asian experiences that both numerically formed and informed the development of the faith, rather than the Western European narrative and history. Unfortunately, this goes beyond the scope of this present work.

repurpose itself for its mission. The church in each shift could not remain as it was and have a future. Neither can we. Discipleship must be reexamined and lived as a significant testimony to the transformative power of the Jesus we love and serve.

Snapshots of Discipleship Practices

Bosch's framework is a seminal contribution in considering the church's adaptive engagement in mission. While recognizing and valuing the importance this framework has played in subsequent writings on mission and history, I am going to suggest my own modified version of these paradigm shifts which seem to make better sense of the way the church refocused itself as a discipling movement which I will be discussing in this chapter. They are:

- Early Eastern Church;
- Medieval Roman Catholic;
- Protestant Missionary;
- Enlightenment;
- Postmodern;
- Ecumenical.

My reasons for suggesting this adapted version of the six paradigm shifts relates to how I understand the relationship of the approaches to discipleship that seemed to be true of the epochs of history I suggest. Hence my revised suggestions to the nomenclature of these possible paradigm shifts better represents, in my view, the focus of discipleship in each age.

Earliest Christianity

The first Christian engagement of discipleship may seem to be a bit of a challenge due to the rapid changes that these earlier followers faced. We have brief summaries in the book of Acts to some of the potential ways in which the church grew and developed its approaches, but there are very limited details. We may reasonably assume that the earliest believers, who were primarily Jewish converts, continued to follow a pattern of community formation based on the learned practices of the synagogue,[4] the main

4. See the helpful description of Jewish influences on Christian worship and development in Beckwith, *Jewish Background to Christian Worship*, 39–51.

difference being the development of the centrality and worship of Jesus, and in light of this, the celebration of communion with its theological, spiritual, communal, and psychological significance.[5]

It is also likely that these first Christians understood discipleship more succinctly, since many rabbis had their own disciples who attached themselves to these teachers and in their shared life journey would literally follow them, learning by example, by innuendo, in formal and informal ways.[6]

Hengel makes some important observations about the leadership and disciple-making practices of Jesus.[7] First, Jesus was not in effect a rabbi, as he did not follow any school of learning, thereby standing outside the traditions of Judaism. He further notes that unlike other disciples who followed after their masters by learning their particular view of Torah over many years, this was not what it meant for Jesus' disciples, whose "following after" implied a commitment to the kingdom and not just the teaching.[8] He finally notes that the calling by Jesus to follow him was a unique practice, as there are no rabbinic examples, which were normally of the student inquiring to follow after the rabbi.

The ongoing formation and agreement of the New Testament documents also played a part during this dynamic period. It is likely that as some of the letters and gospels were agreed, these became tools to influence and shape these disparate communities in providing some guidance into how to conduct themselves as new disciples. This is especially so in the formation of the early Christian communities, as many of these documents are written to churches rather than individuals.

It was not long before this all became more focused and therefore formalized into a form of catechistic teaching, ultimately leading to the setting up of schools[9] and formal practices often associated with baptismal rights.[10] Sittser provides this helpful indicator of its importance to the emerging Christian movement:

---

5. See the important contribution by Dunn, *Parting of the Ways*.

6. Marriner, *Following the Lamb*. See esp. ch. 2, "Discipleship in the Ancient World," for some key reflections on how this relates to the context of discipleship in the first century.

7. Hengel, *Charismatic Leader*, 42–57.

8. Ibid., 54. Hengel notes "following after" has primarily the concrete sense of following him *in his wanderings and sharing with him his uncertain and indeed perilous destiny.*

9. Frend, *Early Church*, 82, indicates that in 180 CE, Pantaeus set up such a school in Alexandria, which was later headed up by Clement who significantly developed it.

10. One of the earlier studies on the importance of the catechumenate is Folkemer, "Study of the Catechumenate," 286–307.

The church, facing problems and challenges as it spread through the Roman Empire, developed a rigorous training program, known as the catechumenate, to form people in the faith and to prepare them for baptism. This training program communicated very clearly that conversion implies a commitment to discipleship and that discipleship is not for the few but for the many, not an option but an expectation, not an addition to conversion but an essential feature of conversion.[11]

Ferguson equally suggests that catechesis was indeed central to the initiation of new Christians in these early centuries. Beginning with the Didache and especially the apologies of Justin Martyr, he seeks to demonstrate that this was more than just proper core teaching, but contained a strong emphasis on the value of communal lifestyle.[12] Kreider similarly notes the communal process, reminding us that this experience created a sense of displacement as the convert began the long journey to transformation:

Once they had become catechumens, they had become "liminal persons," persons "on a journey from the centre of the city, so to speak, to its fringes." And this process could last years. Even if the three year requirement is a (late third century?) emendation to the Apostolic Tradition, it is clear that catechetical process would take a long time . . . the vital thing was transformation: as the Apostolic Tradition puts it, "if a man is keen, and perseveres well in the matter, the time shall not be judged, but only his conduct."[13]

In the writings of the *Apostolic Tradition*, we find indication of the kind of processes that may have taken place with those seeking to become new followers of Jesus.[14] In sections 15–18, Hippolytus outlines a process of the journey for the new catechumens. After being brought before the teachers, their lives, conduct, and work experience are examined, all around issues of character and a willingness to desist in certain occupations or experiences. Then they were invited to hear the word, followed by a three-year period of instruction, then followed once again by a time of hearing the gospel. After this, they were then prepared for baptism and entry into the church.[15]

---

11. Sittser, *Catechumenate*, 181. He helpfully notes the growing body of scholarly literature in exploring the place and importance of the catechumenate and its effect on the discipleship of these early believers.

12. Ferguson, *Early Church at Work and Witness*, 18–51.

13. Kreider, "Baptism, Catechism," 321.

14. Hippolytus, *Apostolic Tradition*, 41–43.

15. Kreider, *Worship and Evangelism*, 18–19.

It therefore seems likely that the intentional process of formation, through the means of the catechumenate, developed as well as enculturated these early Christians into the kind of radical followers found in a community where risk, adventure, generosity, and mission[16] were normal expressions.[17]

Rise of Monasticism

A further kind of development also took place in spiritual formation with the rise of the monastic expressions of faith. As Christianity experienced rapid growth amid the various obstacles of persecutions, theological debates, and growing heresies, concern began to be felt that compromise was causing the faith to become too closely identified with the empire.

In response to this, some believers sought to physically remove themselves by going to solitary places, thereby adopting an ascetic and individual approach to living the Christian life (*eremitic*). By the second century, Syrian believers became hermits, living in isolation, and were entirely celibate in their commitment to following Jesus.[18] Perhaps the best example is the third-century ascetic Antony (d. 356 CE). In Athanasius's book about his life, he tells the story of his withdrawal into the desert, his struggles with temptations, then becoming a hermit at age thirty-five, and for the next twenty years his asceticism shaped him into someone who could live in total solitude.[19] Antony thereby became a model of the disciplined life, eventually overcoming his inner demons and finding peace. He became one of the most well known of the desert fathers.

This quiet, individualistic approach was only one such method of discipleship. The other, which eventually became the predominant expression that developed, was intentionally communal in nature (*cenobitic*). While at first it was men who engaged in this practice, known as monks (*monochos*), later developments included women. This expression would ultimately lead to the development of various expressions of monasteries that span the Western world.[20]

16. Kreider notes that the effect on the catechumens was transformed lives. This had a significant missional impact as it developed alternative habits and distinctive reflexes. Kreider, "*Ressourcement* and Mission," 248.

17. Stark raises some intriguing sociological insights into the rapid growth of this emerging Christian movement in his *Rise of Christianity*.

18. Chadwick, *Church in Ancient Society*, 398.

19. Dunn, *Emergence of Monasticism*, 1–7.

20. McGrath, *Christian History*, 33.

> Anthony founded Christian monachism in the opening decade
> of the fourth century. He stressed the semi-eremitical life. The
> cenobitic community was launched into the Church by Pacho-
> mius (c. 315), who also made southern Egypt the centre of his
> work.[21]

Dunn notes the vital importance of asceticism as an expression of discipleship:

> Asceticism is usually defined in negative terms—often as a re-
> jection of sex, or food or both but might more productively be
> seen also as a discipline or collectivity of disciplines which aim
> at the transformation of the self and the construction of a new
> one. Framed in opposition to the dominant society around it,
> asceticism is not to be understood merely as a process of rejec-
> tion but also as one involving not only the construction of a self
> but also of a new set of social relations or understanding.[22]

These individual and communal expressions were a clear means of separation in order to enable these followers of Jesus to remain focused, dedicated and pure in their devotion to the growing Christian faith.

Urban to Rural and the Mission of the Celts[23]

Even though Britain was part of the Roman conquest, and thereby an out-post of the empire, with the eventual collapse of the Roman Empire, the Christians now faced a new challenge. Prior to this, Christianity in its devel-opment had been predominantly an urban movement. The pagan[24] invad-ers from Gaul eventually deconstructed this by bringing their own rural contextual framing. While facing persecution was nothing new for the early Christians, the loss of influence, property, homes, and therefore identities created a sort of vacuum.

The Celtic mission, spearheaded by Patrick in Ireland, was to become the next incarnation of missional development.[25] Numerous and nameless missionaries were sent out to share faith, build community, and disciple

---

21. Hardinge, *Celtic Church in Britain*, 153. See also the discussion in MacCulloch, *History of Christianity*, 200–210.

22. Dunn, *Emergence of Monasticism*, 6.

23. A good, clear introduction can be found in Bradley, *Celtic Way*.

24. Pagani—a term used to describe the rural peoples.

25. McGrath, *Christian History*, 75–76.

these new believers.[26] Central to this, for our purposes, is the consideration of their approach to discipleship within this new missionary context.

The Celts, like the Assyrian churches, drew heavily on the desert fathers for much of their theology and spiritual formation.[27] The combination of asceticism as well as traveling for preaching and healing, encouraged these monks to risk the uncertainty of the journey. This was coupled with a strong contextual expression that was consistent with Celtic life and practice. As Bradley notes,

> Celtic Christianity spread so rapidly through the British Isles partly because its evangelists tailored it so well to the norms and needs of a rural and tribal society. In the rather inelegant jargon favoured by academics it was a particularly good example of religious inculturation with the church adapting itself to the culture in which its was operating.[28]

This enabled the Celtic church to flourish, as it was able to adapt to its surroundings, which made the Christian story both appealing and easily recognizable. He further notes that this was not too difficult for them, as they were from the same background and culture as those they were seeking to bring to faith.[29]

The catechumenate continued to be central to their discipleship. Preparations for baptism were not inconsistent to the expressions found within the Roman rites. In addition, the importance of nature, of the arts, and a deep sense of prayer and spiritual warfare deepened the life of the believers. Pilgrimage, or *peregrinatio*, reflected the inner journey of discipleship by being expressed outwardly in an emerging participatory sending out practice, often by traveling in their small coracle boats and allowing the winds of the Spirit to take them wherever they may go.

Perhaps the best known example of the Celtic saints, Columbanus (543–615 CE), was a living example of one who embraced all of these values. Traveling across mainland Europe, he and his fellow traveling monks established new monasteries in France, Switzerland, and Italy. His many sermons reflected his meditation on Christian *wanderlust* and pilgrimage which typified the spirit of discipleship within the Celtic age.

---

26. Robinson, *Rediscovering the Celts*, 32–33.

27. Bosch, *Transforming Mission*, 231–33. See also MacGinty, *Influence of the Desert Fathers*, 85–91.

28. Bradley, *Celtic Way*, 20.

29. Ibid.

Further Medieval Developments

The framing of learning that had been brought about in previous generations, primarily through the schools and catechumenate, gave way to a more divisive setting, which began to develop. The true disciples were now those who could commit to the various orders whereby they could devote themselves wholeheartedly to the Christian enterprise.[30]

A wide variety of intentional communities, and their rules and values, began to emerge. They were in fact a community of monks and nuns committed to isolation and solitude. It is remarkable that even children as young as six for nuns or ten for monks could be oblated (*oblatus*), or gifted to the monastery.[31]

Within this context, there was a clear need for guidelines or rules of life to provide healthy boundaries in spiritual formation. One significant example is the rule of St. Benedict.[32] This framing of life according to rules of Christian conduct and lifestyle was at its heart a school for those beginning the Christian life.[33] This kind of discipling created very clear outcomes with almost military precision.

The importance of these communities was not purely about the maintaining of the faith tradition, but was equally valuable in the formation of the wider society. Eventually they would become great places of learning as well as fostering culture and civilization. In Britain in particular they were often gifted land by landowners to aid in their provision of spiritual leadership and of conversion of the populace.

While life in the monastery provided a strong learning context, with great focus on scholarship, the wider engagement of uneducated laymen also needed a framework for discipleship. They had not been called into the life of the monk or nun, so their own discipleship was crucial. It is here perhaps that the form of church architecture and the use of stained glass windows were important didactic tools for discipleship.[34] In addition, the

30. Dyas, *Pilgrims Were They All?*, 43, notes, "The monastic life, whether solitary or coenobitic, soon came to be seen as the highest calling for a Christian, a status it would continue to enjoy for the next millennium."

31. Brown, *Rise of Western Christendom*, 223.

32. Various online language translations of the rule can be found at http://www. osb.org/rb.

33. Ibid., 225.

34. Horman, *Art of the Sublime*, 66–68. He notes, "In the medieval period the intention was to convey a sense of correct belief and an intimate knowledge of the mythology on which it was founded" (66).

medieval development of the English mystery plays were greatly influential in their extensive cyclical usage.[35]

As the church became more powerful and thereby more central to life, churches gave way to Gothic cathedrals. These incredible edifices proclaimed a sense of heaven on earth, with their use of light, size and decorative arts. As Janzen notes,

> Not only did the art and architecture of the Middle Ages reflect a theology of the nature of God, they were also used more didactically to instruct the populace in the stories and doctrines of the faith.[36]

These impressive buildings provided a sense of grandeur thereby reinforcing the greatness of God. But the Christian texts were still inaccessible, as they were mostly in Latin, the language of scholarship. As previously noted, it was the use of the buildings and their art, in particular the stained glass windows, which were the didactic tools to tell and retell the biblical and gospel stories.[37]

Noteworthy as a form on enculturation for discipleship, the English medieval mystery plays were a form of annual cultural entertainment as well as a tool of basic discipleship. The four cycles (York with 48 plays, Chester with 24, Wakefield/Towneley with 32, and Coventry / East Midlands with 42) became a main part of community life, by both informing/teaching the biblical stories and forming and reinforcing within the community the Christian narrative as the British and European story.[38] As Happé notes,

> The plays were written as part of a theological message, and were intended, no doubt, to be an act of teaching and worship combined. Such were the vigour with which they were executed, and the popularity which accrued to them that many other minor objectives grew up: but essentially the plays were meant to celebrate the Christian story from the Creation to Doomsday, with two central peaks in the Nativity and the Passion of Christ.[39]

With the advent of the Reformation throughout Europe, these plays were initially adapted, and then quickly fell out of favor.

---

35. One of the best collections is Happé, *English Mystery Plays.*

36. Janzen, "Art and Architecture, Instructional Use of," in Kurian and Lamport, *Encyclopedia of Christian Education,* 72.

37. Ibid., 72–73.

38. Happé, *English Mystery Plays.*

39. Ibid., 10–11.

Reforming and Radical

The Reformation is usually seen as the watershed moment for the development of Protestant Christianity.[40] Martin Luther is widely noted as the key figurehead in spearheading this transformation, with his engagement of reform from reading and translating Romans and advocating the Protestant cry of "justification by faith." Zwingli, Calvin, and other lesser-known leaders also significantly added to the fervor that enabled change to occur.

Nothing, however, helped to foster the emergence of the Reformation experience more than being able to have the Bible in one's own language. With the advent of Gutenberg's printing press, this new technology enabled Bibles to be produced and distributed quickly. The slow and demanding writing out of the text had given way to the mass production of the Scriptures quickly and efficiently. The often illegal practice of smuggling these handwritten portions of biblical text in the vernacular of the people into one's country would begin to come to an end.

Even though access to the newly translated Bible became an essential part of Reformation discipleship, it was not only this desire for the Bible that was needed. The growing middle classes were often more educated than some of their clergy, and their thirst for knowledge and spiritual reading was growing. Commentaries and other key spiritual texts were soon made available. This included the highly influential work of John Calvin. His *Institutes of the Christian Religion* provided a kind of a systematic theological framework that would help Bible readers to deeply engage with the newly produced Scriptures.

Availability of the Bible was not only a catalyst for a spiritual revolution, but equally began to deconstruct and create new narratives for the nation-states of Europe. Authority soon began to shift from the lone voice of the papacy and the king to *sola scriptura*, the Bible as the sole authority, and to a lesser extent, the Bible reader and scholar as the interpreter of the text, thereby deconstructing the old order and creating a new authority. This then paved the way for even greater cultural change. As McGrath notes,

> In part, the radical developments of the sixteenth century are to
> be explained on account of the changing social context of western Europe, which was creating new pressures and possibilities
> for cultural and religious change.[41]

Hill takes this even further when he says,

---

40. See McGrath, *Christian History*, 159–70, for a good summary of the key issues.
41. Ibid., 154.

> The availability of the Bible in English was a great stimulus to learning to read; and this in its turn assisted the development of cheap printing and the distribution of books. It was a cultural revolution of unprecedented proportions, whose consequences are difficult to over-estimate.[42]

While the Reformation brought about revolution to matters of faith, church architecture was equally transformed. Henry VIII's dissolution movement removed and destroyed many works of art and artifacts. Simplicity rather than opulence became the order of the day. In particular, the place of the Bible as over against the Eucharist or Mass became a central focus not only in the architecture of the church building, with the pulpit often replacing the altar, but also in the development of spirituality, particularly in many of the subsequent nonconformist churches. This engagement with the Bible and being able to read and understand, or even listen and understand, was part of a growing development in discipleship.

Of especially noteworthy importance are the radical reformers. Theirs was an intentional focus on the importance and simplicity of following the teachings of the Bible. This kind of active engagement ultimately brought them into continual disrepute. At the heart of their discipleship was a radical commitment that included the cost of one's life.

> "None can truly know Christ unless one follow him with one's life" wrote Hans Denck in 1526, a year after his excommunication and banishment from the Lutheran city of Nuremberg on charges of heresy.[43]

A key catalyst was the issue of baptism, and especially the strong conviction that infant baptism was heretical. Estep notes that for the Anabaptist, *sola scriptura* led to the logical implication that baptism, being central to discipleship, was for adult believers alone. Many of the earliest writings of these pioneer leaders centered on this issue[44] which became blue touch paper to the wider Christian community, leading to regular and systematic condemnation and abuse.

Their discipleship was not only reflected in their shared life, baptismal practices, and teachings, but also in the simplicity of their church architecture. That being said, unlike many other emerging Protestant expressions, these marginalized Anabaptists did not, in the end, discount or destroy art, seeing it as a form of idolatry, but continued to engage in its practice,

42. Hill, *English Bible*, 12.
43. Biesecker-Mast, "Spiritual Knowledge," 201.
44. Estep, *Anabaptist Story*, 201–36.

thereby continuing to tell the gospel story, as well as their own, within a visual context.[45]

Of strategic importance for them was a serious engagement with the teachings of Jesus, in particular the Sermon on the Mount (Matt 5–8). They intentionally sought to live their communal life by these teachings, developing some of their core practices, including Jesus as the model of living, not swearing oaths, and pacifism (loving your enemy).[46]

Protestant Revivalism and John Wesley

John Wesley, a devout Anglican, sought to know God by engaging in a variety of spiritual practices, including regular spiritual reading and weekly communion, along with his strong desire for inner holiness. His commitment to the Holy Club while at Oxford was an intentional shaping experience, almost a kind of peer mentoring with his other young colleagues, including his brother, Charles, and George Whitefield, the great evangelist who was a key leader in the North American Great Awakening. These experiences may have been the seeds of his strategy for later discipleship through the class meetings that he would develop.

His apparent failure as a missionary to the Native American Indians in Georgia made him ask hard questions of himself and his calling. That, coupled with his fear of travel by sea, meant that he was seemingly more attentive to the presence of the Moravian believers on board the returning ship. This inevitably made him more receptive upon receiving an invitation to their meeting at St. Algate's Street. It was at this meeting that he received his personal experience of his heart being strangely warmed.[47] This experience was crucial to Wesley's enduring theology and subsequent discipleship, to help keep believers in faith through practice and experience.

In terms of discipleship, the genius of Wesley was not primarily in his prolific preaching, writing, and travels, which even today are an outstanding achievement, but in his understanding of the need to help provide a clearly organized discipling process for the thousands of new believers who would eventually form into the Methodist denomination.[48] To do this, he focused

45. Janzen, "Art and Architecture, Instructional Use of," in Kurian and Lamport, *Encyclopedia of Christian Education*, 73.

46. A good overview of Anabaptist beliefs and contemporary engagement can be found in Murray, *Naked Anabaptist*.

47. This brief description is summarized from his own journal, which can be found at http://www.ccel.org/ccel/wesley/journal.html. See also Snyder, *Radical Wesley*.

48. Snyder, *Radical Wesley*, 34–36.

on two things. First, he focused his attention on discerning and developing key leaders who could offer leadership, especially from among the laity, who were then released to preach and lead. This was quite a prophetic stance, as it was based on the rediscovery of the Protestant doctrine of the priesthood of all believers in terms of it becoming a concrete expression. His second important contribution was his infrastructural model of intentional discipleship, the class meeting.

Werner notes the vital importance of this kind of accountability for these early believers:

> It was the small group setting termed by Wesley as the "class meeting" (or "meeting in class") that provided the primary context for the Methodists to grow in their inward and outward holiness. The class meeting, by Wesley's design, was the main unit of Methodism. . . . Class meetings did this by providing accountability: accountability to Wesley, to each other, and to Wesley's standard of both works of piety and works of mercy. Thus the class meeting became Wesley's method for behavioral change.[49]

Clearly this kind of small group accountability became a powerful tool to form these newly awakened believers into disciples. This was much more than merely a way of engendering piety. At initiation, there was a three-month probationary period before one actually became a member of a class. At each weekly meeting, there were serious personal questions that needed to be addressed. Those who did not continue to engage well were summarily removed. Discipleship in this context focused on core spiritual disciplines to grow and sustain faith.

Wesley published *The General Rules* on May 1, 1743, which governed each meeting. It was incumbent on the leader of each class meeting to know the members of their class well, and to have the courage and discipline needed to ask very specific and direct questions. Some of the questions sought to inquire and comment on the observable behaviors of each person in light of how this was connected to the inner life that was developing. Other questions included exploring personal trials within the life of each member and their success or failure in facing them, as well as further instruction or reinforcement of the public preaching.[50]

Sustainable discipleship is a crucial outcome from the Wesleyan approach. The radical insights of finding ways of forming healthy communities, as well as focused and determined accountability structures, enabled

---

49. Werner, *John Wesley's Question*, 69.

50. Ibid., 73–74.

this movement to provide a new foundation of Christian engagement throughout the ensuing decade.

Enlightenment Discipleship

With the advent of the telescope and microscope, new vistas into understanding the world and our place in it began to emerge. With these new tools, fifteenth- and sixteenth-century thinkers such as Copernicus, Bacon, and Descartes began to deeply explore and thereby reimagine the world. By the following century, the thinking of Locke, Spinoza, Leibnitz, and Newton had found an acceptable place within the newly established worldview of the Enlightenment.[51] These voices and their influences enabled the progressive advancement of modernity, particularly through the scientific lens. Immanuel Kant (1724–1804) epitomizes this age of reason in his oft-quoted statement:

> Enlightenment is man's leaving his self-caused immaturity. Immaturity is the incapacity to use one's intelligence without the guidance of another. Such immaturity is self-caused if it is not caused by lack of intelligence, but by lack of determination and courage to use one's intelligence without being guided by another. "Sapere Aude! Have the courage to use your own intelligence!" is therefore the motto of the enlightenment.

This secularizing of culture ultimately led to a focus on that which was objective and measurable as being ultimately real, thereby human reason and the empirical method became the modus operandi. This was not, as in previous centuries, the product of special revelation, but was found within the natural order, and thereby was the inheritance of everyone. This shift in worldview moved the focus much more to the enlightened individual and, therefore, the beginning of modern secular culture into greater focus in the public sphere. Reason increasingly replaced revelation, thereby separating values and beliefs into a more subjective element.[52]

The end result of this process was how Christian communities would engage within this new paradigm, now that their power and centrality had been effectively removed. Three broad approaches can be suggested. For some Evangelical believers, an extreme response was to ignore and/or withdraw, thereby seeking to sustain the previous paradigm. Revelation and biblical inspiration were the only things that mattered, so human reason

51. Bosch, *Transforming Mission*, 262–74, provides a clear and succinct summary.

52. Hollinghurst, *Mission-Shaped Evangelism*, 158–64.

was rejected as authoritative, in a type of reductionism.[53] This led to what is termed fideism. Fideists reject human reason and rely on the Word of God as the only authentic source of revelation and authority. Discipleship continued to focus primarily on personal piety and a devotional engagement with Scripture.

At the opposite end of the spectrum, Protestant Liberal theology began to emerge in the early nineteenth century, embracing reason as the primary source of authority. Higher biblical criticism encouraged the use of critical tools to explore the Bible, raising questions about the historicity and miracles and the relevance of the supernatural. This ultimately reformed faith and belief for the modern person, producing a kind of synthesis. In this context, discipleship took a more cultural approach,[54] so that faith was both reasonable and palatable for modern men and women.

The final response we might call negotiation. Revelation and reason were drawn together in a kind of creative tension. Scholarship and faith were not exclusive, but were focusing on different things. While not developing until the early twentieth century, Evangelicals, Catholics, and eventually Pentecostals began to make greater use of reason and critical tools while seeking to maintain a strong and passionate faith.[55] One of the dangers for discipleship was a growing professionalization of leadership and learning, so that the primary experience for many in their discipleship experience was the weekly sermon at church, whereby the trained and learned leader would bring this learning to the congregation.

The cultural watershed of the 1960s saw an increasing secularization where faith was marginalized and reduced to being mainly private and subjective, having little place in the modern world.[56] During this time, the sociologist Peter Berger wrote of the impact of modernity as the removal of the sacred canopy in Western culture. While this may be generally true of modernity, where God is no longer essential or necessary to nation-states

---

53. This seems to be the case for extreme Anabaptist groups such as the Hutterites and Amish, as well as other more fundamentalist forms of Christianity. For them the Bible was infallible and held all authority. It could equally be argued that this became the case for forms of Catholicism, whereby the pope was infallible and authority was held within the church. It is important to note that modern scholarship began to be embraced within Catholicism after Vatican II.

54. One recalls Schleiermacher's recasting of the gospel in his work, Schleiermacher, *On Religion: Speeches to Its Cultural Despisers.*

55. Hunter, "What Is Modernity?"

56. Robinson, *Honest to God,* and *Now That I Can't Believe,* became highly popular works which demonstrated how faith could be expressed within the modern world. Miracles, revelation, and faith are all reexpressed through the lens of modernity for the generation of the 1960s.

and individual modern life, the rediscovered earlier writings of Bonhoeffer, as a prophetic voice, brought challenge to this kind of thinking.

Bonhoeffer began to express his defiant expression of faith against the growing narratives of the emerging Nazi regime, itself a form of secularism. For him, faith was essential in challenging the acquiescence of the German national church to Hitler's growing, evasive power, as well as taking a positive, nonviolent approach by taking action to help the marginalized Jews.

For Bonhoeffer, two formative practices of discipleship within modernity stand out. The first was a rediscovery of Christian community. His own experience as the leader of the Finkelwalde seminary of the confessing church provided a context for his own living together with a group of training ministers. Much of his reflection is contained in his short work *Life Together*. Within the cultural milieu of the enlightened individual, Bonhoeffer brings a radical rediscovery of the significance of sharing life together, including regular expressions of developing faith.

The second insight was a radical reengagement with the life and teaching of Jesus. Bonhoeffer's now classic and seminal work, *The Cost of Discipleship*,[57] challenges the kind of personal and private piety that has emerged within the culture of modernity.

He brings both of these elements together when he states,

> The renewal of the church will come from a new type of monasticism which only has in common with the old an uncompromising allegiance to the Sermon on the Mount. It is high time men and women banded together to do this.[58]

It is apparent that these expressions can equally be found within the Celtic, Monastic, and Anabaptist traditions. The radical revisionist experience that Bonhoeffer brings comes from the intentional focus on the life and teaching of Jesus, and in particular the sermon on the mount as a sort of handbook for discipleship.[59]

Postmodern Voices[60]

During the 1980s the advent of the personal computer and the internet has brought another significant technological and cultural shift to the challenge

---

57. *Cost of Discipleship (Nachfolge)*. This is effectively what this book is about.

58. From a letter to his brother Karl-Friedrich, January 14, 1935.

59. Bonhoeffer, before his execution, handed his well-worn copy of Thomas à Kempis's *Imitation of Christ* to his executioners.

60. See Grenz, *Primer on Postmodernism*.

of discipleship. Through the use of this technology, new awareness and engagement of various cultural, historical, and ideological forms of information have become available to anyone, which has raised significant issues about the accepted beliefs and narratives that have shaped modernity and indeed expressions of faith and spirituality.

The French philosopher Jean-François Lyotard expressed his belief in the "incredulity towards metanarratives." This statement implies that any big stories were merely constructs of those who told them. This clearly related to the modern story of progress and colonization. Reason was now no longer king. Authorities were now no longer trusted, as they had been both the arbiters of promise and the conveyers of destruction. The same science that produced life-providing medicines also produced death-destroying wars and bombs. Healing verses Hiroshima. It also related to the belief in the metanarrative of the biblical story.

Soon a skeptical attitude toward all claims of ultimate truth was being expressed. This lead to the realization that without a cogent, logical framework for life, there were no fixed moral codes. All stories, beliefs, ideas, and ethics were culturally determined, as well as being equally valid. Life was not a logical discourse, but a random set of conflicting experiences. It was up to the individual to choose which bits they wished to believe and allow to shape their own life. This produced a "pick-n-mix" approach to life. The information highway had brought the world's thinking, experiences, beliefs, and contradictions out in the open. It was up to each person and/or community to select which was best for them.

While there are always some who find this cultural change extremely difficult and produce a resistance mentality, not all of postmodernity should be of concern. In terms of discipleship there are some noticeable elements which may prove helpful.

The first is a reengagement with the arts. As is often the case, in art we find the pioneering thinkers who express new ideas by using the canvas of their experience to reflect their stories, beliefs, and culture. For many years it was religious art that dominated the cultural landscape. As the enlightenment took hold, secular objects became the focus. As postmodernity began to be expressed as early as the 1930s, expressions of art were the avant-garde of the pioneering change to challenge cultural assumptions.

For Western discipleship, moving away from purely objective reasoning and reengaging all the senses provided a more holistic framework for new forms of spirituality and formation. The Eastern church has always understood how important art has been, in its magnificent use of icons and images. The Western church is now rediscovering this in expressions of being church and in alternative forms of worship. This visual age invites such participants to explore faith as a multisensory offering.

The second element of helpful engagement with postmodernity is a wider embracing of spirituality. The past, present, and future converge in seeking engagement with God. Various blogs, websites, artists, and emergent churches have rediscovered ancient forms of worship, creeds, liturgies, and music, as well as creating a wide variety of new sounds and approaches.[61] Like an orchestra full of a variety of instruments, the worldwide expressions of creative worship are being drawn together, producing a new cacophony of sound and experience.

The final piece is a rediscovery of community. As with the voice of Bonhoeffer, the importance of community has once again reemerged. The lone individual of modernity has begun to loose its voice to the myriad empowered voices of ordinary people,[62] freely expressing themselves, and seeking to be taken seriously. A fresh discovery of how community (be it family, neighborhood, city, or nation) forms and reshapes our lives is emerging, as we learn to share the journey together. While the experts are still around, theirs is more a facilitating role in seeking to bring out the best of what God is developing.

Ecumenical Worldwide Discipleship

While in our view the period we call postmodern may be a helpful and creative period of ancient and modern/postmodern forms of discipleship finding expression, there are two particular challenges that may be considered.

Multicultural and Intercultural Challenges

First, the great picture in worship in Revelation 7 is of all tribes, nations, and peoples gathering round the throne of God, expressing themselves as cultural peoples in worship and as a community. This picture is more than just a vision of the future. With the continuing growth of mass migration, especially within Europe, the opportunities to become an inclusive intercultural church are now possible. Small as well as large congregations have discovered the challenges, opportunities, and joys of being places of welcome, which has transformed their experience of what it means to be

61. A number of good examples can be found in Gibbs and Bolger, *Emerging Churches*.

62. Murray Williams and Murray Williams, *Multi-voiced Church*.

church. This presents a challenge to our perceived and preferred ways of do-ing things, but it equally presents a great opportunity in expressing a greater visual about the kingdom of God. Where else on planet earth can peoples from various cultures, ethnicities, and experiences find a sense of family, of belonging, and thereby become a prophetic symbol of a new future.

This has been at the forefront of our own recent speaking, teaching, thinking, and practice. We have together recently authored a book on the intentionality of such an enterprise within the framework of creating mis-sional communities and church planting, entitled *Forming Multicultural Partnerships*.[63] We also work together in a UK network of churches which is exploring what it could be like to develop into a missional movement informed and transformed by engaging in the multicultural experience.[64]

These are relatively small beginnings, and present great challenges in terms of discipleship across cultures, generations, and ethnicities.

Branded and YouTube Discipling

The second issue may be more prevalent among younger disciples. The avail-ability of numerous online resources can bring about a sense of branding of a Christian type or style. Finding the latest song on YouTube, then playing and singing it at the next gathering, is not necessarily a bad thing. We have done it ourselves, often with good outcomes. The point is that one's sense of identity and informed discipling can then be primarily expressed from a particular theological, cultural, and sociological framework, which enforces as well as limits good development. The type can become the brand, which ultimately is the measure of whether this is "good." This in the end may be a hindrance to creating effective missional disciples since it lacks the local context to help offer critique.

There is no desire to dismiss such valuable assets, since it is a privilege to have such great resources readily available. It is rather noting a subtle kind of development, due to the viral nature of online experiences, which then creates trends without sufficient discernment either theologically or contextually. This has, of course, always been present, as each culture, generation, and people group have preferences that they wish to express in worship and discipleship. The concern being expressed here is the lack of

---

63. Hardy and Yarnell, *Forming Multicultural Partnerships*.

64. The Fellowship of Churches of Christ in Great Britain and Ireland. While many denominations and networks have great and encouraging examples of multicultural churches, we are considering what an entire denomination could be like if this were the case.

sufficient critical reflection, so the well-known leader or camp vindicates the content, therefore justifying its use in one's local setting. The danger is the oft-noted rise of Christian consumerism.

The benefit of having such a wide pallet of resources to draw from provides a potentially rich tapestry that can help to develop followers of Jesus into maturity. It will take thoughtful, engaged leadership that seeks to understand the opportunity of intentionally engaging with such resources, which can help to develop and lead a new generation of missional disciples.

Conclusion

Making use of the broad framework of Bosh, this brief overview has selectively focused on a few expressions of discipleship throughout the history of Western Christianity. No doubt some readers will be critical of such a simplistic survey and quickly note others that could or should have been included.

What this approach has hopefully alerted us to is an awareness that taking note of contextual issues for discipleship is crucial in seeking to develop an authentic approach for mission.

The question for us and for our time is, what is it about current Western Christianity that has caused so much concern and indeed neglect around discipleship?[65] Perhaps more importantly, what has caused an active participation in non-discipleship?

One observation to be made is that the approach to the process of formation may have been part of the dilemma. Often, and this is especially so within Western culture, it has been focused on learning and gaining knowledge rather than the transformation of a whole person's life. If you only believe these things . . . repeat these words of the creedal statement . . . This was clearly not the way in which formation was developed in many of the key examples above.

The second core challenge has been the place of the Western Judeo-Christian worldview as an assumed framing for European life. The great growth of the faith in relation to the state and the powers that be, inevitably lead to the long span of the Christian story and memory as the only viable narrative for society and life. This was *the* legitimization story of what it meant to be European. This can be seen in the position of the church in politics, in its buildings, art, language, and in many cases framing of everyday way of life (through the Christian calendar). The effect of this meant that other interpretations or worldviews or stories had to be told in relation to this overarching and framing understanding, be they other readings of

---

65. Kreider, *Origins of Christendom in the West*; Murray, *Post Christendom*.

Christianity or even other faiths. The postmodern, post-Christendom paradigm and worldview has now pushed this to a point of no return.

Bosch notes the prophetic comment of Hendrik Kraemer, who stated,

> We are called to a new pioneer task which will be more demand-
> ing and less romantic than the heroic deeds of the past mission-
> ary era.[66]

Learning to become disciples in this new world environment is crucial not only for our survival, but to learn to become authentic disciples in
our own generation, while also leaving a legacy for the next. The following
chapters will explore how we might go about this in the light of our post-
Christendom context. The practical theology of this book, beginning in the
next chapter, seeks to relate ancient passion and conviction for Jesus with
contemporary challenges and opportunities.

---

66. Bosch, *Transforming Mission*, 8.

Section 2

A Biblical Basis for
Missional Discipleship

This section aims to provide some broad brushstrokes to the biblical basis of discipleship. It is largely based on New Testament backgrounds found in the Synoptic Gospels, John's gospel, the Pauline emphasis on the imitation of Christ, and critical reflections on the importance of a reign of God theology, which shapes the disciple's present life in the light of the future life.

Chapter 2

Following Jesus in the Synoptic Gospels

By Dan Yarnell

Introduction

Some of the earliest recorded expressions of Christian discipleship come from the writings of the Synoptic Gospels.[1] These eyewitness accounts both inform and provide a context for discipleship.[2] It is these particular "gospel" writings, likely to have first been a type of evangelistic tract,[3] provide us with some important viewpoints on how discipleship may have been encouraged, engaged in, and fostered in the emerging early Christian movement.

The Synoptics are especially important as their own theological frameworks and written perspectives provide some examples of contextual expression, suited to the needs of the communities they were produced to help. Each provides its own unique flavoring, while making use of the core sayings, miracles, and teachings of Jesus. It is these that will help to inform this chapter and hopefully provide some reflections on how their continued use can inform our own missional discipleship beliefs and practices. It is important to remember that these writings were written against the backdrop

1. There are of course important materials within the noncannonical gospels, especially the *Gospel of Thomas*, but exploring this goes beyond the scope of this work.

2. See especially Bauckham, *Jesus and the Eyewitnesses*, for a recent contribution in exploring this viewpoint.

3. So suggests Moule, *Birth of the New Testament*, 122.

of the empire, and some of this political overtone can be seen in their composition. This is important to take careful note of, as they were composed within a pre-Christendom narrative, which can provide some useful indications of how we might engage with them in a post-Christendom narrative. The Johannine contribution will be considered in the next chapter.

Matthew's Discipleship Framework[4]

Various scholars have noted the seemingly intentional compositional nature of Matthew's gospel.[5] While not wishing to suggest a particular pattern, it has been noted by Wilkins that there may in fact be a didactic framework for developing a focus on discipleship. He notes,

> Matthew has emphasized the goal of the believers' life of faith through the discipleship stories directed to the μαθηται. Matthew's gospel is at least in part a manual on discipleship. With all of the major discourses directed to the μαθηται, with the term arranged in such a way that most sayings directed to the term have become teachings on discipleship, with the positive yet realistic enhancement of the picture of the disciples, and with disciples called and trained and commissioned to carry out the climactic mandate to "make disciples" in the conclusion of the gospel, Matthew has constructed a gospel that will equip the disciples in the making of disciples.[6]

Of prime importance in formulating a focus on discipleship is the collection of Jesus' sayings in chapters 5–7, which we identify as the Sermon on the Mount. It is not possible in this book to go into any significant detail on the Sermon on the Mount. Readers should consult appropriate commentaries and studies.[7] Instead, it is worth noting two things which relate to discipleship.

---

4. Morhlang notes, "One of the evangelist's prime concerns in writing the gospel is to spell out what it means to be a μαθητης of Jesus" (*Matthew and Paul*, 74).

5. These varying literary viewpoints are helpfully summarized by France (*Matthew: Evangelist and Teacher*, 142–52). The most famous, often noted in more popular writings, is the work of Bacon, who saw a framing of five sections, which would then act as an aide-memoire to the five books of the Torah. Bacon, *Studies in Matthew*.

6. Wilkins, *Concept of Disciple*, 221.

7. These include Guelich, *Sermon on the Mount*; Betz, *Sermon on the Mount*; Talbert, *Reading the Sermon on the Mount*; as well as commentaries on Matthew.

The first is the structure of these various statements and teachings within these chapters. It seems that Matthew may have provided his readers with a type of discipleship manual.[8] As Luz notes,

> When in 28:20—again on a mountain—Jesus charges the eleven disciples to teach the nations to keep everything "I have commanded you," the thought is probably of the Sermon on the Mount. Thus it is also the central content of the Christian missionary preaching.[9]

One of the noteworthy elements of Matthew's focus on discipleship is that what is required is a sense of perfection of character and maturity (5:48). The kind of righteous and just living needs to surpass that on display of the Pharisees and teachers of the law (5:17). This, it seems, is why Jesus goes beyond the letter of the law, seeking to transcend the kind of life style that focuses on the outer elements and gets to the heart of the matter. This is foundational to an understanding of the Sermon on the Mount. As Mohrlang notes,

> Though both learning and teaching are involved, it is this element of obedience which is most central to Matthew's understanding of discipleship and which he is most concerned to emphasize; and it is this that lies at the heart of the demand for "deeper righteousness" in the Sermon.[10]

An interesting aspect of the mixture of sayings and mini parables in the sermon is the continued focus on the motives that generate the behaviors of Christ's followers. Obedience comes from these motives as much as other behaviors that do not live up to the beliefs, values, and qualities that underpin what believers may or may not do well. An important parable focuses on the need to build the disciple's life on sure foundations. Clearly the sure foundation is allegiance to Christ as master and Lord. This is clearly referenced at the end of this sermon with the three examples of choice: the two gates, the two trees with fruit, and the two foundations for houses. In each of these a choice is presented and obedience is required in order to live well.

Even more interesting may be its relationship of Christ as the one that the gates of Hades cannot prevail against in Matthew 16, in the declaration of Jesus' messiahship at Caesarea Philippi. In this passage, the powers of evil cannot prevail against Christ's ekklesia (community). An interesting correlation may be considered to exist here between the qualities, values, and

---

8. Famously noted by Bonhoeffer in his *Cost of Discipleship*.

9. Luz, *Matthew 1–7*.

10. Mohrlang, *Matthew and Paul*, 75.

beliefs that motivate Christ's disciples, and Christ himself who embodies the source of influence and power in the disciple's life. The church as the Christian community (*ekklesia*) can only be sustained and maintained by lives rightly motivated to be obedient to Christ. In other words, the church does not make disciples as part of its programs, as one aspect of many other functions it carries out, but it is actually the disciples who make the church true to its real calling, to become Christ to the world.

We might argue here that the God of mission shapes disciples to be a missional community to the world rather than the church and its structures making disciples and sending them out to make other disciples. The house built on the rock is constructed based on a vital connection to Christ the model disciple. It is much more than a simple foundation, it is also a real motivating power and influence that comes from a living connection with Christ. The church does not own mission and neither does it manufacture disciples, but faithful followers motivated by the God of mission by his Spirit create a church that can vibrantly participate with the Spirit of Christ in his mission. Motivation of the disciple's life is the foundation to the missional church's effective participation in God's mission to reconcile the whole world to the reign of God.

Come, Follow, Go[11]

Here we have another kind of framing of this gospel. These three commands seem to form a kind of paradigmatic expression of key statements of Jesus which the early disciples may have been aware of.

Come

The calling of the first disciples were those who responded to the invitation to come. Throughout this gospel this word *come* becomes an important statement to the life of a disciple: come all who are weary and need rest (11:28); the invitation to Peter to come out of the boat and step onto the water (14:29); inviting the little children to come (19:14); *come* follows after possessions have been sold (19:21) and the invitation to the faithful and obedient during the final retribution (25:34). As noted in chapter 1, a normal rabbi would have been more likely to have a would-be disciple go to them without a specific invitation. The idea of a rabbi initiating an invitation

---

11. I am grateful to Tim Herbert for pointing this out to me.

to new disciples seems countercultural and unique. Yet this invitation from Jesus calls us into the journey of discipleship.

This is part of what is at the heart of what motivates the disciple to faithful service in the *missio Dei*, to make yet other disciples. It is based on a continued invitation of the Spirit of the Lord beckoning both the disciple and new followers to "come follow me" as Jesus beckons and leads the way. This is why the church, in its pioneering phases of growth, is not really in control of mission through its ecclesiastical structures, but rather it is based on gatherings of people who share a common identity who gather together, to encourage one another and to care for each others' needs. When churches become institutions they then often lose a sense of the pioneering Spirit's call—"come follow me." Instead the "come" quite often becomes "come to our services and do things our way."

Follow

This second focal point follows on from the first. It is clearly seen as part of the original invitation of Jesus to the first disciples, "Follow me" (4:19), and throughout Matthew we see summaries of both the disciples (4:20, 22) and the crowds following him (4:25; 8:1; 12:15; 14:13; 19:2; 20:29). However, following carries much more weight than this, as these references are more than just the physical movements of people. The heart of authentic disciple-ship for Matthew is about following Jesus, in facing up to the demands of discipleship that Jesus presents. An example of this is found in chapter 8, where the would-be followers all have their excuses, but Jesus takes no notice and informs them that following means facing up to the challenges of change and letting go. The following chapter then introduces the reader to the tax collector Matthew, who immediately leaves his work in order to adhere to his new master, Jesus.

Chapter 10 takes this further, as the returning disciples who had been sent out by Jesus, upon returning, find some very challenging statements about the future and their allegiance. Here Jesus informs them that the one worthy is the one who takes up his cross and follows. Chapter 16 picks this up again in more precision, just after Peter's confession and subsequent rebuttal.

It seems that for Jesus, as Matthew portrays him, following is more than just a physical movement, but involves the deeper commitment to embrace the kingdom values and live them fully, whatever the cost. This seems to reinforce much of the teaching found in the Sermon on the Mount.

Go

This final imperative is especially noted as the ending of Jesus' ministry in Matthew's gospel, as well as the foundational understanding of Matthew's view of discipleship.[12] The so-called great commission begins with this statement for the disciples to fully enter into the continuing ministry of Jesus, by going into the whole world, much further than Jesus was able to achieve in his short ministry. Scholars have been quick to point out that this imperative is supported by the two further phrases, so in going, baptize, and in going, make disciples. This seems especially appropriate in the light of recent theological conversation around *missio Dei* theology, where the apostolic nature of Christian mission is being reimagined, especially for the church in the West.

Go, however, is not merely limited to this passage; as with *come* and *follow*, we find other key statements from Jesus that indicate the important contribution to our understanding of participatory discipleship within Matthew. These include: going the second mile (5:41); the command to the centurion that in going his faith was enough for the healing of his servant (8:13); and the first commission of the Twelve to go to the lost sheep of the house of Israel, proclaiming the good news of the kingdom (10:6–7).

Throughout Matthew's gospel, then, we see this pattern of come, follow and go. This may be another kind of framing that would support the idea of an approach to this gospel as a tool to develop and train new disciples in their ongoing contextual mission.

The Relational Values of Discipleship

Another key focus of discipleship that we find in Matthew is the high value of relationships that is expressed in various sayings and miracle stories. This may be highly relevant if the audience are those who have recently converted from Judaism and need to know that they are part of a new community. Of the various statements throughout this gospel, including the important section on caring for the little ones, chapter 18 is the most pronounced.

Inevitably in his own ministry, the disciples of Jesus would have faced times of relational challenge. Jesus' physical presence would have been the catalyst in dealing with needed reconciliation. When he was no longer present among them, then some guidelines that were both familiar and focused on maintaining the high value of relational accountability would have been required. It is here that the word "church" (εκκλησια) is found on the lips of Jesus in this gospel. Aside from any debate about the originality of this

12. So France, *Matthew: Evangelist and Teacher*, 261.

coming from Jesus, the issue of this text seems to be in seeking to maintain a healthy community and ways of dealing with the challenges when things go wrong. This seems to make the best sense of the only occurrence of this word on the lips of Jesus. For Matthew, then, it seems that discipleship finds its best expression in a discipled Christian community.[13]

The Test of Discipleship

Chapter 25 has been seen to be a controversial text and produced various viewpoints, including a universalist approach (doing good to everyone), a particularist (these are Christians who are suffering).[14] Some of this may relate to the hermeneutical approach in seeing this focusing mainly as a text on the Parousia and within a primary eschatological framework. Within Matthew's framework, this seems highly unlikely. It can be read as a prophetic encouragement and challenge to the emerging community of disciples and how they relate to those among them who, perhaps due to persecution or isolation from their former faith community, now find themselves. The challenge here is that the sheep are the true disciples who will intentionally engage and support those within the community in their time of need, much as had their master, Jesus. The goats will avoid and disengage in this process, perhaps out of fear, or at least out of neglect, and therefore will not express the discipled life of Jesus within their community.

Making Future Disciples

The final chapter of Matthew's gospel provides the clarion call of actively participating in the *missio Dei* by going out to make new disciples. As noted above, the imperative to "go" is in relation to baptizing and teaching them to obey. It is here we begin to see the continuation and expansion of Jesus' ministry. Being sent out into the whole world (εθνη) expands the horizon of the kingdom mandate that Jesus began with his focus to the house of Israel. Baptism and obedience is the way in which Jesus accomplished this in his

13. Donaldson, "Guiding Readers—Making Disciples," 46.

14. France, *Commentary on Matthew*, 354–58, provides a good summary of the variety of positions by various scholars who support both views, but comes to the conclusion that this is not primarily about the response to human need in general, but to the need of the disciples in particular. He notes in support of this view the earlier language of Matthew which spoke of the little ones as members of the disciple community (10:42; 18:6, 10, 14).

life and ministry, it is the way the disciples expressed their journey with Jesus, and it is the continuing expression for the entire Christian community.

This is in fact what it means to follow: to express the new life that Jesus offers from a *missio Trinitatis* framework.[15] The Father, Son, and Spirit working in partnership and helping this new emerging "church" made up of these new disciples to grow into such maturity that this becomes the hallmark of their life and witness.

Herein is the heart of our study. Making disciples is foundational to the future of the kingdom, but in the West, it has been a bit hit or miss. Matthew's contribution is a challenging reminder that discipleship is both essential and normal.

Mark's Focus

In the minds of most scholars, Mark is central to the entire understanding of the Synoptics, not only by being succinct in his approach, but as the likely foundations to the creation of both Matthew and Luke. In addition, the implied audience is considered to be new believers and an emerging church with a Roman setting. More recent studies have reminded us that while Mark does indeed present his own editorial theology, he is writing narrative, and this reading must not be overlooked. In particular, according to Williams,

> Mark's Gospel is a call to discipleship. A true interpretation of Mark must not ignore or obscure its rhetorical purpose, but instead must convey its message in such a way that the call to follow Jesus will be heard again.[16]

Scholarship has often noted how central discipleship is for Mark. While this gospel is short and to the point, there are some paradigms that inform the reader about the way in which discipleship should be manifest in their lives and communities.

The Twelve as a Paradigm for Discipleship?

Hurtado is one of many scholars who has noted that for Mark, the Twelve are portrayed as having both a positive and a negative paradigm for discipleship.[17] For much of the gospel, however, there is a way in which they

15. Hirsch and Hirsch, *Untamed*, 88–89.

16. Williams, "Discipleship and Minor Characters in Mark's Gospel," 336.

17. Hurtado "Following Jesus," 17–25; Kingsbury, *Conflict in Mark*, 89–117; France, *Gospel of Mark*, 27–29.

are presented to the reader that indicates that their response is not the way to follow Jesus. A couple of examples should suffice.

The first miracle at sea (4:35–41) is one of the indications that all is not well with the disciples. After the onslaught of a squall, which brings about the rapid filling of the boat with water, the disciples are both afraid (v. 38) and untrusting of Jesus' ability as well as the results of his actions (v. 41). Fear of the circumstance as well as fear of Jesus does not present a very enduring picture of what discipleship is all about.

A second example (8:14–21) demonstrates in a didactic example where the disciples misunderstand the warning of Jesus about the "leaven of the Pharisees and Herod," thereby demonstrating in the words of Jesus their "hardness of heart." Once again, not a promising example for the readers.

However, while in overall agreement, Donahue suggests that the place of the Twelve in Mark's thought equally implies a positive model for mission and discipleship.

> The twelve who will respond immediately to Jesus' command function as models of faith and at the same time form a new family around Jesus which is a substitute for the natural family.[18]

He further notes,

> The Jesus who speaks through the gospel to the Markan church is not a Jesus who lived in isolation. The first public act of his ministry was to summon disciples who were to follow him and to participate in his mission. Those first called are soon joined by others who form around Jesus a community which he empowers and instructs. In the call of the disciples the radically communitarian dimension of Christianity is vividly affirmed. Discipleship involves not simply hearing the summons of Jesus, but engagement with others who heed that same summons and embody a response to it in their lives. To "be with" Jesus is to be with others in community.[19]

This apparent dichotomy is part of the real tension that Mark demonstrates in indicating the challenges of being a disciple. At times, they are positive examples of the life of mission and community, whereas other parts of Mark suggest they are not to be copied in their approach. This seems to ring true in most of our own discipleship, as we can find this kind of dualism in our own experiences.

18. Donahue, *Theology and Setting*, 18.
19. Ibid., 19.

Greatness and Servanthood in Discipleship (10:35–45)

The center of Mark's gospel can be found in this important and distinct experience which Jesus shares and at the same time is at odds with his disciples. In a similar way to the framing of Matthew's gospel, Mark has a noticeable rhythm of moving toward this key event, and then focusing the remainder of his gospel to Jerusalem and the final hours of the life of the Master. In this third passion prediction, Jesus states and then embraces the calling to become the ransom who will sacrifice his life for all.[20] While there should be no confusion as to the implications of what Jesus is saying, sadly, in the midst of this is the vying for position by the two brothers James and John.

The core issue here seems to be about favor and identity. This is quite a fundamental issue within discipleship. Knowing who we are, how we belong, and therefore being recognized is quite a human need. The counter-cultural value that Jesus brings is noting that the position of who is greatest in the kingdom is that of being a servant.[21] It is this that Mark's gospel notes as being central and core to discipleship, first being modeled by Jesus himself, and then by implication for all disciples.

There is then in this text an invitation and a confrontation for the disciples. The invitation is to express servanthood as the appropriate framework for discipleship. This is the heart of the ministry of Jesus, and the invitation is addressing the Twelve in how they will respond to their own discipleship. But here is the rub, it is only Jesus who can ultimately express servanthood as the divinely appointed sacrifice who can give his life for many. As Lane notes,

> The parallel themes of Jesus' suffering in fulfilment of the will of God, misunderstanding, and the call to true discipleship exhibit emphases which Mark regarded as so essential for his community to understand that he made them the heart of his Gospel.[22]

---

20. Moloney, *Mark*, 85–86.

21. This value not only challenges the disciples' understanding of power, but the Roman cultural framework, as well. Christal notes, "Mark's Gospel informs his community, who lives under the power of the Roman Empire, about the unexpected and astonishing way of Christian discipleship within the realm of God's reign" (*Disciples and Discipleship*, 62).

22. Lane, *Gospel of Mark*, 293.

FOLLOWING JESUS IN THE SYNOPTIC GOSPELS

Pax Romana or Pax Deo?

Central to the Hellenization process[23] begun by Alexander was the importance of the *Pax Romana*—the Peace of Rome. This controlling narrative enabled all citizens and conquered peoples to enjoy a sense of potential coexistence, as well as a sense of toleration. This is clearly seen in the way the Jews were treated by the Romans. Overall, they had restricted freedom, but in this restriction, they were able to express their life and faith and to flourish. This did, of course, present its own set of challenges as second, third, and subsequent generations were enticed to become Roman citizens, often throwing off much of their cultural and indeed spiritual heritage, or at least reinterpreting it. The strong resistance of Zealots for a more radical and revolutionary approach as well as the complete withdrawal of the Essenes, focusing on a more apocalyptic interpretation and experience, were the two competing extremes of response. However, the core challenges lay within the more centralized approaches of the Sadducees and Pharisees. In both instances, disciples were produced, but none were considered by Jesus to fully express what authentic discipleship looked like. "For I say unto you that except your righteousness shall exceed the righteousness of the scribes and Pharisees, you shall in no case enter into the kingdom of heaven" (Matt 5:20).

The coming of Jesus and the fostering of the early church in the writings of the Apostle Paul indicated a different paradigm, the *Pax Deo* (Peace of God).[24] Jesus, as the giver of peace (John 14:27), and Paul, in declaring the peace of God (Phil 4:7) and the God of peace (Phil 4:9), provide a different focal point. This would have been liberating as well as challenging for Mark's readers. The centrality of the cross noted above would have been incredibly challenging in itself, and would not likely be seen to be the way of peace. Yet this gospel in particular notes the centrality of the cross as core to the journey of discipleship.

Luke's Focus—the Gospel (and Acts)

Like a great symphony, the contribution of Luke to our understanding of discipleship is greatly enhanced as we have his second movement found in the book of Acts. It therefore seems sensible to consider their contribution together as one furthers the other in a kind of synergetic relationship.

---

23. See especially Hengel, *Judaism and Hellenism.*

24. This is in contrast to the observation by Vallée that the traditional Roman worship was a means of maintaining the *pax deorum* (peace of the gods). *Shaping of Christianity*, 101.

At the heart of the contribution of Luke is the realization that discipleship is the journey of a costly venture.[25] Building on the work of Mark, Luke brings this emphasis to the story of Jesus and life of the disciples. Unlike Mark, the disciples in Luke are seen in a much more positive light. As Longenecker notes,

> For Luke views the disciples as modeling the essential characteristics of Christian discipleship. It is not their failures he highlights. Rather, what he emphasizes are the new commitments, orientation, and lifestyle that they reflected in their lives by association with Jesus their Master.[26]

Fitzmeyer notes that whereas Mark seemed to focus his understanding of discipleship in light of a seemingly imminent eschaton, Luke develops his focus more in the present. How do we live as followers of Jesus today seems to be implied by Luke in both his gospel and in Acts.[27]

We can see the use of this imminent focus when we consider the following key texts:

4:21	*"Today* this Scripture is fulfilled in your hearing." This beginning of Jesus' ministry in his home town of Nazareth indicates that something is presently taking place.
13:32–33	When speaking to Herod's servants, Jesus notes that his casting out of demons and performing cures happens *today* and tomorrow, but on the third day this work will finish and be completed.
19:5	Jesus calling to Zacchaeus to come from the tree, thereby expressing a welcome to him, which is then reciprocated as Jesus indicates he must stay in your house *today*. Within this imminent experience of Jesus, Zacchaeus demonstrates generosity by giving away half to the poor. It is this action which causes Jesus to then say to him, *today* salvation has come.
22:61	For Peter, before cock crows *today*, he will deny Jesus three times.
23:43	To the thief on the cross, Jesus indicates that salvation is not just a future eschatological event but will take place immediately, as he states, *"Today* you will be with me in paradise."

All of these indicate the importance of the immediate experience. However, the most significant of the statements is Luke's editing of the simple invitation from Mark on discipleship. "He called the crowd with his

---

25. Sweetland, "Following Jesus," 109–10.

26. Longenecker, "Taking Up the Cross Daily," 57.

27. Fitzmeyer, *Gospel according to Luke (I–IX)*, 235. See the further discussion in du Plessis, "Discipleship according to Luke," 58–71.

disciples, and said to them, 'If any want to become my followers, let them deny themselves and take up their cross and follow me'" (Mark 8:34). It is here that Luke brings the addition of "daily" to this condition of discipleship. It seems then for Luke, that the need for the day-to-day experience of following is a necessary requirement of discipleship.

Discipleship for the Rich and the Poor

Various scholars over the past few decades have noted the focus in Luke's writing on the marginalized and subsequent empowerment.[28] These include the important role and contribution of women, the welcome and embracing of children, but one of the most poignant seems to be the focus on the poor. Luke has a greater usage of the word "poor" (πτωχος) and its derivatives, but there are particular frameworks in Luke that seem to indicate how vital this is for his own theological contribution about Jesus.

Luke 4:16–30 and the Mission of Jesus

Drawing on the prophetic writing of Isaiah 61:1–2a, Jesus begins his ministry by indicating his Nazareth Manifesto by indicating that his own reading of the Isaiah scroll, which was read in his own local context, was to be the *raison d'être* of his entire ministry. Here we see the emphasis on those who are poor, marginalized and broken as a primary focus on his ministry.

Prophetically Challenging the Status Quo

Luke suggests that the coming of Jesus is in itself a prophetic and subversive act. In chapter 1, the songs of Mary and Zechariah each indicate a sense of reversal of fortunes in the activity of God in the coming of this child. In his birth, the good news is not presented to the rich and powerful but to lowly shepherds (2:8–20). Rome, the political center of the empire, is not the place of arrival of this king, but rather Bethlehem. Could this be a kind of typology of the shepherd of Israel promised by Zechariah 11?

Along with the manifesto noted above, within this gospel there are direct challenges to the rich. One such example comes from the beatitudes as found in the Sermon on the Plain (6:20–22). "Woe to the rich" echoes

---

28. The literature is quite voluminous on this issue. A good, clear overview can be found in May, "Rich and Poor," 800–810. Also Seccombe, *Possessions and the Poor*, and Green, "Good News to Whom?," 59–74.

repeatedly, as a contrast is set up between those who are poor, and therefore by implication authentic disciples, and those who are rich, and therefore must face this prophetic challenge to their discipleship being called into question. For Luke, discipleship is a costly journey. Could this be part of the reason for Luke's gospel, to help those who were coming to faith to confront the challenges that might prevent an expression of authentic discipleship?

The Need to Care for the Marginalized as Part of the New Community

The contrast to this prophetic viewpoint can be found in the birth of the church as a new kind of community. Luke does not use the word church in his gospel, but the forming of the discipleship around Jesus, which includes the multicultural mix of peoples and viewpoints, predicated a fuller demonstration in the birthing of the church at Pentecost. The inclusion of women and men, rich and poor, fostered the development of forming disciples across social, ethnic, political, and religious boundaries. The two Lukan summaries (2:41–47 and 4:32–39) indicate an intentional sharing of life and goods, creating a unity of purpose.[29] It is noteworthy that these descriptions indicate the shared life of discipleship that would sustain them (even sharing their goods) as well as release them in mission and prophetically challenge the powers of empire and religion. Perhaps this is why Acts has become a paradigm for centuries of followers of Jesus as what church is meant to be.

The inherent dangers of wealth, power, success, acceptance, and identity are regularly indicated by Luke as potential obstacles to authentic discipleship. That being said, it is important to note that there is an important contribution for the rich in Luke's understanding of discipleship. In the parable of the unjust steward (16:1–13), we see something of Luke's concern for the right use of possessions, thereby demonstrating Luke's attitude to wealth. "Making friends with unrighteous mammon" seems to indicate that for Luke, wealth in and of itself is not evil; rather, as Pilgrim notes,

> that the disciples are exhorted to make friends with mammon seems to imply a matter of right or wrong use, not total rejection. Mammon is unrighteous then, either because it is so often acquired wrongly or because it represents such a grave seduction for humanity . . . the way to make friends with mammon is to use one's wealth in the service of love.[30]

29. Pilgrim, *Good News to the Poor*, 147–59. Barrett, *Acts*, 33–36, 65–68.

30. Ibid., 128. Bailey helpfully denotes the importance of understanding the Middle Eastern cultural perspective in interpreting these verses (*Jesus through Middle Eastern Eyes*, 332–42).

These issues of compassion and care while making good use of wealth continue to present challenges for the would-be disciple today, both in the post-Christian West, with our numerous resources and Christendom heritage, as well as within the developing world, in the fostering of a prosperity gospel and in the challenges of covertness. As migratory movements of people bring many more Christians to the West, these challenges are hard to avoid. Some important partnerships around theological understandings, strategic development, and openness to humility and learning from each other may be able to help us all steer through this turbulent environment.

Spirit-Led Mission

A second focus which is often noted is the importance of the role of the Spirit within the Lukan corpus. At its heart, we are confronted by the vitality and uncertainty that this creates. The spirit who empowers Jesus at the beginning of his ministry in his baptism also leads him into the wilderness to face his own demons. Empowerment and risk could be seen to be the hallmarks of the work of the Spirit in Luke.

This is especially so in the books of Acts, where we see the Holy Spirit shaping, pushing, confronting, empowering, welcoming, and blessing this newly formed emerging community. Discipleship becomes more than merely believing, being baptized, and then learning to be together. Confrontation, becoming uncomfortable, challenges to inherited theologies, being forced into persecution, and embracing change are all hallmarks of his work. This is to help facilitate the development of the ongoing mission of Jesus by these disciples into the world.

A watershed moment is indicated in Acts chapter 10. This kind of second conversion of Peter on the rooftop demonstrates many of these kinds of workings of the Spirit; to bring the infant church into a new manifestation of life and hope. For Peter, to consider acting on the vision he received was quite a risky step. This is a seemingly direct challenge to his inherited theology. What Jew would even consider rising and killing unclean animals, when these are directly forbidden? The appearance of Cornelius's servant, the subsequent coming of the Spirit on the Gentiles, the response of baptism, all confirm that it is the Spirit who is in charge of the mission of the church and therefore ultimately of discipleship.

Conclusion

How might this brief, selective overview of contributions from the authors of the Synoptics inform our journey of discipleship after Christendom? We would like to make a few observations:

Intentional and Informed Values

At the heart of the ministry of Jesus is not only a clear sense of identity and purpose for his mission, but the underlying values that shaped his life and work. These values are clearly expressed in his various approaches to people and situations. Generosity, kindness, trust, compassion, honesty, vulnerability, and transparency are some of the obvious examples. These enabled him to handle the varying challenges to his leadership, to his relationships, and to his focus on his mission. He could demonstrate welcome to children and broken people, to outcasts and enemies, but he would equally confront hypocrisy, wrong forms of power and abuse, especially from those who were meant to be setting a good example. This seems to be behind the statement in Matthew about our righteousness surpassing that of the scribes and Pharisees (Matt 5:20). These leaders seem to have been blind to how their actions and responses were informed by the underlying values they had consciously or unconsciously adopted.

In considering our own discipleship, we need to give consideration to the importance of our own values which inform and ultimately transform our expressions of ministry. Some of the most difficult ones will have been shaped by our culture and history. This is where cultural blindness may create havoc in our attempts in expressing authentic discipleship. We need our sisters and brothers from other cultures, traditions, and experiences to aid us in this journey. We may never be fully aware of how limited we are, but with the help of an intentional formative community, we certainly stand a better chance of meeting our intended aim—to be like Jesus.

Contextual Awareness

We have noted that each of the gospels has its own specific context, the authors shaping and forming the stories, miracles, and teachings of Jesus for their own audience and theological framing. Understanding that each of the Synoptic writers had a focused approach to discipleship helps us to engage with these texts in an informed and honest way. This is not only for hermeneutical transparency, but to aid us in our own theological reflections and our active participation and expression of the life of Jesus.

Intentionally giving more consideration to our own local, national, and global/glocal contexts should help us frame a more appropriate discipleship response. Just as the gospels do not clearly present a program of activities for would-be disciples, we must also take seriously what discipleship means within the cultures where we are expressing God's mission. We do need good examples of modeling and noting good practices to learn from, but our multicultural, pluralistic framework should warn us not to think there is a one-size-fits-all approach. Authentic discipleship will be formed and expressed in its own context while equally being shaped by Scripture, traditions, and the leading of the Spirit.

Endurance and Perseverance

At the heart of discipleship is a journey, from death to life, from darkness to light, from slaves to free, from being alienated to being in relationship. This sense of movement and growth is foundational to a mature discipleship that will express itself and actively and intentionally encourage others. The journey for Jesus was one of total surrender and obedience as he lived his life each day with all the challenges to his leadership, his values and ethics, his sense of identity and purpose. This was also the journey of his followers. Matthew illustrates the importance of teaching and obedience, notably in the Sermon on the Mount and in the commissioning of the Twelve who would continue the ministry of Jesus, Mark indicates that often the disciples were not very good at understanding and seemingly missed the point, but they did find a way through their brokenness to keep going. Luke then notes the particular issues that faced the expansion of the kingdom as disciples from new cultures were added, along with the challenges of riches and wealth.

In all these particular ways, the heart of discipleship was being expressed. What is somewhat amazing is that with all the challenges that faced these disciples, there was that sense of persevering and enduring until the end. There was an awareness that theirs was a journey, not just a simple decision. Authentic faith is faith that endures. Maturity comes from staying the course, not just in the sense of being faithful, but also in being fruitful. Perhaps we need to reconsider this for those of us in the West who often want quick results.

Supporting the Weak, Different, and Marginalized as an Inclusive Community

It may be obvious, but the development of Jesus' discipleship community was quite unique by any standard. An apostolic team of twelve chosen men, various supportive women, and various other followers expressed a type of open community. It seems that most of the disciples were not well educated, the place of women in that society was highly limited, yet Jesus forms a safe place of hope and belonging with a clear sense of vision and mission. This is also echoed in the book of Acts, where we see the forming of new intentional communities across cultures and ethnicities. Here is a model of the kingdom on earth.

In addition, it is a place of healing. Brokenness and failure is not rejected, but finds within this new community a healing of body and spirit, sometimes physical, often spiritual and relational, and thereby it aims to bring new life. The poor, widows, and orphans, the elderly, the unloved and rejected all find a place at the table and in each others' lives. It of course is not a utopia, for any human society has its serious challenges, which may be why there is so much of Jesus' teaching around right kinds of leadership, support, and encouragement for the marginalized.

We have noted the importance of this in a previous work,[31] but it is worth noting that one of the most missional expressions in our divided world can be a community of various peoples, ages, cultures, and ethnicities who are expressing a life together, being formed and transformed by the story of Jesus in their discipleship. This kind of unity, which we see with the followers of Jesus and in the continuing life and work of the early church is something we could intentionally seek to express in becoming a discipled, cohesive community.

Are There Limits in Discipleship?

Does discipleship have any limits? Clearly in the Synoptic gospels Jesus called people to himself and then to his missional journey of following. There were those who found the call too difficult, others who were distracted, discouraged, and dissuaded. The ending of the Sermon on the Mount indicates there are two sets of choices and the way of the disciple is not an easy one. To deny self, take up our own cross, and to follow is foundational in all the gospels. These are clear limits if we are to take the sense of Jesus as Lord at all seriously.

31. Hardy and Yarnell, *Forming Multicultural Partnerships*.

Although with a few clear exceptions, Western Christians during Christendom have regularly known various forms of cultural Christianity without clear intentional discipleship. This has led to a kind of non-discipleship, to forms of nominality and little transformation or radical challenge of the status quo. In our post-Christian environment, this legacy has found us in a time when the Christian story is either widely unknown or highly distrusted. Finding new ways of expressing discipleship urgently needs to be found. We cannot go back to some golden age in the past. That doorway is decisively closed. We might learn from the Synoptic authors, who each found ways to communicate the story of Jesus to their audiences in order to develop discipleship. In doing so, we may find we can be brave and honest enough to take the risks of subverting the cultural narratives and learning to express God's mission in and for our generation.

Chapter 3

John's Gospel and Discipleship

By Andrew R. Hardy

Introduction

There are many notable scholarly works on John's gospel that have advanced our understanding of its literature, history, theology, and interpretation. In this chapter we will focus on the topic of discipleship. John shares about 8 percent of its contents with the other three gospels. The question has been copiously raised, "Why is it so different from the other three?" Is it based on a real historic deposit of Jesus' teaching, given that the style of its presentation and language is so different compared to the other gospels?[1] Brown has argued that it is based on the testimony of the so-called beloved disciple who was probably one of Jesus' early followers.[2] Does it function as more of an interpretation of the meaning of Christ's life and mission?[3] The way that this question is addressed has varied between key Johannine scholars like Brown, Cullmann, Martyn, and Richter.[4] Dodd paid

---

1. Bauckham, *Jesus and the Eyewitnesses*, 126–29.

2. Brown, "Johannine Ecclesiology," 388.

3. Cooke, *New Testament*, 362.

4. Brown, "Johannine Ecclesiology"; Cullmann, *Johannine Circle*; Mattili, "Johannine Communities," 294–315. Martyn's work is not readily available in English.

great attention to its historical literary and cultural backgrounds.[5] Does it represent a different kind of Christianity than that reflected in the Synoptic Gospels?[6] Does its focus on knowledge rather than simple faith in Christ, representing some kind of Gnostic Christianity, or a Christian response to Gnosticism—some scholars seem uncertain.[7] Could it perhaps be the case that similarities in language and symbols between John and some of the Essene community's writings mean that John's church was founded by Essenes who converted to faith in Jesus the Messiah?[8] Some of these ideas are more controversial than others.

Hurtado suggests the church behind the community was recovering from a breach in their fellowship that entailed some of their members leaving the Johannine church/es.[9] He also suggests that part of the split occurred between Jewish members who believed that Jesus was divine and those who did not.[10] He notes that the Johannine church seems to have had a vibrant experiential faith, in which they enjoyed charismatic communion with God.[11] It is interesting that Hurtado suggests a rift in the Johannine church due to a difference of interpretation regarding the nature of Christ.[12] A difference of interpretation regarding Christ's nature as divine, or human, would have made a difference in the way that his first or later disciples regarded him.

Brown, Martyn, Richter, and Cullmann were interested particularly in the prehistory of the gospel's formation and the groups behind its architecture. Given that Brown et al. suggest that the gospel came to be written based on a Jewish community that made up its church or churches,[13] it is important to also consider other groups it sought to define itself over against. Brown suggests the following about the situation at the time of the final redaction of the gospel:

> When the Gospel was written, at least a quadrilateral situation existed:
>
> • The synagogue of "the Jews";
> • Crypto-Christians (Christian Jews) within the synagogue;

5. Dodd, *Interpretation of the Fourth Gospel.*

6. Guthrie, *New Testament Introduction*, 274.

7. Koester, *Introduction to the New Testament*, 185.

8. Drane, *Introducing the New Testament*, 203.

9. Hurtado, *Lord Jesus Christ*, 402–7.

10. Ibid., 404–6.

11. Ibid., 400.

12. Ibid., 404–6.

13. Brown, "Johannine Ecclesiology."

- Other communities of Jewish Christians who had been expelled from the synagogue;
- The Johannine community of Jewish Christians.[14]

It would seem that each of these groups had a part to play in the church/es to differing extents, even if to critique or challenge their beliefs and practices. Brown also suggests that there was a Samaritan group of Christians in the church/es.[15] It seems that the church/es was/were seeking to define themselves over against four groups:

> *Mosaic-Prophet-Christians.* Rejecting the idea of a Davidic Messiah, a group of Jews, resembling the Ebionites, proclaimed Jesus as a prophet-like-Moses.
>
> *Son-of-God-Christians.* Part of this Jewish Christian community developed a higher Christology of Jesus as the préexistent, divine Son of God, a figure who came down from heaven bringing salvation.
>
> *Docetist-Christians.* Some of the Son-of-God Christians interpreted the Evangelist's high Christology in a docetic way: Jesus' divine origins were so stressed that he became a totally divine being whose earthly appearance was only an illusion.
>
> *Revisionist-Christians.* A redactor who was decidedly anti-docetic rewrote the *Grundschrift*[16] by making additions (1:14–18; 19:34–35) and composed First John as an apologetic defense of a theology of Jesus as the Son of God come in the flesh.[17]

These were the probable background communities that were likely addressed, corrected, or whose beliefs were accepted into what might be called the Johannine tradition. It would seem that the "beloved disciple's" testimony was preserved as a kind of guiding narrative to help the so-called Johannine church or church/es to define their Christology. It was deemed to be a high Christology that posited Jesus Christ to be the divine Son of God. As we will discuss in brief below, Hurtado has done much to demonstrate an early devotion to Jesus as one to be given worship similar to that offered to Israel's God.

14. Ibid., 382–83.
15. Ibid., 390.
16. German word meaning "Ground Script."
17. Ibid., 383.

Implied Types of Disciples

Each of the four groups would have represented a different view of what a disciple should base their beliefs and practices upon. In the case of the Mosaic Prophetic Christians, the view of Christ may have been of a new Moses-like figure, who was sent to prepare for the final realization of Israel's hopes, which included the kingdom of Israel being restored and the demise of Roman power and governance. The Son of God Christians seemed to hold to a similar divine-man Christology like that found in Philippians 2:1–10 and Colossians 1:14–15, et al. In this case the preexistent eternal Son of God had come to reveal what the Father of Israel and the created world was like. The goal of discipleship here could have been to model the Johannine churches on a similar intimacy of relationship with the Father as the God-man himself modeled. The intimacy also probably included a grounded belief that God wanted his people to live out their spiritual lives honoring the material world as the place of divine interest, mission, and action. The Docetic kind of Christians probably disdained the material concentration on God's works in the world and wanted to spiritualize their faith so as not to include the material world, or life in it. Theirs may have been a very otherworldly focus including an ascetic spirituality. The revisionist group may have overreacted to the challenge posed by the Docetic element. As a result, they may have become rather inward looking and defensive. In turn this may have meant that the love and fellowship of the group was somewhat stilted and paranoid toward outsiders. This chapter assumes that the Son of God Christians and the Revisionist group were the ones who made up the membership of the Johannine church/es.

The scholarly assessments that posited these groups is likely to have been somewhat accurate. They come from an earlier period in gospel studies that focused attention on literary-historical criticism, form criticism, and in Brown's case a preference for redaction criticism. In this chapter a reader-response method will be used that in some ways works quite well alongside a redaction critical methodology. It will be left to the interested reader to define these terms for themselves.

This chapter will focus on three matters. First, a brief survey of the differences in interpretative horizons of Jesus and those Jews who were hostile to him will be considered—as they are displayed in the text of the gospel itself. In this instance, John's account of who Jesus was, his words, and the questions raised by disbelieving Jews in this gospel's narrative will provide some interesting insights. Second, a consideration of the gospel's account of the disciples' views of Christ will be considered, with a goal being to understand how early disciples were shaped as a community of followers. It is to be noted that individual women and men play an important part in the gospel's narratives and discourses. It is probable that the members of the Johannine church/es gave prominence to both sexes in leadership. Third, the relevance of the gospel to contemporary disciples will be considered.

Who Is Jesus?

The question is as old as the Christian faith itself. Each gospel seeks to address it in their own inimitable way. Hurtado has not been slow to recognize the divine Logos Christology presented in the gospel.[18] Neither has Dunn.[19] The classic opening passage found in John 1:1–18 has been recognized as a kind of wisdom literature, which probably formed a kind of creed for the Johannine church/es.[20] This creed clearly draws on common themes that can be traced back to Old Testament sapiential literature, like that found in Proverbs 8:22–31.

In Proverbs, wisdom is metaphorically personified as a feminine exemplification who stands at Yahweh's side during the creation of the world. It is common to call this personified companion "Lady Wisdom." In John it is the "Word" (Greek *Logos*) who is the one through whom God creates the cosmos.[21] The sapient nature of the Logos, the Son of God in John's theology, has he/she stand at God's side. This Logos is said to be God in nature. The Logos became "flesh."[22] Indeed the Word (Logos) is identified as Jesus Christ,[23] who is said to have come from the very heart (side or bosom) of the Father.[24]

Feminist scholars have reflected on the feminine aspect in relation to the creed of John's opening passage compared to the wisdom literature. They have argued that the creative and generative aspects of God's nature have important things to say about women made in God's image, as the bearers of new life created in a female's womb.[25] Given that John's gospel has been a rich source mined from the earliest period of Christianity to theologically reflect on the nature of God, this is important to consider

18. Ibid., 349–426.

19. Dunn argues for an adoptionist Christology in the New Testament, but he also recognizes that John's gospel assumes a divine Christ. Dunn, *Unity and Diversity*, 20, 48, 233, 236, 240, 243, 249, 260, 262, 278–81.

20. Brown, *Introduction to the New Testament*, 338.

21. Ibid.

22. John 1:14.

23. Brown, *Introduction to the New Testament*, 353.

24. John 1:18.

25. Fulkerson et al., *Oxford Handbook of Feminist Theology*, 33.

seriously. Trinitarian doctrine has most readily been deduced from this gospel. In terms of feminist theology, the Trinity finds the feminine and masculine represented in the Creator, based on John's clear reliance on wisdom literature.[26] This kind of theological reflection is also supported by Genesis 1:26, as mankind is made in God's image as female and male. This recognition was not lost sight of in the sapient Logos tradition of Johannine memory. This theological recognition is important, as we might argue that disciples after Christendom are shaped in the *imago Trinitatis* (image of the Trinity).[27] Female and male disciples are equal in the Trinitarian family—as sons and daughters of God. Edwards comments:

> Some female characters . . . have been of special interest to feminist scholars. These often consider John especially sym-pathetic to women . . . , sometimes arguing that he depicts an "alternative" Christian community in which women share fully in leadership.[28]

This is important to consider, given that much of human history has been dominated by patriarchal power structures that have often abused the rights of the female sex. Patriarchies of this type have rightly been challenged and overcome increasingly in the late modern period—among native Western women particularly. In some of the multicultural diaspora communities, made up of migrant women from around the world now living in the West, the struggle often begins as they see the freedoms that Western women enjoy. The Jesus presented in John's gospel honors individual women and men in dignified communication, which is an aspect of the gospel that has not had much attention drawn to it in the male dominated theological literature.

A message of John's gospel seems to be that Jesus values female and male disciples equally, as does the Father. This recognition of mankind as female and male is important to how Logos theology in John is to be under-stood, in its literary and historical context.

An interesting angle is that the Logos is said to have become a human in the person of Jesus Christ. Against the backdrop of a Jewish or Gnostic Docetic understanding of the gospel, there seems to have been the denial by a group that contested God could not have really become a human creature.

In other words, Christ could not be a divine-human being, because otherwise how could an infinite God be contained in such a vessel made of corrupt matter? The gospel clearly does not fudge the issue on this matter.

26. Ibid., 32, 33.
27. Hardy, *Pictures of God*, chs. 3, 4, 8.
28. Edwards, *Discovering John*, 106.

There are several instances when Christ's identity is merged with that of God. It is nowhere better to be located than in John 8:58, where Jesus identifies himself with the "I Am," who met Moses at the burning bush in Horeb.[29] John's Christ predates Abraham, as well as being the agent through whom the original cause of creation (God) effected its action.[30]

The God-man embraces the male and female aspects of their creation in the *imago Trinitatis*. The creative aspects of what it means to be men and women made in God's image is to be redefined by the God-man, who has become human. In the gospel, the meetings that Jesus has with individual women and men represents how he seeks to transform them to become children of his Father. What are the implications of this nascent divine-man Christology?

Once more the gospel leaves the reader in no doubt. Jesus declares to Philip that to have known him is to know the Father.[31] This christological insight has profound implications for how "Logos" might be understood etymologically. Logos may be identified with the divine artificer Wisdom, who was at Yahweh's side at creation. It is Lady Wisdom, who as it were, speaks creation into being. It is She-He that is used to imply the language of thoughtful design that constructs and brings creation to birth. The masculine and feminine aspects of the *imago Trinitatis* are to be reconstructed in the human soul and the community of the church. Disciples share a creative capacity to help shape new disciples to become like Christ. Just like in the Genesis creation story,[32] God speaks and the words form a world that can be understood by those made in Trinity's image.[33]

In like manner believers have a part to play in helping to shape new followers as new creations to be made in Christ's image. Psalm 19 is a creation psalm that declares the created order itself communicates knowledge of the Creator who made it. Romans 1:20, coming in a passage that speaks of pagan distortions and misunderstandings of who God is, declares that the world provides clear evidence of its Creator. Logos Christology probably links Lady Wisdom to the intelligent design of the world and mankind and its birth at creation, as well as its ongoing birth as a recreation in Christ. Christ comes to restore men and women to the creational image of God. Indeed, the language is plain enough:

29. Exod 3:1–12.
30. John 1:1–4.
31. John 14:9.
32. Gen 1 and 2.
33. Gen 1:1–5.

> The true light that gives light to every man was coming into the
> world. He was in the world, and though the world was made
> through him, the world did not recognize him.[34]

It may be claimed that John's Logos Christology, coming with this
heritage of intelligent creative design associated with it, powerfully implies
that Logos needs to take its definition from this background. The following
definition is therefore suggested by the writers:

> John's Logos Christology presents Jesus the God-man as the one
> who provides the interpretation of what God is like. He provides
> a living relatable picture of God to those he interacted with on
> a personal and communal level. Logos Christology implies that
> Christ the disciple-maker came to transform women and men
> into what they were originally designed to be, image bearers of
> the Trinity family's likeness. The Christian community that lives
> as a family based on God's love is a missional model for society
> to interact with in order to obtain an interpretation of what God
> as Father, Son, and Holy Spirit are like. The people of God are
> a shopping window that puts the invitation to become part of
> God's window on display.

John's gospel does not ever use the term Trinity. However, it attests to
the tri-personal nature of God. The Son of God is personified in Christ the
God-man.[35] The Father[36] and the Spirit are also included in the Johannine
Godhead.[37] Each of the persons are given an identity, although the Spirit's
identity is somewhat subsumed into that of Christ.[38]

The Logos Hermeneutic of John

The divine Logos is said to have come from the Father's "breast," or "bosom,"
(John 1:18). The breast is the location of the heart, which to the ancient Near
Eastern biblical mind-set represented the seat of human emotions and life.
It is the conscious part of the human psyche. It is as if John were saying,
"the God-man knows God on a deep intimate heart level." In biblical terms
the heart represents the place of the deepest life of the soul. It is the seat of
all that motivates a person, or in this case the Father of the universe—God

34. John 1:9–10 NIV.
35. John 1:14–18.
36. John 1:18.
37. John 4:24.
38. John 16:13.

himself. Jesus comes from the heart of a compassionate Father, to provide the deepest possible interpretation of what God is like in his nature of love and forgiveness. Jesus and the Father are one in their relationship and intimacy according to John 17. John's Christ provides a window into the meaning of God's heart.

With Christ's appearance, no fuller revelation of what God is like can be given. This is vital to the theology of discipleship in John's gospel. Disciples after Christendom can look to Christ to find the ultimate meaning of life in him. No fuller revelation of what God is like can be exposed beyond it. These are bold claims indeed, but the gospel seems clear enough to be understood in this way. The Logos hermeneutic is that Christ interprets what the Father is like—in terms of his nature and purposes for humankind and the cosmos.[39]

Nowhere better is the heart of Christ revealed, and therefore that of the Father's, than in John chapter 17. Christ is about to depart from his disciples. His priestly prayer sets out the goal of the mission of God to be the sharing in the oneness of the Father's, Son's, and Spirit's union. This union is also for his disciples to enjoy (in some mysterious manner). Newbigin captures an important insight from this chapter, which disciples after Christendom would do well to reflect on:

> The sending of the disciples into the world is not an empty gesture. They are chosen and sent in order to "go and bear fruit" (15:16). And so the prayer of Jesus extends beyond the first disciples to include all who will come to believe "through their word." The disciples are to be present in the world, not withdrawn from it. But presence is not enough; they must also speak, for faith comes by hearing. There can be no believing that Jesus is the messenger of God unless the name of Jesus is spoken.[40]

Newbigin offered a particular critique to the way discipleship may be conceived related to John's vision of it. As a missiologist and contextual theologian he understood that it was not enough for the church to have a presence in a neighborhood based in its own church building. It required that the people of Christ intentionally make themselves present to the people of the communities they lived in. Moreover, Newbigin's vision of contextually based discipleship required that there be a realistic compassionate Christian presence, that on the one hand acted as if believers were Christ himself to the people, serving them, praying for them and seeking to help them in every good way possible. On the other hand, this also meant offering a compassionate critique of the prevailing culture which would call

39. John 3:16–17.
40. Newbigin, *Light Has Come*, 234.

people to repent and turn to the Lord for salvation and renewal. Bevans calls this the countercultural model of contextual theology,[41] in the sense that the gospel of Christ seeks to transform the ungodly structures of society to become subject to the reign of God.[42] This is vital to Newbigin's theology as well,[43] and it must be too the missional disciple's.

Four Views of God and Christ in John

The speaking of Jesus' name is a speaking into the very nature of Jesus as the revealer of the Father's heart, in terms of John's portrayal of it. The name of Jesus means Yahweh saves. It also takes on the special sense of being a revelation of what Yahweh the Father of Israel is like. There are four visions of what the Father is like in the gospel. The first is the one the writer of the gospel provides, in his well-known theological narrative theology. The second is based on what Jesus reports about himself and the Father. The third is based on what his contemporaries that did not believe in him had to say. The fourth is what the disciples discovered about him. In this latter instance, their discoveries tell us much about how we might understand the claims of Christ on us as his followers.

1. John's Vision of Jesus

> The law was given by Moses; grace and truth came through Jesus Christ.[44]

There seems to be a deliberate dichotomy intended by John regarding the difference between the Christ event and the giving of the law through Moses. It might be called a dialectical tension. Moses' law does not give access to the interpretation of the Father's heart. It provides a legal and ritual definition of what is required to follow Yahweh. Until the appearance of the Logos, who gave the law to Moses,[45] there is only a partial revelation of what God is like. The legal and ritual definitions have become highly traditionalized by the time of Jesus. This may have also been true of the Jewish community that moved from Judea to Galilee after the destruction of the temple in 70 CE. There seems to have been a rift in fellowship between

---

41. Bevans, *Models of Contextual Theology*, 117–38.
42. Ibid.
43. Ibid., 117.
44. John 1:17 NIV.
45. John 8:58.

a more traditionalized Jewish group, and the charismatic, grace-focused community of the Johannine churches, that saw Jesus as a revelation of the Father's heart. The law described here may be particularly focused on the Shema, as a main creedal statement of the Hebrew faith.[46]

It forbade the worship of more than one God. The Shema is still considered today by Orthodox Jews to be the central creedal statement of the Torah. It could be that John intended to draw a distinction between how Shema-focused Jews that had left the church, and those who embraced Jesus as divine, interpreted what Christ had revealed about the Father and his special relationship with him. Those that left the church may have done so in protest over the divine Logos Christology of the Johannine church. A strong legalistic adherence to the Shema, as the creed of the Deuteronomic Torah, may have caused a group to align themselves against the view of Christ—the divine Son sent by his Father.

Hence the term AntiChrist[47] may apply to those who deny the divine Logos Christology of the Johannine church. This view may be further established as credible, as directly following verses 16–17, John completes the Johannine churches' creed, declaring:

> No-one has ever seen God, but God the One and Only, who is at
> the Father's side, has made him known.[48]

Christ provides "grace" and "truth" as a message directly from the "Father's heart." Antichrist sets another view instead of the divine Logos Christology in place, i.e., that Christ is some kind of embodiment of a knowledge sent from the Father about God, but he himself is not divine. It is possible an Angel Christology may be implied here. We know that there was speculation in Jewish apocalyptic of this type. The book of Hebrews in chapter 1 addresses this kind of view probably held by some early Jewish messianic believers. This would fit well with an adoptionist view of Christ that scholars like James Dunn has averred—and in some similar sense was formulated by Arius in the early fourth century. In these schemes of thought Jesus is somehow adopted by God, as his special agent before he entered the world, or by the divine voice at his baptism in the Jordan. In contrast John declares Christ to be divine.

Christ the bringer of grace and truth replaces the law and its rituals and festivals, indeed its temple and its cultus—by virtue of Christ being the center of God's revelation, the temple is no longer to be the focal point of

---

46. Deut 6:4.

47. 1 John 2:18.

48. John 1:18 NIV.

God's presence.[49] We find this brought to the foreground in John chapter 2. Christ is the grand telos of the temple and its cultus.

God is now to be interpreted in the light of Christ's life, death, resurrection, and presence at the Father's side in heaven. Of particular significance is John chapter 8, in which Jesus reveals his true identity to the religious authorities. Christ is none other than the "I Am" that Moses met at the burning bush.[50] According to Blomberg this has been challenged in recent studies that have demonstrated that after 70 CE, angels and exalted humans could be associated in this manner, not just God. However, this is a contemporary scholarly assessment rather than a historic one, in terms of other opinion.[51] Christ is the Lord that gave the law to Moses their forebear. Yet the Jewish authorities do not know him. They interpret the Hebrew Scriptures wrongly. Jesus shockingly declares that their interpretation of the words of Moses come from "their father the devil."[52] He declares that Moses wrote about him, but this has been missed by adopting a wrong hermeneutic, that does not recognize Christ as the Son of Yahweh in Israel's ancient Scriptures. This claim is considered blasphemous. The Jews pick up stones to kill him.[53] Their Shema theology has failed to embrace the revelation of the Father's heart provided for them—through Christ the hermeneutic of it.

Christ interprets what God is like as a communion between himself and the Father. It includes the Spirit as the one who advocates on behalf of Christ, so that Jesus might be universally present with all who believe after his departure back to the Father.[54] The community that Jesus founds is based on his followers knowing the truth about what God is like, as well as receiving his free gift of grace—providing them with eternal access to live with the Father and as part of his family.[55]

---

49. The book of Hebrews testifies to this trajectory in New Testament thought, which arguably John's gospel also resonates with. See on Heb 9:23–26.

50. Exod 3:1–8.

51. Blomberg, *Historical Reliability of John's Gospel*, 149; Barrett considers there is no relationship here to Exod 3:14 (*Gospel according to St. John*, 352); Brown clearly agrees with more contemporary assessments of John's divine name appellation of Jesus in John to himself (*Gospel according to John I–XII*, 366–67). Both authors agree that a postmodern assessment has to be open to the authenticity of this testimony.

52. John 8:44.

53. John 8:59.

54. John 14:18–27; Smith, *New Testament Theology*, 139–46.

55. John 17:3; Morris, *Gospel according to John*, 719–20.

2. Jesus' Self-Consciousness

We have related what Jesus says about himself in the passage in John chapter 8. There is more yet to be disclosed. Jesus only does what he sees his Father doing.[56] He provides a model for his followers to do what he as their Lord does.[57] Nowhere more clearly do we see a startling picture of what Christ and his Father are like than in John chapter 13. The Lord washes his disciple's feet. He then tells them that they are to follow his example. The correspondence between what this passage reveals about the nature of the Father and Son and chapter 14 is vital to grasp.

Christ informs Philip that to have seen him is to know what the Father is like.[58] It requires that we correlate this insight with the picture of God provided by Christ as he performs the task of the servant in John chapter 13. Christ may be claimed to portray the Father as the one that serves creation. God's power is not based on the exercise of totalitarian dictatorship but on the act of sacrificial humility and love. This quality of God's self-giving nature may be considered a definition of how the Father, Son, and Spirit live in relationship together and toward their creation. Gift-love and sacrifice define how they live in union as persons joined in the one being of God.

The disciples are called to become "one" even as Father and Son live in such a union. It may be termed a model of the experience that Christ wants his followers to share. This seems to be suggested by what Christ is reported to have said at the end of chapter 13. It would be by the examples of the disciple's mutual love for one another that the world would know they were his followers.[59] Jesus is conscious of who he is and what his Father is like. He self-consciously models his union with the Father to his disciples in the act of foot-washing. The blessing of the paschal meal is part of the blessing of salvation and eternal life, that will be derived from the sacrifice of the God of the cross.

Jesus invites his followers to model their community on the same kind of sacrificial gift-love that defines God's loves for creation—as an active process of sacrificial service that gifts creation with abundance of life.

Jesus' self-conscious knowledge of the Father is important to understand. The Greek word for "to know" (*ginosko*)[60] relates to experiential knowledge. It does not relate to rational knowledge. Jesus has an ongoing intimate

---

56. John 5:19.
57. John 13:12–15.
58. John 14:7–9.
59. John 13:34, 35; Ryle, *John*, 263–66.
60. Kittel, *Theological Dictionary of the New Testament*, s.v. "ginosko" (689–714).

experience with his Father with whom he is in constant communion. His Father does not rest on the Sabbath and neither does the Son.[61] Jesus does all the Father is doing. He also communicates all that the Father has sent him to do to those who will listen.[62] The disciples are also to experience a knowledge of God that comes from an intimate open connection with God through his Spirit. The Spirit is to be Christ's representative after his departure.[63]

Just as the Father and Son are one, so are the disciples to become one in them.[64] That is, they are to become intimately connected as children of God in the Trinitarian family through the Spirit.[65] The Spirit will provide them with ongoing access to revelations of the Father's will for them to participate in.[66] The Spirit is sent to be the helper at their sides, as well as their intimate inner friend and connection to Father and Son.[67] This speaks to the deep intimacy that Christ has called for his followers to enjoy. We are to have a close bond with God, something like that enjoyed by Christ with the Father and Spirit. Christ the God-man connects humanity to God and God to humanity. It is portrayed in John as a deep mysterious connection which Jesus likens to his own relationship with the Father.[68]

Without this close experiential bond of revelation knowledge, the Christian missional community will be unable to really shape any disciples to become like Christ. We can only follow a Jesus who is pneumatologically present. The church cannot manufacture that for itself. John's churches did not manufacture it. The gospel seems to have been written for churches that enjoyed a deep intimate oneness through the agency of the Spirit with the risen Lord.[69] First John informs us that they had a spiritual charism that taught them all things.[70] We too need that charism. Jesus promises he

61. John 5:17.

62. John 17:1–5.

63. John 16:12–15.

64. John 17:21.

65. John 14:25–31.

66. John 16:12–15.

67. John 14:25.

68. John 17:1–5.

69. I make this suggestion based on the theological expectations set out in the words of Jesus in John 17 where oneness like that between Father and Son is to be enjoyed by the disciples. Moreover, this is to be correlated to the promise of the Spirit and Father and Son coming to make their home in the hearts of disciples and in their discipleship formation communities—see John 14:23.

70. It is likely that the First Epistle of John was sent to the church close to the time that the gospel was written. First John 2:27 has this to say about the Spirit's work in the believer's life practices in the Johannine churches.

will continue to communicate with his followers through the Spirit as need arises.[71] Jesus self-consciousness as the Son of God was based on an intimate experiential connection with his Father.[72] His contemporary disciples may too experience a similar knowledge which includes assurance that they belong to the Father's family.

In John 17, Jesus' own close relationship with his Father is brought to particular focus. This important chapter helps us to understand the deep intimate bond that exists between the persons of the Trinity.[73] Even more amazingly, it seems this chapter was provided by John to help followers to appreciate that they are to be a deep, meaningful part of the divine family. We are to experience the oneness of a similar intimacy that Jesus the God-man has with his Father. This may be considered part of the intimate self-understanding that the Johannine churches enjoyed as part of the horizon of their Christian communal life experiences.

3. The View of the Ruling Religious Dynasty

Clearly the divinity of Christ, although assumed in the gospel, was not accepted by Jewish leaders nor probably realized by the disciples during Jesus' ministry. It is highly unlikely that the "beloved disciple," as a key source and witness for the later gospel redaction, would have considered Jesus divine in the time of his earthly ministry. John weaves this fact into his narrative in the light of those Jews who have probably left his churches, due to rejecting a divine Logos Christology. In other words, contents in the gospel were included to meet the needs of believers in the Johannine churches. It has been claimed, quite understandably by Jewish people, that John's gospel seems to be anti-Semitic in nature. It may have been used historically at times to favor a hostile view of Jewish people. However, it is not accurate to suggest that all Jews in John's gospel are treated with hostility, nor that the gospel is anti-Semitic. To begin with, Jesus and his disciples are clearly identified as

---

71. John 16:12–14.

72. John 5:19, 20.

73. A critique that some theologians make of John's gospel is that it does not have a fully developed Trinitarian theology. Some argue that it is rather based on a binatarian theology. It is true that the relationship between Christ and the Father are most clearly brought to light in the gospel, but the Spirit is also given its own personal identity, described in John 4:20–26 where it is said "God is Spirit." Moreover, the Spirit is described as Counselor in John 14. There is a tri-personal language in the gospel but it is not developed in a systematic way such as one might find in the later church councils.

Jews.[74] Jesus is called Rabbi.[75] The Baptist declares Jesus to be the Lamb of God, who will "take away the sins of the world."[76] This is a Jewish symbolism. So who are the Jews that resist Jesus and his ministry?

It seems they are quite often identified with the Pharisees (e.g., John 9). In John the Pharisees seem to be taking over Judaism, which is quite unlike their portrayal in the Synoptic tradition. Pharisees are powerful and influential enough to exercise authority over other Jews in John's gospel. They are called "rulers" or "officials" of the synagogues. They are able to cast out the blind man healed by Christ from the synagogue and to intimidate his parents to deny knowledge of his healing or original condition as a blind man.[77] Once more this is not the picture provided of them in the other gospels. They have the authority to expel those who profess Jesus from the synagogues. To some large extent it seems that John's gospel does not mean to vilify the Jewish nation, but rather to demonstrate a failing on the part of the leaders in Judea to recognize Jesus as the Messiah. This speaks volumes related to the historical situation of the Johannine church as well. They had been probably expelled from the synagogues in Galilee by a strict Pharisaic party following the Council of Jamnia. The appellation of "Jew" does not always equate with a negative image of the Jewish people, or the followers of Christ in John. However, it is important to note that John is careful not to call Galileans or Samaritans "Jews."[78] Not all Pharisees were treated with the same negativity in the gospel. Smith comments:

> Thus Jesus, his followers, Galileans, and perhaps Samaritans are Jewish, but they are not "the Jews." There are also people explicitly called "Jews" who are not enemies of Jesus. Prominent among them is Nicodemus, a ruler of the Jews (3:1), who keeps coming back to Jesus, speaks for him (7:50), and helps bury him (19:39). . . . The people who mourn Lazarus with Mary and Martha are said to be Jews, although they also are not hostile to Jesus. Moreover, throughout John's Gospel "Israel" and "Israelite" are used in a positive sense. Thus Nathanael can be called "truly an Israelite in whom there is no guile" (1:47) and Jesus is hailed as "king of Israel" (1:49), a title whose entirely positive

74. The fact that John the Baptist a Jew points to Jesus as the Lamb of God is testament enough to this thesis. And Jesus' response to Nathanael that he is a true son of Israel is yet another. See John 1.

75. John 20:16.

76. John 1:29–34.

77. John 9:13.

78. See ch. 6 in John's gospel.

connotations contrast with "king of the Jews," which has a negative and sarcastic ring on the lips of Romans (e.g., 19:3).[79]

What is it that the resistant rulers do not believe regarding Jesus? First,
they do not believe in Jesus' messianic claims, that figure prominently in the
gospel.[80] Jesus is cautious and unwilling to declare his identity in the Synoptic Gospels, but in John he often defends it in roundabout ways. Second,
the rulers recognize his claims of a seeming equality with God, which they
resist and accuse him of blasphemy for. We never find Jesus making such
bold claims in the Synoptic Gospels. Third, they do not accept that he is
the prophet to come predicted by Moses. In this case the question is raised
with John the Baptist regarding his own identity. He clearly states he is not
the Messiah or the prophet like Moses who is expected to come.[81] Fourth,
and similarly to the second point, the Jewish rulers and importantly chief
priests, insist that Jesus must be crucified because he claimed to be the "Son
of God."[82] The fact that the "chief priests" who represent the temple cultus
call for Jesus' execution is important. It is they that perform the rites of the
temple that Jesus is about to surpass as the Lamb of God.

There is a strong post-temple theology in the gospel, as Christ is now
considered the advocate at the Father's side in the heavenly temple. The gospel
is clearly written after 70 CE. This makes the advocatory role of the Spirit of
immense importance to disciples, as it is the Spirit who mediates and communicates between the disciples on earth and the heavenly Christ at the Father's
side. Hence guidance on the mission of Jesus is to be obtained by disciples
discerning what the Spirit mediates to them, to inform their understanding
of their mission in participation with Jesus. Ironically the plaque placed over
Christ's head on the cross declares the culmination of the mission Christ has
been sent to complete, "Jesus of Nazareth, the King of the Jews."[83]

Christ has redefined the concept of Messiah to make him the divine-
man. He is, therefore, the fulfillment of God's plan to save the whole world
through the Jewish nation, and with this culminated view in mind, the Jews
will no longer be the agency, the nation, for global salvation. Now missional
disciples will be the new Israel. This is confirmed earlier in John's gospel to
be part of the Johannine theology, as Jesus declares to the Samaritan woman

79. Smith, "Judaism and the Gospel of John," in Charlesworth, *Jews and Christians*,
76–96.

80. John 8:48.

81. John 1:19–28.

82. John 19:7.

83. John 19:19 NIV.

that salvation "is through the Jews."[84] In Jesus' death the temple is no longer the focal point of God's soteriological and atoning activity—from now on people can worship God in "Spirit and truth" anywhere and at any time based on Jesus the Messiah's provision of access to the Father's heart of love and compassion.[85]

The negative appraisal that John associated with Jewish religious leaders distinguishes Jews in general from Jewish authorities. It is interesting that the Pharisees are most commonly associated with resistance to Jesus in the gospel.[86] It is likely that those who left the Johannine church were Pharisees and those influenced by them.

Hurtado goes further, suggesting that at one point the Johannine Christians were accepted by Jewish leaders of synagogues resident in Galilee after the destruction of the temple. However, as Johannine Jewish Christians became more convinced about Jesus' divinity, they had probably been painfully expelled from the synagogues.[87] Hence those followers who embraced the divine Logos Christology paid a heavy price by being expelled from among those who did not share the same kind of high Christology that they did. It may be said that disciples after Christendom find themselves on the margins of a society that does not believe in the divine Christ. Such claims will often be greeted with skepticism. However, the Gospel of John passionately avows the divine God-man, and in the light of his claims on the disciple's lives there is much to be learned in the contemporary situation.

4. Individual Disciples

A whole book in its own right could be produced to do justice to all the individual encounters of persons with Jesus in John's gospel. Each of the narrative accounts bring to existential consciousness something about the nature of discipleship and what it asks of us. John's gospel seeks to drill deep into our consciousness. It beckons us to reflect on how Christ seeks to transform different aspects of our psyches. It would be to do an injustice to the gospel to try to simply take a shallow look at each instance where Jesus communicated something of importance to individual disciples. Hence two instances will be considered. That of Jesus' mother and the story of the woman at the well. We will get much more out of deeper reflection on these two stories than shorter

84. John 4:22.
85. John 4:21–25.
86. See on John 6, 7, and 8.
87. Hurtado, *Lord Jesus Christ*, 402–7.

consideration of more. However, here in brief, are the individual snapshots John provides us with of individuals who met with Jesus:

- Andrew and Peter: John 1:35–42;
- Philip and Nathanael: John 1:43–51;
- Jesus' Mother: John 2:1–11;
- Nicodemus: John 3:1–15;
- A woman at a well: John 4:1–26;
- An official: John 4:46–54;
- Peter: John 6:60–65;
- An adulterous woman: John 8:1–11;
- A blind man: John 9;
- Mary and Martha: John 11:1–37;
- Pilate: John 19:9–11;
- Mary Magdalene: John 20:1–18;
- Thomas: John 20:24–29; and
- Peter: John 21:15–23.

4a. Jesus' Mother

John 2:1–12 represents the first instance where a woman comes into the gospel story. Mary and Jesus are at a wedding in Cana of Galilee. Mary has probably kept high hopes in her heart that Jesus would soon embrace his destiny (my assumption). The story assumes that she knows that her son has the ability to do remarkable things. She would not have drawn his attention to the lack of wine at the feast otherwise. Jesus response that his "hour" has not yet come also presupposes that there has been more than a limited self-consciousness of his special life purpose, assumed at least in the narrative world of the gospel. The story seems to suggest that mother and son have communicated about his mission previously. Of course this is a narrative construction, but it is not without plausibility to have been historically factual.

The way Jesus addresses his mother is rather strange. He calls her "woman"[88] as he did the woman at the well.[89] This is unusual in terms of the

88. John 2:4.
89. John 4:21.

customs of the period. A good son would normally address his parent with the respectful title "mother" or "father." Perhaps John is suggesting a turning point in Mary's and Jesus' self-consciousness here. Perhaps Christ now wishes to help his mother make the conscious transition from being his mother and guardian, toward helping her to see herself afresh as one of his disciples.

There is an important angle to the transition that Mary has to make in terms of how she regards Jesus, which as a narrative artifact is interesting to observe. John is potentially addressing a similar transition that occurred in the Johannine church, where some regarded Jesus as fully divine, whereas others had not reached that conclusion. There was a change in perspective in the community that is probably mirrored in Mary's change in outlook. Paul wrote to the Corinthians about a similar change in perspective that he had experienced (and that all of us may experience):

> From now on, therefore, we regard no one from a human point of view; even though we once regarded Christ from a human point of view, we regard him thus no longer.[90]

The hermeneutical horizon for how Mary regarded her son was being transformed. She was to go through a process of moving from seeing herself as his mother to coming to consider herself to be one of his followers. This would be a journey for her, no doubt. He was to become for her the divine Son of the heavenly Father. She needed to transition from seeing him as a man of the earth to being God's one and only Son. The Johannine church had likewise been through this sort of transition.

In terms of disciples after Christendom, we must do more than simply see Jesus as a man that lived a good, if not perfect, life. He is the Son of God. He has ultimate claims on our lives. A challenge faced post-Christendom is that we live in a secular culture that has a focus on the individual, i.e., "me first." This is a very anthropocentric view of human nature. The danger of this kind of individual humanism is that we estimate Christ to be our equal, a man like us rather than God and therefore our Lord.

Contemporary disciples may be encouraged to have a change in the ways they interpret the meaning of Christ to their lives. Like Mary, his earthly mother, we need to come to see him from a divine perspective rather than an earthly one. The Johannine churches also needed to make this transition. Mary had probably long meditated on what it meant that she would give birth to one who was to be called "the Son of God" (my view).[91] Mary's faith was

---

90. 2 Cor 5:16 RSV.
91. Luke 2:19.

being heightened and transformed in readiness to embrace the son born of her as her God. Mary clearly had faith in her son's abilities (my view).

In John's narrative framework she instructs the attendants at the wedding banquet to do whatever he "tells you."[92] The miracle of the water turned into wine represents the transition where Jesus enters into his ministry. This is the first sign he performs that causes his disciples to believe in him.[93] It also helps his mother to model what those close to Jesus, that is his followers, will do. They, like Mary, put their faith in him to do what needs to be done in order to intervene in the human situation—so as to transform it. Mary's instructions to the attendants were an act of faith. Mary models faith in the divine Son of the heavenly Father, beginning to make her own psychological adjustment (my view) to now see herself as one of his faithful followers. It is Mary's faith that triggers Jesus to exercise his divine power to perform this first miracle of transformation.

This miracle has sacramental significance. The miracle of wine may represent the blood of the covenant which Christ is to spill on Calvary. This is reinforced by the blood and water which pours from his side pierced by a soldier when Jesus was on the cross.[94] It is interesting how his mother appears again at the cross to witness these things, as another narrative construction.[95] The wedding banquet may also more broadly represent the bride of Christ and his people, who will drink this new wine and declare it better than any served or experienced before. Each of these narrative artifacts may be deliberate attempts by the writer of the gospel to make theological inferences.

Such is the quality of the God-man's sacrifice. In symbolic terms, John may be making a play on the wedding feast as a representation of the messianic banquet, which popular Jewish apocalyptic represented would take place when the Messiah restored the kingdom to Israel.[96]

Jesus declared to Mary, at the wedding feast, that his hour had not yet come and for the messianic banquet to begin. Later in the gospel she reappears with him at the cross. The cross is considered pivotal in John's theology. It reveals the love of Father and Son in action as the Son completes

92. John 2:5.

93. John 2:11.

94. John 19:34.

95. John 19:27.

96. See the summary of Pope Francis's general audience, June 8, 2016, https://press.vatican.va/content/salastampa/en/bollettino/pubblico/2016/06/08/160608c.html;   in this summary bulletin the Vatican press discusses the relationship of John's use of the wedding feast in Cana as a typology for the messianic banquet.

the divine mission he has been sent to achieve.[97] John comments that Jesus knew all things were now finished. The plan of God to save the world was ready to be resoundingly completed.[98] Mary stands with her mother's sister, Mary wife of Clopas, Mary Magdalene, as well as the beloved disciple at the foot of the cross.[99] She is present to witness the far larger miracle of the death of Christ that completes the work given to him by his Father.

The miracle of water transformed into wine is contrasted with the miracle of the atonement. Blood (symbolized by wine at the wedding) pours from his side, with water, when the Roman soldier pierces his side. His blood transforms ordinary human life (water) into refreshing and life-giving wine. Those who stand with the crucified God-man are these women and this one man, who the gospel writer claims Jesus loved.[100] Indeed the source for the witness of the gospel is that beloved disciple, we are told at the end of the gospel narratives.[101]

The cross is the most intimate moment of life. It envisions the departure of the one brought to life from the womb of Mary. She stands at the cross to witness the end of the power of death, by virtue of the life-giving grace of the Son of God. He must die in order to rise again and bring to birth new life. Soon Christ will emerge from the womb of the tomb in resurrection life, bringing to birth eternal hope and eternal life for his followers. One of the Marys, Mary Magdalene, witnesses the resurrected God-man, who has emerged from the womb of the tomb (Mary Magdalene is reminiscent of Jesus' mother in name), to bring to birth the new future he has won for all of his followers.[102] Birth is an intimate experience that means pain. Pain and suffering for the Son leads to joy. Jesus declared to his disciples that they would experience pain and sorrow at his departure. They would later find joy with his resurrection and the coming of his Spirit—making him a deep, intimate part of their lives.[103]

Christ has an intimate relationship with his followers. It was three women and one male who were closest to his heart during the last hours of his existence. They did not abandon him in his darkest hour. Jesus gave his earthly mother, now one of his disciples, into the care of his beloved

97. John 17:1–5.
98. John 19:28.
99. John 19:25–27.
100. John 19:26.
101. John 21:20–24.
102. John 20:11–18.
103. John 16:16–24.

disciple—John.[104] Jesus loved to the last, but in order to complete his mission he must now return to the Father in heaven, leaving his earthly mother in the care of John. In essence she represents all followers who Jesus gives into the caring hands of each other in the Christian faith community.

He came from the Father's heart and made it known. Now he returns to that intimacy, so that his followers might receive another helper who will be with them and will dwell in each of them "forever" and will be at the center of the Trinity-shaped community of followers on earth.[105] It is as if John means us to understand that intimacy with the Father is to be obtained by being close to the sacrificial heart of Jesus. Only by Jesus returning to the Father may that intimate connection be made by the coming of the universal Spirit of God into each heart and as the binding force of love in the Christian missional community.[106]

Hence all may be one with the risen Lord. Jesus informs Mary Magdalene, as she clings onto his ankles after his resurrection, that it was imperative she let him go so that he might return to his Father.[107] Disciples after Christendom are called to have deep intimacy with the God of the cross and with one another as they model that same love as togetherness in a community shaped by the Triune family's love. It is on the cross that the heart of God is revealed for all to behold. It is in the resurrection that they are transformed to become heirs of eternal life.[108]

The Father is in Jesus, revealing his passionate love for the world for which he has given his only Son as a gift.[109] He means that every reader should reflect long and hard on what the sacrifice of the God of the cross means to the way his followers should live as a community and in terms of how they share that love with those who they seek to disciple. Those closest to Jesus gather around the cross. How do we evaluate our relationship with Christ? How well do we know him? What is the level of our intimacy with him? We do not find the other disciples at the cross. However, we find Nicodemus and Joseph of Arimathea, secretly for fear of the authorities, requesting to take his body in the darkness of the night to a tomb.[110] The love of the women, and the beloved disciple for Jesus, makes them fearless as they stand alongside him for all passing by to behold.

---

104. John 19:25–27.
105. John 16:7.
106. John 16:7.
107. John 20:17.
108. John 5:24.
109. John 3:16.
110. John 19:38–41.

Another contrast to be found in the crucifixion narrative is between the Jews who require Pilate to crucify Jesus and the love of Mary and the others. The Jewish authorities declare to Pilate, "We have a law, and by that law he ought to die, because he has made himself the Son of God."[111]

The Shema declares God to be one God. The law of Moses demands that those who worship idols be put to death.[112] Has not this man Jesus made himself more than an idol, by claiming to be the divine Son of God? John possibly draws a contrast here between the Shema hermeneutic of the authorities, who have rejected the divine Christ based on their interpretation of it, and the women and man at the cross who embrace his act of love and grace.

The contrast may be between legalistic adherence to a way of life, compared to the revelation of Christ's intimate relationship with the Father. Once more, John may be replaying the difference between the hermeneutical horizons of those who seek to keep the law of Moses compared to those inspired by the grace and truth that comes through Christ. Perhaps John seeks to declare that the community of authentic disciples is to be shaped around the vulnerability of the God of the cross, who gives up all in his self-sacrifice to save a fallen humanity. Jesus declared to the disciples after the Paschal meal:

> A new commandment I give you, that you love one another;
> even as I have loved you, that you also love one another. By this
> all men will know that you are my disciples, if you have love for
> one another.[113]

Missional churches that shape disciples need to share an intimate love with Christ and one another, based on the vision of the heart of Christ's sacrificial love for the Father and them. It is a Trinitarian love, that is shared by Father, Son, and Spirit—brought to life and sustained in a community that shapes itself based on the presence of that love in their midst through the Spirit of Christ.[114] Missional disciples must no longer regard Christ from a human point of view. He is their Lord and the source of their mission. It is Christ's reign that they live under, and to which they point people to embrace. It will be the quality of the love inspired by the presence of the Spirit between people, in the missional church, that will cause contemporary disciples to care for each other deeply. It will inevitably have a magnetic effect. Jesus declared:

---

111. John 19:7 RSV.

112. Lev 20:1–5.

113. John 13:34, 35 RSV.

114. Hastings, *Missional God, Missional Church*, 293–306.

"And I, when I am lifted up from the earth, will draw all men to myself." He said this to show by what death he was to die.[115]

One important way others see Christ lifted up is in his followers living sacrificially and graciously together. The missional church that disciples people effectively is one where the love dance of the Trinity family[116] is acted out by the Christian community. Christ informed his disciples that this can only happen if he was present among them through the Holy Spirit as his representative.[117] This will be evident when it happens. It will cause people to seek to consider becoming part of this alternative society, modeled by God's people.

Late modern youth, and young adults, are highly attracted to small, genuinely caring communities, where people authentically care about each other (see chapter 8 for more background). They need to belong to a group for a long time before they believe its truths. People need to really feel they genuinely belong and are authentically cared for, often for quite a while, before they start to experiment with putting their trust in Christ. The strength of a missional community that is small is that it will be possible to invest in small numbers of those who want to explore the presence of God. John's gospel invests not so much in crowds as in an emphasis on Jesus' teaching ministry; it highlights the importance of the few and the individuals Jesus interacted with. There is much to be gained from reflecting on his mother and what she can reveal about her Lord. The small band gathered at the foot of the cross represents those who come closest to the heart of the Father revealed through Jesus.

4b. A Woman at a Well

The longest recorded interaction in John with an individual is to be found in John 4:1–26. This is important to recognize, as it is a Samaritan woman who had a triple injunction on her life—when it came to Jewish men interacting with her. She was a woman that no self-respecting Jewish male would be seen alone with in public. She was a Samaritan that Jews considered outcast from Israel's covenant promises. She was also associated with loose morals, having had five previous relationships with men and now living with one who was not her husband.[118] Jesus crosses three boundaries in this story,

---

115. John 12:32–33 RSV.

116. Hardy, *Pictures of God*, 178–83.

117. John 17:20–26; ibid., 190–218; 268–92.

118. John 4:16–18.

meeting this woman who was on the extreme margins of Jewish toleration. She would not have been permitted any kind of approach to a devoted Jewish male in this period. She is outcast in terms of the culture of the period. Yet Jesus offers her respect and acceptance by talking to her.

There is yet another angle to this narrative. Some notable marriage arrangements in biblical literature begin with a meeting by a well. This is the case with Isaac and Rebekah,[119] Jacob and Rachel,[120] and Moses and Zipporah.[121] There is the possibility that John is making an important theological statement about Jesus here. He may be portrayed as the bridegroom of the new Israel that includes the Samaritans and the Gentile world in the messianic banquet mentioned earlier. This is further strengthened because Jesus tells the woman that the temple on Mount Zion, and the Samaritan temple on Mount Gerazim will from now on not be the location of worship of Yahweh.[122] A new event horizon has occurred. The new horizon of human encounter with God will be possible at any time and in any place, without the need to go to a temple or a priest to represent human interactions with God. The Spirit of Christ is from now on to be at work among all nations, tongues, and peoples—by implication. The argument has been made that the Samaritan woman is actually a metaphorical representation of Samaria's historic flirtation with numerous gods.[123] In this case, it is as if John is saying that from now on the Samaritans have been redeemed and included to be God's one true people. This is further reinforced by the fact that this woman is the only person in the gospel narratives who is directly told by the Lord that he is the Messiah.[124] Jesus honors her above any other disciple, except Peter, who in the Synoptic tradition at Caesarea Philippi recognized that Jesus is the Christ.[125]

There is an interesting contrast in this story to that of contemporary disciples. The woman is publicly known by her peers to be a person of loose morals. She has not been able to hide it from them. She certainly cannot hide from the all-seeing eye of the Lord. In order for her to be refreshed by the living water on offer, she must first recognize her situation and change her life. In terms of our present Western secular situation, people are able to privately pursue their lives for the most part without public knowledge or censure for their sins. It is possible to hide them from our peers because of our private

119. Gen 24:10–51.
120. Gen 29:1–14.
121. Exod 2:15–22.
122. John 4:19–26.
123. 2 Kgs 17:29–34.
124. John 4:26.
125. Matt 16:16.

lives. Late modern Christians enjoy the privacy and secrecy of their private homes. The challenge of this story is that the God who calls us to follow him reaches into these private spaces and calls us to leave behind those things that have become replacements for the Lord. Jesus declares to the woman:

> But the hour is coming, and is now here, when the true worshipers will worship the Father in Spirit and truth, for the Father seeks such as these to worship him.[126]

How might we understand this saying? It could be interpreted to mean that in order for God's Spirit really to transform us, we have to be willing to allow him access to all the inner rooms of our souls, shining his light into each nook and cranny.

The goal is to remove all that is not holy or pure. In other words, we need to honestly seek the Lord, asking him to reveal those things that need to be brought to wholeness in us, which will include disposing of the detritus of our sins. Worship has to do with the things we attach worth to. The question is, do we attach more worth to things, friends, lovers, or our jobs than we do to Christ? The story of this woman demonstrates Christ's intentional respect for her and her situation. He is not there to judge but to heal and restore her and the Samaritan people, who follow in her footsteps. In this story, based on her personal testimony, the Samaritans come to meet the Lord:

> Many Samaritans from that city believed in him because of the woman's testimony, "He told me everything I have ever done." So when the Samaritans came to him, they asked him to stay with them; and he stayed there two days. And many more believed because of his word. They said to the woman, "It is no longer because of what you said that we believe, for we have heard for ourselves, and we know that this is truly the Savior of the world."[127]

The narrative of Jesus' mission to Samaria also has much to add to the theology of the universal presence of God's Spirit, true of the post-Pentecost church. Sheldrake makes some essential observations about the Trinitarian and incarnational importance of how Jesus called his disciples to fresh places, to find and bring the catholic (universal) presence of God there:

> Our reflection on catholicity moves from God as Trinity to the Church and world through the medium of Christology. The catholic "space" that is shaped by God-as-Trinity finds expression in our time and space through the incarnation. Thus, the focus of catholicity in space and time, without which it remains

126. John 4:23 NRSV.
127. John 4:39–42 NRSV.

insubstantial and diffuse, is the person of Jesus Christ as the living fullness of God. In Christ, "the whole fullness of deity dwells bodily, and you have come to fullness in him, who is the head of every ruler and authority" (Col. 2:9–10). And "From his fullness we have all received, grace upon grace" (John 1:16).

In so far as the catholicity of God is mediated through Jesus Christ, it is important to note in reference to the New Testament that an important feature of Jesus' practice was to push people, not least those closest to him, away from familiar places into locations they found disturbing. To put it another way, the actions of Jesus redefined the nature of what was "centre." He regularly moved beyond exclusiveness of the traditional Jewish land to reach Gentiles in outlying areas. So, for example, there is a suggestion of tough words being needed to force reluctant disciples into the boat to cross to Gentile Bethsaida in Mark 6:45. It is in places on the edge, and among those considered God-forsaken by many of his contemporaries, that Jesus knew his identity as Messiah must be revealed. He healed the demoniac on the East Coast of the Sea of Galilee in the land of the Gerasenes (Luke 8:26–39). He crossed into Tyre and Sidon to heal the daughter of a Syro-Phoenician woman and to commend her faith (Matt. 15:21–28). He healed in the Decapolis. In Mark 8:1–10 he fed a multitude on the eastern or non-Jewish side of the lake. "Ever dragging his disciples away from the familiarity of home, he declares present the power of the kingdom in the alien landscapes of another land."[128]

The interaction with the Samaritan woman, and the response of her peers to Christ, demonstrates how Jesus treats those on the margins with great respect. He enters incarnationally into their territory as the universal reign of God begins to break in. The woman is an unlikely gatekeeper for this Samaritan community. Her testimony leads to a mass response by her peers. Disciples after Christendom need to keep on pushing the boundaries of the places they seek to incarnate in, as the mobile missional body of Christ in fresh places and spaces.

Conclusions

The Gospel of John aligns women and men as equals in the body of Christ. In terms of Free Church Ecclesiology, we would suggest that the Christian community, like that of John, is built on the intimacy of Father, Son, and Spirit with their children. Individuals were shaped by the Lord on an

128. Sheldrake, *Spaces for the Sacred*, 68–69.

intimate level personally and in communion in Christian communities. It was also to be through their relationships with each other that disciples were to be shaped by one another. The Spirit of the Trinity shaped this ancient Johannine community of women and men to live united in their diversity. They each shared mysteriously in the love dance of a similar perichoresis of the Godhead in some way.[129] It may be suggested that in the Johannine churches, there was a positive expectation of intimacy of believers with their God and one another. There was a breathing in and out of the fresh breath of the divine fellowship, modeled by Christ's relationship with his Father in this gospel's narratives. In a similar way believers in the Johannine churches were potentially encouraged to treat each other with a mutual love—based on their experience of communion with their God. Jenson has helped develop what is known as communio ecclesiology. It is important to understand what it is, as it relates well to the Johannine theology of discipleship formation as a communal activity. Cary explains it:

> Communio ecclesiology asserts that the foundation, model, and goal of the church's communion (koinonia) is the koinonia of the triune life. Since participation in the Trinitarian life is at the root of communio ecclesiology.[130]

This type of "communio ecclesiology" is interestingly implied in Niemandt's missional ecclesiology:

> Mission begins in the heart of the Triune God. . . . Mission is an extension and amplification of God's very being. Missional theology builds on the understanding that God is Trinity and missional. Mission is participation in the life of God. It is to be caught up within the dynamic sending and being sent that God the Holy Trinity has done and continues to do.[131]

Missional disciples after Christendom may encourage each other to be shaped in churches somewhat like those of the Johannine churches. "Communio ecclesiology" is a form of missional ecclesiology that links every disciple of the kingdom to the Trinitarian family and its reign in their lives. Missional churches should clearly engage in the Trinitarian communion in order to be able to be inspired, motivated, and guided by the heartthrob of God's love for the world. Missional churches need to view themselves as agencies that send out every believer to participate in the Triune mission in what they do in their everyday lives.

129. Hardy, *Pictures of God*, 184–207.
130. Cary, *Free Churches and the Body of Christ*, 41.
131. Niemandt, "Trends in Missional Ecclesiology."

Chapter 4

Imitation of Christ and Pauline Discipleship
(*Imitatio Christi*)

By Dan Yarnell

> In the history of the church the imitation of Christ has become
> both a very important matter and a very controversial one.
> Hence, it is not surprising that commentators and interpreters
> center much attention on this phrase and seek to derive its very
> last implication from it.[1]

Thus writes De Boer in his significant exegetical study on the key
Pauline texts. From the models of saints and martyrs, to the publication of Thomas à Kempis's *Imitation of Christ*, to the more recent WWJD
movement, the importance of the person of Christ as a model exemplar
in the lives of ordinary believers and communities is writ large. This is not
really surprising, as we are not like the early disciples who were able to share
their lives and the missional journey of Jesus on a daily basis. Our challenge
is to engage with our own understanding of Jesus and express how this may
impact our own discipleship today. This does bring some important contextual challenges, which we will consider below.

The recent publication by Will Gompertz, the BBC arts editor, suggests that in the world of art, as well as other creative environs, imitation is
essential. He notes,

---

1. De Boer, *Imitation of Paul*, 161.

Anyone involved in any creative pursuit starts off by copying, be it a ballet dancer or a structural engineer. It is how we learn. Children listen to music and try to play it back note-perfect. Would-be-authors read their favourite novels in an attempt to learn a particular style. Painters spend their early years sitting in chilly museums copying masterpieces. It is a form of apprenticeship. You have to imitate before you can emulate.[2]

Background

It seems quite appropriate therefore to ask the vital question, "What is the power of imitation?" Are we really influenced by the examples of others, for good or ill? Does an example or model adversely affect our own understanding and life choices? Can a historical figure or spiritual leader from the past have any effect on contemporary postmodern people?

The immediate answer seems to be "yes, of course." There are seemingly numerous examples of how the influence of a significant person has developed and aided the actions and reactions of humanity over generations for good. Equally, cultural expressions of being seen to be a public spectacle presents an example of the negative reinforcement of imitation—what not to be like. Various forms of punitive punishments have helped to reinforce this, from the medieval practice of being placed in the stocks, or being tarred and feathered, to one's name representing a form of ridicule or mistrust, thereby becoming a scapegoat. Some historical examples include Leon Trotsky, blamed by Stalin for the problems in Russia; Andrés Escobar for the 1994 World Cup defeat from his own goal, leading to him being shot, and Gaëtan Dugas, the young flight attendant for the spread of AIDS.

Imitation and Social Learning Theory

Albert Bandura is considered to be the father of modern social learning theory. This was developed from the now famous Bobo doll experiment, in which young children mimicked destructive behavior in beating up a doll, not through reinforcement or reward, but in imitating the behavior they had observed. Bandura called this observational learning. In his primary work (1977) he posits the suggestion that children are exposed to a variety of examples of behavior that may influence them. These behavioral models offer stimuli to influence and provide a framework that, under certain

2. Gompertz, *Think like an Artist*, 86.

conditions, can be explored and tested to see whether the child wishes to follow this suggested pattern.

Some of the strength of Bandura's work is related to his methodological approach. He set clearly measurable frameworks to consider how certain stimuli could affect children in a particular environment. This enabled him to empirically measure findings with a degree of certainty to see whether there were any discernible patterns.

Critiques of this approach have noted that observation is not exclusively about behavior, but must equally be cognizant of the place of genetics in determining overall influence. This includes individual biological states, variations of learning abilities, and physiological responses.[3] More recently, observational learning theories have been strengthened by the discovery of mirror neurons and their capacity to help reinforce certain behavioral tendencies.[4]

After various ongoing critiques of this approach, as well as his own maturation of thought, he subsequently modified his theory in 1986. He renamed it Social Cognitive Learning Theory, even though continuing critics note that it is not a unified theory overall and does not consider the importance of maturation of an individual over time. What is important for our purposes is the instructive nature of Bandura's focus on imitation. He notes,

> The people with whom one regularly associates, either through preference or imposition, delimit the behavioral patterns that will be repeatedly observed, and hence learned most thoroughly. . . . People can acquire abstract principles but remain in a quandary about how to implement them if they have not had the benefit of illustrative exemplars.[5]

This would seem to indicate that while imitation as a process is inherent throughout life, it is especially among the developmental cycles of children and youth that the potential of influence is the greatest. It is during this period of human development when youth often look to others as role models, be they historical, mythical, or contemporary. This is often why significant others in positions of authority are suggested as examples of how one should emulate key characteristics of their life.

As suggestive as this is, surprisingly it is not always clearly the case. A recent study by Bricheno and Taylor focused on the popular assumption that male teachers are highly influential role models among primary and secondary male pupils. While there were some notable elements of influence, the study found that the role of a male teacher was less influential

3. Ross, in *Praeger Handbook of Education and Psychology*, 55.
4. Mazur, *Learning and Behavior*, 291.
5. Bandura, quoted in Chung, "Paul's Understanding," 306.

than that of a family member.[6] This is in contrast to the UK government's partnership with the Premier League FA project entitled "Playing for Success," an after-school scheme run since 2007 in hundreds of local centers, demonstrating that this scheme of influential football players as role models on young boys has had significant and demonstrable effects on their educational performance.[7]

While this study may raise a note of caution, it does not remove the importance of the moral life of another as someone that can express what it means to live a "good and therefore exemplary life." It is here, when we consider the ethical value bases that inform the models of morality, that we find the importance and use of imitation.

Greco-Roman Models of Exemplar

The concept of imitation was clearly known within the ancient world.[8] The seminal idea of a "great man," who is to be revered and emulated, can readily be found.[9] Whitmarsh, in commenting on the role of Plutarch's *Parallel Lives* and its influence for imitation, notes,

> The theory that mimēsis might be of positive benefit to the state is enacted in Plutarch's biographical works . . . [his] interest is thus not so much in referential description as in the construction of an ethical subjectivity that is designed to improve and educate the reader.[10]

This idea is not just found within the poetic and philosophical writings. The important and thorough study by Judge details how, in the city of Ephesus, the use of statues of influential men sought to inform and instruct the normal civic populace as examples of virtue and ethical choice that should be followed. If the image became forgetful, there was appropriate textual commentary to remind them, thus continuing the influence that these exemplars could offer future generations. This visual illustration of the use of statues of great leaders can still be found today in most major cities of the world, as, for example, in Trafalgar Square in London.[11] This

---

6. Bricheno and Thornton, "Role Model, Hero, or Champion?," 383–96.

7. Sharp et al., *Playing for Success.*

8. Samra, "Biblical View of Discipleship," 5n14; Wilkins, *Discipleship in the Ancient World*, 11.

9. Harrison, "Imitation of the 'Great Man,'" 213–15, who offers numerous examples.

10. Whitmarsh, *Greek Literature and the Roman Empire*, 54.

11. I.e., Nelson's Column.

seems to reinforce the value of "honor culture" that was so prominent in the Greek East and Latin West, and fostered the role of civic ethical behavior.[12]

It seems highly likely that this would also be influential for the writings of the Apostle Paul, as he may have recalled these examples, which would be well known practices, and how this kind of "power" image might be part of his own thinking as he explored the imitation paradigm.

Rabbinic Expressions

As noted briefly in chapter 1, many of the rabbinic disciples sought to emulate their masters in very thorough and precise ways. A disciple would not only seek to master the wisdom of the rabbi, but would almost entirely emulate their life so as to not pollute the core teaching that they had received.[13] This may be the reason why a disciple would often be known by the name of their master. A kind of symbiotic apprenticeship would develop and keep alive the living tradition of that rabbi's teaching of the Torah through the written and oral experiences of the disciple.[14]

Ladd, however, notes the differences between Jesus and the rabbinic practices of discipleship wherein he states,

> Discipleship to Jesus was not like discipleship to a Jewish rabbi. The rabbis bound their disciples not to themselves but to the Torah; Jesus bound his disciples to himself. The rabbis offered something outside of themselves; Jesus offered himself alone. Jesus required his disciples to surrender without reservation to his authority. They thereby became not only disciples but also *douloi*, *"slaves"* (Mt. 10:24f.; 24:45ff.; Lk. 12:35ff., 42ff.). This relationship had no parallel in Judaism.

He goes on to note why this was likely the case,

> Discipleship to Jesus involved far more than following in his retinue; it meant nothing less than complete personal commitment to him and his message. The reason for this is the presence

---

12. Harrison, "Imitation of the 'Great Man,'" 214, notes that this aspect has not been widely discussed by classicists and New Testament scholars.

13. Hengel, *Charismatic Leader*, notes the observable tendency for the pupil to learn the *halakhah* from the everyday behavior of the teacher (53, with various references).

14. So Ab 5.21 suggests the regular course of training: "with five years on scripture, ten on the Mishna, thirteen of fulfilling the Commandments, and fifteen on teaching" (Hengel, *Charismatic Leader*, 53n56).

of the kingdom of God in Jesus' person and message. In him, people were confronted by God himself.[15]

Following Jesus

What is somewhat surprising is that there is quite limited evidence found within the gospels that Jesus suggests an imitation approach from his own disciples. Hengel notes how little the idea of imitation or example actually plays within the gospel tradition. For Hengel, the focus for Jesus is not so much mimicking his everyday behavior as it is to the inauguration of the kingdom of God and the will of God.[16]

This is of course not to say that some of Jesus' sayings do not either imply or suggest such an approach. While there are some expectations that are implied in the ministry and teaching of Jesus, we do not find him regularly stating we should imitate him. Instead, what he does do is offer the imperative invitation to follow him. He invites us to journey with him in our following, and what is implied is that this engagement will enable transformation as our community is sharing life with our Master. This is quite a unique approach, as it is not the disciple who takes the initiative, as would be the case with rabbinic disciples, but rather Jesus who speaks forth the word of invitation and welcome.[17]

There is one place, however, where there is a specific command of Jesus that encourages the practice of imitation, namely foot-washing. In the Gospel of John we find the following specific command:

> After he had washed their feet, had put on his robe, and had returned to the table, he said to them, "Do you know what I have done to you? You call me Teacher and Lord—and you are right, for that is what I am. So if I, your Lord and Teacher, have washed your feet, you also ought to wash one another's feet. For I have set you an example, that you also should do as I have done to you. Very truly, I tell you, servants[d] are not greater than their master, nor are messengers greater than the one who sent them. If you know these things, you are blessed if you do them." (John 13:12–17 NRSV)

During the time of Jesus, when guests would arrive, the host was expected to make provision for the washing of their feet. Often it would be a servant

---

15. Ladd, *Theology of the New Testament*, 105–6.

16. Ibid., 53.

17. Nepper-Christensen, "μαθητης, ου, ο, μαθητευω," 373.

who would engage in this activity. In this practice, there is no specific religious meaning, but rather a practical expression of hospitality and welcome. This quite common occurrence is, in John's account, given new meaning with the advent of Jesus taking the towel and washing his own disciple's feet. Quite surprising, after the initial shock of these events, Jesus then commands these followers to continue this example within their own discipleship.

Regardless of the particular interpretation of the meaning of this experience,[18] the act of foot-washing has been a more occasional expression of the ancient liturgical practices of both the Western and Eastern churches as a dominical institution. The Reformers seemed to have mostly bypassed this as have some of the Pentecostal churches. It is primarily the Anabaptists and Seventh-Day Adventists who have intentionally engaged in this ancient practice of foot-washing as an expression of worship and discipleship. The practice has never been fully uniform, but did provide, at least initially, a sense of difference from the other Reformers and the Roman Church, thereby creating a boundary set and creating an identity-conferring practice, seeing themselves as the "true church."[19] The continuing expression of foot-washing among Anabaptists et al. is now less about identity (either in imitating Christ or in being set apart from other Christian denominations) and more about expressing Christian humility.[20]

Paul's Imitatio Christi[21]

This then leads us to consider the importance of the post-Jesus writings of the Apostle Paul. The prominence in considering this development is that it is here we encounter and engage with the key terminology that informs an "imitation" approach to discipleship.[22] The epistles of Paul clearly raise the matter of ongoing discipleship with faith communities he writes to.

---

18. Thomas, "Footwashing in John 13," notes that within scholarship there have been various interpretations of the meaning of this practice, including: an example of humility, a symbol for the Eucharist or of baptism, for forgiveness of sins and cleansing, as a soteriological sign, and as a polemic.

19. Graber-Miller, "Mennonite Footwashing," 151.

20. Bender, *Mennonite Encyclopedia*, 347–51, for a good overview of the history and practice with the Anabaptist tradition. Graber-Miller, "Mennonite Footwashing," 151–54.

21. For an extensive list of studies on imitation and the Pauline writings, see Harrison, "Imitation of the 'Great Man,'" 219–20n31.

22. Bauder notes that all of these usages carry an ethical imperatival aim that is directed to specific expressions of conduct. *NIDNTT*, 1:491.

Thessalonians

The phrase "to become an imitator" (μιμητὴς γίνεσθαι) is first found within the Thessalonian correspondence, perhaps the earliest of the recognized writings of Paul. In the first of his two letters, we find two occurrences of the phrase (1:6 and 2:14). Paul, as a pioneer and key figure, expresses his desire for this new infant missional community to become imitators. This is, first of all, an imitation of the apostolic team (*you became imitators of us*), and then becoming an example to the other churches (*you . . . became imitators of God's churches in Judea*) and thereby, an example for others to follow.

What is less clear is what Paul is alluding to when he indicates the need for imitation. Is it their faith that Paul is requiring them to emulate? Perhaps it is their commitment to the mission? Is it imitation of their suffering, as noted in 2:14?

This seems to be what is being suggested, as Fowl notes,

> In both of these references the imitation that is commended is seen in terms of faithfulness in the midst of suffering and distress. This faithfulness is the cruciform life which Paul saw in Christ and took on for himself.[23]

Bruce additionally supports this conclusion. He notes that what made the early Christians an apostolic fellowship was this commitment to following both the teaching of the apostles, as well as their commitment to suffering for the sake of the gospel, thereby multiplying the growth of the kingdom through their own engagement in being good news communities.[24]

Postmodern feminist critiques have rightly noted that there is a strong sense of power and authority that is inherent in the language and approach of imitation theology,[25] though this has been recently challenged.[26] In some ways this seems quite appropriate. Those who have been involved in pioneering mission recognize that being involved in the founding of a new work does indeed carry a sense of ownership and authority. This sense of being a mother or father in God is also noted by the apostle (2:7–10). As

23. Fowl, "Imitation of Paul / of Christ," 430.

24. Bruce, *1 & 2 Thessalonians*, 15, 45; see also Witherington, *1 and 2 Thessalonians*, 72, 251.

25. In particular, Castelli, *Imitating Paul*, who seeks to follow Derrida and Foucault in providing a critique on the abusiveness of power.

26. Harrison, *Christian Origins and Graeco-Roman Culture*, 218, expresses an important note of caution: "Castelli's stimulating monograph on imitation is, in my opinion, too ideologically driven. She comes to the ancient texts and the epistles of Paul with a priori suppositions about the nature of power, overlooking how the subtleties of the honour system shaped power relations in antiquity."

the founding planter and apostle, Paul would be seen to have an authority which may go deeper than simply a sense of copying or mimicking. As
Ehrensperger notes.

> That Paul did claim authority and status as an apostle over the
> congregations he founded is beyond doubt. This is an impor-
> tant issue in the assessment of his imitation language . . . as the
> founder of a community of Christ-followers his status cannot be
> identical with that of his converts. His role and function are dif-
> ferent from the role and function of any of the Christ followers
> in the εκκλησιαι he founded.[27]

There are, in addition, two further examples in the second part of
the Thessalonian correspondence. Here we find the phrase "to imitate,"
μιμεισθαι (3:7, 9). The first occurrence focuses on how this missional community should follow the example of the apostolic team, which is centered
on the lifestyle of providing for themselves, thereby not being codependent
on others as they expressed their life and ministry. This is then followed two
verses later, where this practice of laboring and toiling is indicative of the
expression of being a model for others.

It seems, therefore, that this early engagement with the notion of
imitation is more than just a cursory experience but is integral to the life
and witness of this early apostolic community. The experiences of the early
apostolic team provide Paul with a living testimony of what it means to follow Jesus in their own context, and it is this that he seeks to offer the Thessalonians as an example to imitate.

Corinthians

The Corinthian correspondence moves the discussion on a bit further,
where we find Paul's injunction more explicit as he invites these believers to
imitate him as he imitates Christ (1 Cor 4:16; 11:1). This first use by Paul of
imitation language once again brings into our discussion the importance of
his paternal relationship with this young church. As with the Thessalonian
correspondence, he appeals to his role as a father figure, which then serves
as the basis of the need for imitation.

> The picture is one of a father who has instructed his children
> in proper behavior by his own example. They are to be "like fa-
> ther, like children. . . . It therefore functions as one more item
> in the long argument of 1:10—4:13 that appeals to the servant

27. Ehrensperger, *Paul and the Dynamics of Power*, 144.

nature of discipleship over against their "boasting" and worldly wisdom.[28]

This, then, seems to be a different kind of approach than merely an objective moral exemplar,[29] for there is the highly relational aspect of the language that Paul is using. Of course, this might be seen as more of the stoic teacher/pupil kind true of the first-century culture. One may recall the statement by Seneca, the great Stoic teacher, who encouraged pupils to seek out

> men [sic] who teach us by their lives, who tell us what we ought to do and then prove it by practice, who show us what we should avoid, and then are never caught doing that which they have ordered us to avoid (Ep. 52).[30]

The emphasis here, however, which seems to be similar to its use in the Thessalonian correspondence, is less about learning doctrine and more about the living example of a community that is modeling itself on what has been seen and learned from the apostolic team. While this will be more fully developed throughout this work, it is important to observe that far too often our own Western hermeneutical horizon has limited us in our engagement with these texts, with an individualistic reading being preferred, which then overlooks the importance of the community itself as an exemplar of the *missio Christi*.[31]

The second usage occurs in chapter 11. It is here we find the most direct statement of imitation, where Paul uses his own life and journey as a discipleship model for the church. "Be imitators of me as I imitate Christ."

This call to imitate comes after the lengthy discussion about Christian freedom and cultural engagement found in chapter 10. In many ways, verse 1 seems to be better placed at the end of chapter 10, as a means of summing up the ethos that Paul is seeking to advance.[32]

Kim brings a helpful corrective in the widening debate of whether we interpret the language of imitation in Corinthians from either a stoic and therefore authoritarian approach, much like the teacher and the pupil, or

28. Fee, *Paul's Letter to the Philippians*, 186.

29. Horsley, *1 Corinthians*, 43, notes that while Paul makes use of standard Hellenistic-Roman oratory in suggesting imitating himself as a model of appropriate moral character, Paul is demonstrating something much more subversive, as he argues that his own character is in utter disrepute and the rubbish of the world.

30. Wanamaker, *Epistle to the Thessalonians*, 355.

31. Newbigin famously observes: "the only hermeneutic of the gospel, is a congregation of men and women who believe it and live by it" (*The Gospel in a Pluralist Society*, 227).

32. Belleville, "Imitate Me," 126.

whether, following postcolonial and feminist interpreters, we see and question the sense of control and domination of seeking to mimic ultimately the imperial voice. He helpfully posits a third alternative, seeking an understanding of imitation as a type of embodiment, which reads these texts much more communally. He states,

> It should be understood as a way of life rooted in the image of Christ crucified, which plays a central role in the letter, deconstructing abusive, destructive powers in a community and society and reconstructing a beloved community for all.[33]

What seems to be implied here is the sense of servanthood, sacrifice, and the humility of Christ as the overall ethos that forms and informs the apostle, and therefore becomes a paradigmatic expression of what a Christlike community can become. This suggests a cohesive approach to what discipleship might look like for this young missional community.

Hooker seems to capture the essence of Paul's injunction of imitation most fully wherein she states,

> The whole Christian community should reflect the love and compassion of Christ: there was no distinction here between apostle and community, except that the role of the apostle was to be a subsidiary model. The Gospel was to be proclaimed both by Paul and by the community, not simply through the preaching of the word, but in every believer's life.[34]

Philippians

While not a specific example or statement by Paul of imitation, the so-called hymn found in chapter 2 presents a kind of model that is presented as an aid memoir of the movements of Jesus: beginning from a position of ultimate authority, moving to servanthood and crucifixion, then climaxing in the redeeming work of resurrection and exultation.

Hawthorne helpfully notes,

> There is in this hymn, which sings the praises of the divine who became human, a grand transvaluation of values. For the

---

33. Kim, *Theological Introduction*, 112. A complimentary view is held by Gorman (2001, 2015), who sees the role of cruciformity as the *essential* narrative spirituality of Paul. Gorman suggests that this has been Paul's own experience and therefore he now invites others to participate in following him and thereby engaging in this reality.

34. Hooker, "Partner in the Gospel," 100.

attitude and actions of Christ outlined here clearly show God's ideal pattern for discipleship.[35]

The structural movements of the hymn therefore demonstrate the way in which subversive values are expressed in the life of Jesus, who then becomes the model life for the Philippians, and for all readers of this text.

This, then, seems to be presented by Paul as an attitudinal model for the Christians in Philippi to follow and therefore to emulate. "Let the same mind be in you as was in Christ Jesus" (NRSV). It is not only the life of Jesus that is set before this Christian community, but the deeper attitudinal aspect that caused him to express his obedience in such a sacrificial manner. This is therefore more about enabling the mind-set to affect them more than the specific actions, which in the end are not easily reproducible.

In chapter 3 this becomes even more explicit, as we find the unusual phrase "be imitators together" (συμμιμηταὶ γίνεσθαι). This unique compound moves the focus clearly back onto the community and its life together as a discipled people. Paul, once again, is clearly calling them to imitate him, but this is now more noticeably expressed in partnership. The continuing theme of unity, which seems to dominate the letter, is seen here once again. Fee notes that in each context in this letter where the *imitatio* is expressed, the setting is around the cruciform life, suggesting active engagement in suffering on behalf of the one who suffered for us.[36] While this is very aspirational, it does raise some important missional questions. How does an entire community imitate the life of Christ? Does this imply that it is not possible to imitate Christ without active suffering?

Oakes notes the importance of this section of Philippians wherein he states,

> Philippians is remarkable for the numbers of links that are made between Paul's way of life and that of his hearers. The most pointed call to take Paul's behavior as a model is in 3.17:
> Συμμιμηταὶ μου γινεσθε, αδελφοι, και σκοπειτε τους ουτω περιπατουντας καθως εχετε τυπον ημας.
> The focus is on way of life: περιπατεω. The aspects of his life to which he has just drawn attention are surrender of privileges (3.7–9), willingness to suffer (verse 10), and determination to press on to the goal (verses 12–14).[37]

35. Hawthorne, "Imitation of Christ," 169.
36. Fee, *Paul's Letter to the Philippians*, 1179–80; also see Fowl, *Dictionary of Paul*, 429.
37. Oakes, *Philippians*, 105.

These key aspects are what enabled Paul in his own personal discipleship to emulate his master, Jesus, and it is to these that he points as the elements of what the life of Jesus should be like for the Philippian believers as they sought to imitate him. The hymn of chapter 2 finds authentic expression in the missional life of Paul, and he now provides this as the litmus test for what a Christian community would experience.

The reality of this kind of community is never far from the conflict of the ideal. In chapter 4, we find the conflict between two sisters expressed as an example of the wrong kind of attitude, highlighting its effect on the overall community. This kind of naming and shaming is quite striking in our postmodern age, but it is good to recall that these are letters to genuine missional communities, and the appeal is meant to bring about reconciliation and healing, rather than be seen as a kind of accusatory statement. If imitation is meant to be genuine, then it must affect at the very least these two sisters in faith, who could do well to find in the imitation of Paul the life of Christ being expressed in his own discipleship, which thereby means for them that they need to consider their own struggles and the importance of intentional reconciliation between them.

Ephesians

While sometimes considered by scholars to not be an authentic Pauline text, it is included here to complete the New Testament usage of these phrases on imitation. This final treatment of this phrase is found in this letter. In chapter 5 there is a clarion call for the entire people of God to become imitators of God as beloved children (μιμητης γινεσθαι).

Lincoln notes the implication of such a call wherein he states,

> It would be incongruous to be God's dearly loved child and not want to become like one's loving Father. In fact, the new child-Father relationship not only requires but also enables imitation to take place, as the children live their lives out of the love they have already experienced from their Father.[38]

This call is, in fact, the only occurrence anywhere in the canonical Scripture where the injunction to imitate God occurs.[39] Barth, among other scholars, noted that there are other types of parallel analogies with

38. Lincoln, *Ephesians*, 310.

39. Michaelis, "μιμεομαι, μιμητης, συμμιμητης," in Kittel, *Theological Dictionary of the New Testament*, 4:666–73.

Scripture, including "following Yahweh," "walking in His ways," and to "be holy as I am holy."[40]

While this phrase is unique in the biblical writings, O'Brien notes that the concept can be readily found within the writings of Hellenistic Judaism, especially Philo.[41] This suggests that for the author of Ephesians it is a known concept and therefore is likely being drawn upon in its development in this passage.

The "therefore" (ουν) notes the transition of this section. There continues to be ongoing critical debate as to whether this indicates a marker for a new section, a link to the previous admonitions, or a summing up of the key issues that the author has been developing.[42] The important point for our purposes is how this language of imitating God is being promoted by the author for intentional expression by his readers.

There seems to be some similarity of this with 1 Corinthians 4:14–16, which is framed around the life and ministry of Jesus. But whereas, there the father image was the apostle, here it is God himself who is the exemplar and model. In the context of 4:32—5:2, we now find the admonition to this community to express the Christ-like actions of love and forgiveness, which enable them to imitate God.[43]

Imitation, and therefore discipleship, for Paul is not primarily about one's own private experience. This call to imitate God ensures that the whole community are being intentionally drawn into the paradigmatic shift of becoming a Father-like expression of the new humanity.[44] Becoming god-like is therefore not primarily a kind of esoteric spiritual experience, but rather finds concrete expression from the cosmic dimensions of the lordship of Christ to the reconciling of differing people groups into a new humanity. This then informs practical expressions of living daily life in various social settings and contexts, where being good news is being fully expressed. This must be more than merely aspirational. Like the earliest Christians, the need for patient endurance and patient ferment is often the normative experience in becoming this discipled community.[45]

40. Barth, *Ephesians 4–6*, 555–56; O'Brien, *Letters to the Ephesians*, 310; Lincoln, *Ephesians*, 310–11.

41. O'Brien, *Letters to the Ephesians*, who follows the more detailed study of Wild, "Be Imitators," 128–33.

42. A good summary can be found in Thielman, *Ephesians*, 320.

43. Clarke, "Be Imitators of Me," 351.

44. Stott, *Ephesians*, notes in his commentary that Ephesians expresses the call to become a new society, thereby implying a shift away from a more purely privatized experience of faith.

45. Kreider, *Patient Ferment of the Early Church*.

Limitations of Imitation

At the heart of these various Pauline admonitions is the need for intentional expressions of discipleship. Having said that, seeking to exactly mirror or clone the person we are seeking to model does not seem to be what is being anticipated. Might this imply that there may be some kind of limitation on imitation?

Within some cultural manifestations, expressions of imitation might be challenging. The WWJD movement is a recent example of how one might easily ignore historical and cultural settings and assume that if we just consider what Jesus would do, then we can also emulate this in our own context. An earlier expression of this approach can be found in the popular Christian classic text *In His Steps*, by Sheldon. Both of these approaches leave it up to the imagination of the participant what in fact might be an appropriate response in imitation of Jesus.

Earlier generations were greatly influenced by the seminal classic text *The Imitation of Christ*, by Thomas à Kempis. This continues to be an instrumental and formative piece of literature that posits some similar ideas about reflecting on Jesus, his life, ministry, ethics, values, practices, attitudes, and then seeking to find appropriate expression in one's own life.

What neither of these texts seem to do well is to consider the hermeneutical challenges of expressing a view of what Jesus would do. For example, neither text examines the example of Jesus' confrontational approaches in the gospels and suggests these as imitation models. Other admonitions and examples such as turning the other cheek (Matt 5:39 / Luke 6:29), loving one's enemy (Matt 5:44 / Luke 6:27), or selling our possessions and giving them to the poor (Luke 12:33) are not easily considered. This seems to imply that while the spirit of seeking to express our lives as Jesus would is honorable and perhaps even desirable, what this actually looks like will often depend upon our own cultural choices, actions, and preferences of texts to inform these expressions. As the Latin American theologian Jon Sobrino clearly notes,

> The following of Jesus does not come down to the mere imitation of Jesus. First of all, it is in fact impossible to do exactly what he himself did. Second and even more important, the Christian should not "imitate" Jesus precisely because an intrinsic and essential feature of Jesus' own moral course is its localization in history. Precisely because of this historical localization, a person's moral life is unrepeatable. . . . Discipleship

is not imitation, therefore; and neither is it a reproduction of certain historical traits of Jesus.[46]

The knotty problem of hermeneutics is briefly noted in the above comments. The complex issues that surround interpretation, as well as being an interpreter, is an ongoing challenge for all peoples of faith. If we are to maintain a sense of solidarity and authenticity we will need to discern the imitation of Christ within our own culture and times.

Suggestive Missional Engagement Issues from Paul's *Imitatio Christi*

Following on from the above, what, therefore, is the overall significance of Paul's rallying cry to be an imitator of Christ. What might this mean for twenty-first-century missional disciples?

I would like to suggest the following as some key issues that need to be considered and engaged with:

- Developing a greater awareness of the mind of Christ. This should involve expressing a pattern of life, death, and resurrection as core elements of the discipleship formation process. This may mean a renewed form of catechesis;

- Intentionally becoming countercultural kingdom people, thereby expressing church not essentially as empire building and organizationally, but church as the formation of a community of people, who are then built up and released into their giftings and ministries within the world;

- Reconstructing the Pauline community of "you" (in the plural, so for the entire community rather than an individualistic interpretation) as togetherness and participation in the new kingdom of Father, Son, and Holy Spirit. This is highly important as the new paradigms of society are being transformed by intercultural experiences.[47] The Christian community could be seen to take a lead in finding good expressions of sharing life together;

- Following on from this, finding ways of expressing "imitating Christ" in others as a means of being transformed into Christ's likeness;

- Ultimately this may find a new expression of missional holiness as the sacramental, whole life practice of being disciples both in the church and in society.

46. Sobrino, *Christology at the Crossroads*, 130–31.
47. Hardy and Yarnell, *Forming Multicultural Partnerships*.

This is not an easy task, and it will likely take that special gift of the Spirit, "desperation," to enable the kind of transformative change that enables the imitation of Christ to find new and fresh expressions. As Dunn highlights,

> For any understanding of what discipleship of Jesus is and involves must surely take its lead from the discipleship to which he actually called followers during his life and ministry. Of course, discipleship in the twentieth century cannot be a mere imitation of discipleship in first-century Galilee. That would be playacting at discipleship, motivated by a morbid fascination with first-century trappings rather than by a sincere desire to share the spirit which motivated the first disciples. But discipleship of Jesus must nonetheless draw its understanding of that discipleship from the record of those who literally followed him, otherwise such claims to discipleship can easily become fanciful and subject to distorting pressures from tradition and ecclesiastical vested interest.[48]

---

48. Dunn, *Jesus' Call to Discipleship*, 2

Chapter 5

The Reign of God and Discipleship Formation

Disciples Shaped by the Prophetic Prolepsis
of the Future Age[1]

By Andrew R. Hardy

Introduction

Where is the reign of God? Is the reign of God something we can see portrayed in any physical or institutional form that makes up our present experience of life? Is the reign of God something we experience in our churches, in the worship services or in the way church governance is practiced? What is the location of the reign of God in your life experiences? What are the plausibility structures you look to, to inform your understanding of the reign of God? Is the reign of God the influence of your leaders on you or of God on you? How are your beliefs, words, and behaviors influenced so that you know how to subject your life to the reign of God? Who do you look to, to mentor you and to hold you accountable to the beliefs and practices of the Christian life of discipleship as citizens of the kingdom? God's reign is fundamental to Christian discipleship formation and it is based on our faith and confession that Jesus Christ is Lord.

---

1. *Prolepsis* means "anticipation."

The coming of the reign of God was prophesied by Old Testament prophets like Daniel, and more particularly in the intertestamental apocalyptic literature.[2] Paul clearly articulated that no one speaking the name of Christ by the Spirit could curse Jesus, the Lord.[3] The reign of Jesus as Lord is based on Christ's real presence in the human soul by his Spirit.[4] So where is the kingdom of God for you? How do you bring your life into harmony with the demands of following Jesus the Lord? The kingdom of God is actually an ongoing relationship with God as king who we are subject to in love to trust, obey, and to serve.

Kingdom of God and Discipleship: Plausible or Not?

In the first-century Greco-Roman period, Christianity came to birth in the midst of the plausibility structures that existed in the ancient Near Eastern culture, which made the language and practices of discipleship plausible to most societies of the period.[5] Moreover, the language of the kingdom of God fitted within a worldview where kings ruled kingdoms and people saw themselves as subjects of a king and his kingdom. The social location of people, either poor or rich, located them to a large degree as subjects of a king or master somewhere. The plausibility structures of the first-century period were based on accepted norms and values, where people were socially located in positions prescribed to them from birth. Hence it was plausible to speak of the kingdom of God as God's reign over his people, meaning it was quite natural to believe that God rightly would expect his people to be his subjects to do his will.

Peter Berger discusses the meaning of plausibility structures in the context of the sociology of religions.[6] Plausibility structures are to be found among all cultural groups in any given society. They are built within the context of each sociocultural situation, as well as being based on accepted systems of meaning that most of those in a given culture accept as the norms and values, by which they define their lives. Hence they enable them to make sense of the world around them.

People commonly accept standardized meanings that make the structures of their society work well, so that they can live in relative harmony

2. Davies, "Apocalyptic," in Rogerson and Lieu, *Oxford Handbook*, 397–419.

3. 1 Cor 12:3.

4. 2 Cor 14:1–5.

5. Vaage, "An Other Home," 741–61; Longenecker, *Patterns of Discipleship*, chs. 1–3.

6. Davison, "Fundamentalism and Relativism Together," in Berger, *Between Relativism and Fundamentalism*, 25.

with one another.[7] Plausibility structures include beliefs and meanings that people hold in common and use to define their lives.[8] For example, in late modern society, the scientific method is broadly plausible. It has proven results that benefit citizens: such as technology that provides electricity to homes and devices like televisions. Hence late modern people trust that science provides some well-tested things that they can rely on.

Plausibility structures are based to some degree on realistic expectations that people in society have confidence in, because they work. But not just any old idea has plausibility. Those things that have some broadly accepted norms in law, customs, and social structures act as a kind of social glue, if they have a proven and accepted track record that works quite well.[9] Hence in postmodern Western society, the metanarrative that the Christian faith and belief in God was normative for the people of a Christendom age, is no longer accepted as normative for the majority of late modern people.[10] The new plausibility structure is that all claims to truth, whoever makes them, Christians, atheists, Muslims etc. are relative. No one thing can be properly called truth, but any number of things might be plausible. So are there no longer any plausibility structures?

One way of answering this is that the prevailing plausibility structure of late modernity is based on relative partial truths. Hence it is harder to convince people of a realm where God reigns supreme, based on his love for the world in a place called heaven, as an absolute setting above all lesser realms. This is because there is less room for absolutes, or absolute beings in a late modern person's plausibility structure. Moreover, a lack of belief in the creation of the world by divine fiat undermines the potential to understand the world to be created by God for a purpose that underpins its reason and purpose for existence.

Can any realm dreamt of by the imagination, artifice, or religious conviction of humankind rightly be thought of as absolute? The French philosopher Derrida deconstructed the structured world of modernity, seeking to demonstrate that structured views of the world were constructed from the perspective of the viewer, rather than by it being possible to find one singular absolute structure all could describe in the same manner.[11] Hence late modern people who accept this view no longer accept absolute truths.

7. Feddes, *Missional Apologetics*.

8. Ibid.

9. Sim, *Routledge Companion to Postmodernism*, 80–84.

10. Ibid.

11. Barker, *Cultural Studies*, 84.

In the case of discipleship formation and the kingdom of God, post-modern people do not readily understand terms like these any more. Discipleship and the kingdom do not relate to the liberal democracies late modern people enjoy, where individuals have the right to form their own beliefs and to live as they see fit. By way of comparison, in the first-century world, discipleship was an accepted norm that was to be found throughout the antique cultures. It was accepted that there were masters who had understood the world alright. It was the role of the less experienced disciple to learn the exact arts that the masters expertly wielded.

In the Hebrew Bible we find the word *talmid* used once to refer to a pupil/learner.[12] A disciple is the rarest of subjects in the Old Testament, in terms of actual nomenclature. *Talmid* comes from the Hebrew verb *lamad*, which means "to learn." Hence in Isaiah 8:16; 50:4; and 54:13, *limmud* was used as a substantive participle, meaning "one who is taught." The scarcity of the direct use of words for disciple in the Old Testament is notable. To what extent were people discipled given the rarity of the term during the time of Israel? One answer is to recognize that for the Jewish mind, God was rightly to be thought of as king. Moving to the Jewish Talmud, *talmid* can be found more copiously in this later collection of documents, although not written in the first century. They are considered to reach back to the time of Christ in terms of preservation of a memory of discipleship practices, that are thought to have existed in Jesus' lifetime.[13] Scholars accept that they broadly provide an authentic nomenclature that spoke to the more common rabbi-disciple relationship attested to in the gospels.[14]

When we consider the gospels, we find the word "disciple" (Greek *mathetes*) used sixty-eight times in Matthew, forty-four times in Mark, seventy-four times in Luke, seventy-three times in John, and twenty-eight times in Acts. Taken in the context of the broader Greco-Roman culture, that Christianity found itself winning Gentile converts among, the term "disciple" was particularly relevant to the common practices used to apprentice younger adults to take on responsibilities in civil society. The copious use of discipleship, where a master-teacher would have followers who were subject to him until they had mastered his teaching, was intrinsic to the plausibility structures that helped Greco-Roman society function.

Hence being a disciple of the messianic king, made Jesus followers disciples of the kingdom. Once disciples had mastered the teaching of their master, they would then take on disciples of their own. These disciples

---

12. 1 Chr 28:8.

13. Longenecker, *Biblical Exegesis*, chs. 1–3, develops this line of thinking.

14. Ibid.

would learn in the same manner as their new masters once had with theirs. Jesus the Master passed on to his disciples the principles of how to equip followers, to be able to make yet new followers under the reign of God. The Pauline and other epistles use the term less copiously, however, the language of discipleship is implied in other ways.[15]

How can we use the terminology "disciple" and "discipleship" in the context of late modern individualistic society, when it is not a commonly accepted social norm? How can the language of Lord as God, one worthy of worship, be grasped in a society where each individual has their own perceived right to determine their destinies?

The question of the relevance of the terms disciple and discipleship (and kingdom and kingship) raises important concerns for the authors of this book, given that it is quite possible that the use of the terminology of "discipleship" is simply not valid in a late modern liberal society. Liberal democracy values individualism, niche market economic forces, and relativity, where free market forces to some extent are permitted to reign. Davison Hunter discusses Berger's critique of the value of any one given plausibility structure and its jargon in the late modern context:

> The first dynamic has to do with the transformation of what Peter Berger calls "plausibility structures." In Berger's view, ideas and beliefs are not merely the province of intellect and will. There is, rather, a dialectic between consciousness and social structure. In his formulation, strong and consistent belief, therefore, presupposes strong and stable social support. Yet the intensive form of pluralism generated by modernity not only means that any shared culture thinned out by virtue of the sustained presence of multiple cultures, it also means that the plausibility structures that provide the social support are also fragmented and weakened. In the end, strong belief and conviction cannot be sustained by fragile plausibility structures. Uncertainty is imposed upon us because no belief is protected from the claims of alternative beliefs; no conviction is left unchallenged by other equally held convictions.[16]

Berger's critique of plausibility structures, no longer being stable units in civil society, is suggestive of a solution to the view that says there is now only one plausibility structure left, i.e., individualism that determines the destiny of each person. It is all down to personal choice and taste. Late

---

15. Ibid.

16. Davison Hunter, "Fundamentalism and Relativism Together," in Berger, *Between Relativism and Fundamentalism*, 25.

modern youth and young adults hold many different beliefs in tension in the melting pot of a multicultural pluralistic Western society. They do this under the rubric of democratic liberalism. The thinly disguised veil of democratic stability in Western society is itself a plausibility structure, which only functions by virtue of it sustaining the many and variable outlooks on life held by people in its pluralistic society. It will continue to function as long as the sovereign God and public opinion welcomes this sense of relativistic outlooks on life, which are considered a stable part of late modern social norms and values.

As long as late modern people approve of each other having the freedom to define their lives and beliefs for themselves, it would seem that this approved relativistic culture is actually a kind of plausibility structure, which is accepted as part of postmodern culture. This freedom to choose one's identity means that a variety of subcategories of plausibility structures exist in Western society, of which not all will be just as strong or weak (for that matter) as other structures.

This in turn means that not all structures offer the same level of plausibility compared to other options on the table. Berger seems overly pessimistic in his assessment that people will therefore no longer affirm beliefs that make more sense to them than other competing claims to plausibility. In actuality there seems to be a highly suggestive interest in spiritual matters among young adults.[17]

It is not a given that Berger is correct that because "no conviction is left unchallenged by other equally held convictions," that it follows that people will not choose to embrace a plausibility structure that provides a metanarrative that can offer structure and accountability to their lives. After all, many Christians do, as do many Muslims and those from other world religions. It does not need to follow that Berger is correct to assert that, "in the end, strong belief and conviction cannot be sustained by fragile plausibility structures."

A structure that offers certainty, in the midst of such a disintegration of "convictions" could itself be plausible, if it offers a credible, sustainable, and realistic hermeneutic for life, which can also be confirmed through phenomenological experiences, such as an experience of the real presence of Jesus might offer. It is not the task of this book to discuss what went wrong during Christendom, as other books in this series trace that well for us.[18] Christendom's plausibility structure was considered too confining to

---

17. Drane, *Do Christians Know.*

18. Murray, *Church After Christendom.*

an emerging liquid modernity.[19] The solidity of Christendom modernity was that it had become static, not open to the future prolepsis of the coming kingdom, or a powerful experience of the real presence of Jesus' Spirit.

Cray has argued strongly that in the context of the pluralistic unravelling of certainty, found in late modernity, that the church can offer a strong, rich, and stable community for people to find plausibility within. However, it has to be far more open to creativity and the ongoing creation of the future kingdom of God. It needs to be based on a very different kind of plausibility structure than that found during Christendom. This difference is not necessarily perceived by those in traditional churches, which still try to live as if the church still held a central role in society and culture. Cray subversively comments:

> The church is not for church. It does not exist for itself. It exists to embody God's purposes for his creation. That may involve actions and statements which can be seen as negative, but they will always have a positive purpose. The most pathological condition a church can reach is when all its energies are taken up with its own maintenance and survival. "Churches are occupied with an obsessive struggle just to repeat the past, to survive or to offer shelter from the storm. . . . Nevertheless, God's intention for the fulfilment of the whole creation is always the church's horizon." This is a pathological condition, because it is precisely the opposite to our calling. "The church does more than merely point to a reality beyond itself. By virtue of its participation in the life of God, it is not only a sign and instrument, but also a genuine foretaste of God's Kingdom, called to show forth visibly, in the midst of history, God's final purposes for humankind."
>
> That is very scary. It is far from most Christians' understanding of the church. It is a long way from the reality of many churches I know. But that is the most biblical statement about the purpose of the church that I have found. "The church is called to show forth visibly, in the midst of history, God's final purposes for humankind."[20]

The key is to participate in the experienced life of the Trinity that is the life and energy of the missional church. To some extent during Christendom the Western church considered its mission finished in the West, and locked away the power of the Spirit of Christ, confining it in its power structures, which among other things disempowered the laity to often become mere liturgical observers. However, it is not to be taken that there were not strong movements within Western society that acted in missional ways.

19. Bauman, *Liquid Modernity.*
20. Cray, *Disciples & Citizens,* 140.

The Wesleyan Methodist movement had a strong focus on the laboring class and the poor, as well as among some of the aristocracy.[21] Their schools and societies are well known to have had a strong discipleship ethos and values.[22] The evangelical zeal of this movement not only brought some degree of revival to the people in the time of the Wesleys,[23] but also in the generations that followed with the world missions movement of the nineteenth century. Other examples could be provided. When the Christian community functions by participating in God's mission, to reconcile a fragmented society made up of disparate communities, every ordinary member can reconnect with the phenomenological life force of the Spirit of Jesus. In terms of this present late modern period it is hoped people will start to look to the real presence of Jesus to transform their lives.

Not a Return to Christendom

The goal of shaping late modern disciples will not be to seek to return to a restrictive Christendom culture, where control of the faithful by a professional clergy might disempower them from exercising their missional priesthood. The priesthood of all believers may also be articulated to include every member ministry, where every believer can act as ministers of Christ in their everyday life contexts. This will also mean that the diverse cultural groups of Western society will need to be discipled. Disciples who come from the rich tapestry of our multicultural society could help to model what the future kingdom will look like to their peers, where all peoples will be gathered to worship around God's throne.[24] A diverse multicultural expression of God's rich and diverse reality is a more fitting goal for people made in his creative image. A diverse world of intercultural expressions in the Christian community is to be found on our doorsteps in the West.[25] Newbigin pointed the missional church toward God's goal,[26] which is well expressed in Paul's Letter to the Ephesians:

> He [God] has made known to us the mystery of his will, according to his good pleasure that he set forth in Christ, as a plan

---

21. Maddow, "Visit the Poor," 37–50.
22. Hunsicker, "John Wesley," 192–211.
23. Ibid.
24. Hardy and Yarnell, *Forming Multicultural Partnerships*.
25. Ibid.
26. Newbigin, *Open Secret*.

for the fullness of time, to gather up all things in him, things in heaven and things on earth.[27]

The church is really an outpost of the continuing in-breaking of the reign of God, where people are Christ's hands and feet sent to serve the world.[28] This is a powerful kind of sacramental theology. Christians should have no difficulty in recognizing that the vision of the reign of God over a renewed earth is the goal of human history.[29] Therefore, central to any faith-based plausibility structure we might embrace, is the love of God that calls each of us to seek to partner together to enrich the world, based on the creative diversity of our numerous cultures working together, in participation with the Spirit of Jesus.

The Christian community needs to provide an alternative vision of what it looks like when multicultural believers seek to participate in creative harmony together.[30] The ancient approach of discipleship formation may not be plausible to a late modern society that distrusts subjection of one individual to another, but it can inform our lives as we learn to trust each other enough, to be open to the perspectives of others. In this case our perspectives on life may be transformed, if we allow ourselves to converse with others who are not from our preferred subculture.

Authentic Discipleship Based on Reciprocal Mentoring

We must be careful not to assume that subjection is only in one direction, i.e., of the less developed disciple (or mentee) becoming subject to a more developed mentor, or discipler. A reciprocal mentoring approach can be very effective to help develop the capacities of parties engaged in equal-power mentoring relationships.

These are mutual mentoring approaches, where two or three people agree to help hold each other accountable. Mentoring may be one way of contextualizing discipleship to the people of late modernity. It is quite plausible for young professionals, or potential future leaders, academics, social activists etc. to take on mentors.[31]

27. Eph 1:9–10 NRSV.

28. Hastings, *Missional God, Missional Church*, 305–6.

29. Wright, *New Testament and the People of God*, 284–302.

30. Hardy and Yarnell, *Forming Multicultural Partnerships*, ch. 3.

31. Lewis, *Mentoring Matters*.

A Plausibility Structure for Mentoring

In the diagram below we may seek to understand the basis to any disciple-making strategy, whatever nomenclature we choose to articulate it. This can be done by considering some core components of the Christian plausibility structure (of course different church traditions represent variances in such a structure).

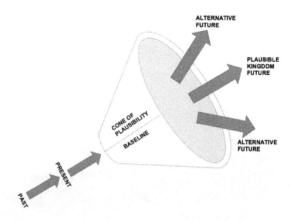

The "cone of plausibility" locates the mentor and mentee (mentee / the reciprocal mentoring relationship) in the *present*. People construct what is plausible to them in terms of their life experiences that largely unconsciously shape their outlooks on the world. Good experiences have become a buzzword category in late modernity. Did you enjoy it? Was it a good experience? Do you think I would enjoy it? The real presence of Jesus may be termed the basis to an abundant Christian life. It is thought of as a powerful presence according to Acts 1:8. The experience of Christ's reality as a deeply felt presence in the human psyche is often fundamental to many Christian accounts of what convicts them to continue in their faith journeys. To come to know God must be part of an abundant life and good experience.

Any account of a person's present plausibility structure has to start in the context of present experiences, even if at times our present experiences cause us to struggle. People still base their assessments of what to try out next, based on *past* memories and how these might inform *present* life decisions. For example, our convictions help motivate our decisions to act. If someone has no experience of a *past* spiritual experience with Christ that feels normative, then it goes without saying they need to experience him in the present, in order to make any kind of assessment of whether he is real and plausible.

It is hard to imagine someone wanting to be mentored to help them explore the Christian life, if they do not have an experience of the reality of the living Christ. The starting point has to begin much further back. The question is how might people encounter Christ? The argument of a later chapter will be that Christians need to incarnate alongside people in their social and personal zones. Friendship will be the starting point to any opportunity to introduce someone to Christ. Assuming that such friendships move on to someone having a personal encounter with the living Christ leading to their conversion, then there will still be the challenge of helping them to construct their own plausibility structure.

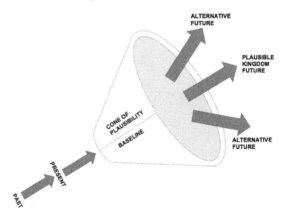

Any consideration where we see ourselves as having a plausible *future* as a follower of Christ, needs to be constructed on the basis of the Christian story. The Christian story aims to shape our identities and outlooks on life based on a history (a *past*) that we accept as a foundation. There first needs to be an acceptance of the historical *past* revelation of the foundations to the story of Christ, as our eternal savior.

This comes from Scripture and a belief in its value as testimony deserving of trust. Hence the revelation from the past is the first *baseline* of a Christian discipleship formation approach. The second *baseline* for discipleship, must be an authentic continuing encounter with the real presence of Christ. This encounter will have a young *past* memory for a new believer, but fragile, or powerful, that it might feel, it is the foundation for a new kind of *past* memory, that will form the basis of the *present* experience and a vision for the *future*. The *future* will need to be prepared for based on the learning of sustainable spiritual practices, that keep the disciple in intimate communion with God. Moreover, it will need to be based on the historic deposit of the Christian faith, of the life, death, resurrection, ascension, and coming of Jesus

Christ. The foundations to Christian belief need to be built on the person of the living Lord, who is still actively *present* with his followers.

The historic deposit of the Christian faith becomes part of the experience of new believers' faith, as they continue to experience the real presence of Christ as a firm foundation for a sustainable *future* life journey. Why all this emphasis on experience and real presence? It is because postmodern people seek genuine experiences that make a difference to their lives. The church after Christendom fails them if it does not mentor them, helping them to develop these. Of course this requires Christian mentors who have these experiences and know how to maintain them in an intimate relationship with the Lord Jesus.

The *cone of plausibility* is important. The continuing presence of Christ with his followers, and his historic reality, are set against a *baseline* that includes three things. First, it casts a vision of the *future*, for the convert to now see themselves as a part of God's eternal reign, as an ongoing experience of life from now into the future. Second, it sets out the *implications* of living in an obedient trust-based relationship, modeling one's life on that of the example of Christ. Third, it needs to be realistic about *alternative futures* that a life in Christ calls a person to embrace, compared to a life that might be shaped by a materialistic and individualistic outlook. Christ remains the only sure way for an eternal *future* with God. People seem to have eternity in their hearts and want a meaningful future. The gospels depict how Jesus called his first followers to count the cost of following him.[32] Part of this evaluation was to consider which *future* they wanted. Would it be one where they followed Christ as the sole arbiter of their destinies or some other route. This counting of cost will always be an important criterion of discipleship formation, which cannot be minimized.[33]

Any discipleship formation strategy that is prudent in its approach needs to challenge the person with the claims of Christ on their lives. This includes helping them to count the cost of following him. Being clear about these three loci in the cone of plausibility is essential to help a disciple to be clear about the boundaries of their Christian *plausibility* structure. Life outside of some important defining Christian beliefs and practices, however well they might be contextualized, would not represent a Christian life. It is important to be clear what these are.

It is when we are not clear about a vision of the future, where God's reign will become the one reality to define the plausible, that we may lose the sense of purpose needed to prepare for the life of that *future*. The concept of realized

32. Luke 14:26–33.
33. Bonhoeffer, *Cost of Discipleship.*

eschatology suggests that Jesus inaugurated the reign of God in the present world, and that believers are part of it already, although it is still to be fully consummated at the eschaton.[34] The final establishment of the kingdom will end all other contender claims to plausibility.[35] Disciples after Christendom are best shaped and formed by a vision of the *future and how it calls them to be shaped in readiness for it.*[36] If it is not part of discipleship formation, then we will not really develop disciples who are preparing to become citizens of the eternal kingdom, by living subject to God's reign now. In other words, we need to teach them to live the life of the future in the present.[37]

Prophetic Shaping of the Eschatological Community of Disciples

Jesus acted as a prophet during his earthly existence. This recognition has been substantiated by a number of New Testament scholars.[38] His ministry may be said to have encompassed more than the prophetic, as he was a rabbi and healer, too. With particular reference to Jesus prophetic ministry, attention needs to be given to the vital role that prophetic parables played in his discipleship formation practices, as a means to help disciples consider what made it important to follow him. The parables about the *future* final establishment of the kingdom of God aimed to create a vision of a plausible *future*, that was meant to inform the disciple's *present* plausibility structure.[39] A good example is the eschatological parable of the Sheep and the Goats found in Matthew 25:31–40:

> When the Son of Man comes in his glory, and all the angels with him, then he will sit on the throne of his glory. All the nations will be gathered before him, and he will separate people one from another as a shepherd separates the sheep from the goats, and he will put the sheep at his right hand and the goats at the left. Then the king will say to those at his right hand, "Come, you that are blessed by my Father, inherit the kingdom prepared for you from the foundation of the world; For I was hungry and you gave me food, I was thirsty and you gave me something to drink, I was a stranger and you welcomed me, I was naked and you

34. Phan, "Roman Catholic Theology," in Walls, *Oxford Handbook*, 221.
35. Beasley-Murray, *Jesus and the Kingdom of God*, 313–37.
36. Ibid., 210.
37. Fee, *Paul, the Spirit, and the People of God.*
38. Witherington, *Jesus the Seer*, 277.
39. Keating, "Idiom of 'Prolepsis.'"

gave me clothing, I was sick and you took care of me, I was in prison and you visited me." Then the righteous will answer him, "Lord, when was it that we saw you hungry and gave you food, or thirsty and gave you something to drink? And when was it we saw you a stranger and welcomed you, or naked and gave you clothing? And when was it that we saw you sick or in prison and visited you?" And the king will answer them, "Truly I tell you, just as you did it to one of the least of these who are members of my family, you did it to me."[40]

This parable has often been taken to refer to the final judgment of the nations.[41] The criteria for a positive or negative outcome to the judgment for the participants in the parable's narrative world will be based on whether they have been engaged in the mission of Christ among the marginalized.[42] The implication of the parable is that the Son of Man is, in a mystical spiritual sense, present with the outcasts of society during the present age.[43] The failure of his people to discern the work of God's Spirit on the margins of society in the present age, counts as not being where Christ is at work. If we have the Spirit of Christ, an implication might be we will be where Christ's Spirit is at work. Hence spiritual discernment of the mission of God is vital.[44] There is indeed much more that we could discuss related to this parable on an ethical and missiological level, which will not be possible to fully address in what follows. The real point is to understand the role of parables as proleptic prophecy in Jesus' disciple-making strategy.

This parable of the *future* is projected back into the *present*, not only for the disciples who were being addressed by the story, or for the Christian community who later received Matthew's gospel, in the first-century period. It is also projected *back* into the *present* for each of us to reflect on. The role of this parable was not to manipulate God's people into doing their duty among the poor, but it was rather a means to help them reflect on the depth of their love for God, which could be expressed as love for the marginalized. How might God's love create capacities in the believer's heart to have God's love for the marginalized and outcasts? In other words, it is asking us to make an ontological assessment of our own heart condition.

Ontology calls us to think carefully about the ground principles to human being at the deepest level. What does it mean for us to be conscious of

---

40. Matt 25:31–40 NRSV.
41. Grindheim, "Ignorance Is Bliss," 313–31.
42. Ibid.
43. Via, "Ethical Responsibility," 79–100.
44. Hardy, *Pictures of God*, 211–32.

our own existence as disciple's of Christ? What is the nature of our Christian consciousness? Without digging into the depths of philosophical ontology at this stage, it would seem fair to say that Jesus calls us to consider the level of our consciousness of his love, compassion, and presence among the marginalized in our societies.[45] This parable of the *future* sets a benchmark standard to measure our *present* heart condition with reference to it. The ethos and values of the *future* eternal kingdom, brought by the divine time machine into the present, needs to help us to develop a deeper conscious-ness and awareness of God's love for the weak and vulnerable in our *present* contexts, where believers might engage in missional ministry to outcasts.[46] This deep kind of love is needed as part of what it means for a disciple to become like Christ.

It helps to shape present-day followers of Christ to take on the ethos and values of the kingdom of God, projected from the *future* into the pres-ent. It shapes the disciple's plausibility structure of what it means to be an authentic follower of Christ, who is challenged to engage in similar prac-tices of love and compassion, which the Spirit of the Lord is already ahead of the church doing in a tragically fallen world.[47]

The very nature of Christ's love, defined for us in this parable, is that we make ourselves vulnerable and open to each new person's situation that we are confronted by. We might ask ourselves often, "How can I see the compassionate face of Christ in this person in this situation?" To develop this capacity, we need to learn how to give compassion in a dignified way to those in need,[48] by learning how to receive help from our peers as they help us in our vulnerabilities in a dignified manner. We ourselves need to be able to identify our need for rescue from our own self-made prisons, so that we might learn how to help those we meet who are imprisoned by situations beyond their control or fathoming.

The foundation to the eternal kingdom is the recognition that we are all poor and vulnerable in Christ's sight.[49] Enrichment comes from serving others and allowing ourselves to be open to being served.[50] We ourselves

---

45. Via, "Ethical Responsibility," 79–100.

46. Roldan-Roman, "Reclaiming the Reign of God," 465–71.

47. Ibid.

48. Palacios, *Catholic Social Imagination*, 36, 48; Palacios's Catholic social teaching is well worth considering for its robust interaction with the issues of social justice and in the light of his understanding of social teaching related to the poor and marginalized.

49. Ibid., 175.

50. "Giving and Receiving" (editorial), *Christian Century* 129 (2012) 7; Gray, "In-carnation," 1–13.

are wounded healers,[51] who can learn to know how to offer help that leads to healing because we have had our own wounds healed. If we know what it feels like to be helped in our weakness, then we may become more sensitized to helping others in theirs. This parable of the *future* was provided by Jesus to help disciples deeply evaluate the quality of their relationship with God, and with those that God continues to suffer alongside. Like Christ, the wounded healer, we might help others in their time of need just as we have been humble enough to call for aid ourselves. This parable is based on a prolepsis (anticipation) of the future age. It places value on genuine sacrificial activist love, that authentically seeks to help the outcasts of society.

The Nature of Prophetic Prolepsis

Prophetic prolepsis was a common device used in the context of first-century Judaism.[52] Prophecies of the future, like those of Matthew 25, were told to project the *future* back into the *present*. We might attempt to use a contemporary popular analogy by referring to Dr. Who's Tardis. When Christ uttered his parables of the *future* it is as if he transported the disciples into the *future*, so that this *future* might inform their *present* and their preparation for the *future* age.

Prolepsis has to do with an anticipation of the *future* in the light of which a person evaluates their *present* moral or spiritual condition.[53] It constructs the follower of Christ's plausibility structure. It aims to propel the disciple to participate with the Spirit of Christ in establishing his reign of liberation in the present world. We pray, "Your kingdom come and your will be done on earth as it is in heaven."[54] Wright has argued that God is already king of the earth and his reign is in a process of ongoing in-breaking.[55] The goal is not to create a negative future vision where people fear that they become part of a lost category of goats (the damned).[56] To emphasize this would be to miss the real matter under consideration in the parable, which is positive, in that it calls us to become people of compassion following the Spirit of Christ to work among the marginalized.

---

51. Nouwen, *Wounded Healer*.

52. Aune, "Understanding Jewish and Christian Apocalyptic."

53. Currie, *About Time*, 39.

54. Matt 6:10 RSV.

55. Wright, *How God Became King*, 38.

56. Although I think we must take it seriously that not all who consider themselves authentic believers will be welcomed into the kingdom.

It is the aim of this parable to transform people of faith in the *present*, to take on positive qualities desirable for the *future* age, as they are inspired to discern the pre-ecclesial work of the Spirit of Christ ahead of the church.[57] The diagram below depicts prophetic prolepsis for us.

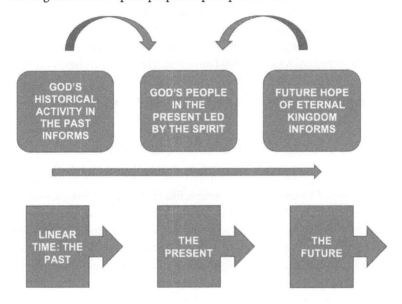

More Examples of Parables of Prolepsis

It may prove helpful for the reader to spend a few minutes reflecting on two other parables found in Matthew 25, to consider some of the challenges they might raise for us, for our churches, or for our approaches to missional ministry in our neighborhoods. One thing worth deep reflection is that the Holy Spirit may be said to be at work ahead of the church, preparing people on the margins of society in our neighborhoods to hear the gospel message. But they will need real help at every level. Christian conversion requires us to dig deeply into our pockets, to often pay a high price to shape people. Conversion is the work of a lifetime. We will need to invest deeply in the lives of those God calls us to walk alongside. They must not become dependent on us, but we need to help to empower them to find the resources on offer to them in Christ to provide for all their needs.[58]

---

57. Newbigin built some of his theology of the Spirit on the concept that the Spirit was at work ahead of the church preparing the ground for the gospel to be communicated and received. See Newbigin, *Open Secret*, 54–58.

58. Blevins and Maddix, *Discovering Discipleship*, 295; Blevins discusses the

A Tale of Ten Young Women

The parable of the ten young women found in Matthew 25:1–13 has been speculated on from numerous angles. One angle is what does it have to say about the real motives and values of these young women. It is of course important not to interpret a parable to mean something not part of its original context. However, in the culture of the period there were certain expectations of family and friends who attended a wedding. In the culture of the period, being prepared was a sign of honor and respect to the groom and his family.[59] The bridegroom, probably a representation of Christ, informs those who were not ready for his arrival. The closure of the door to the feast implied they were not acceptable for admittance. The words "I do not know you" to five of the young women are indeed troubling. What is going on here? What does this parable project back to us about how we should prepare for the messianic wedding banquet?

Overall the parable repeats other calls in Matthew 24 for the believer to watch and to be ready.[60] This seems to represent the need for an expectant attitude in the context of the coming final establishment of the kingdom of God.[61] It could be argued that the real issue of this parable is not the lack of practical preparation of the "foolish" young women, but their lack of relational preparation. The kind of not knowing of the five foolish young women (by the groom) involved in this parable, could relate to a relational lack of intimacy and active interest in those matters most important to the Lord's heart, i.e., the preparation for the wedding banquet of the kingdom.

The bridegroom is the Messiah.[62] The messianic banquet is related to Christ's marriage to the people of his church.[63] In the apocalyptic language of Revelation 19:6–9, those who are part of the eschatological wedding feast of the "Lamb" are those who have "made" themselves "ready."[64] The language of apocalyptic is being used in Matthew chapters 24 and 25.[65] It is therefore appropriate to mine this story from the hermeneutical perspective of the

---

importance of empowering different ethnic groups to be able to sustain themselves.

59. Walvoord, "Christ's Olivet Discourse," 99–105.

60. See Matt 24:44.

61. Walvoord, "Christ's Olivet Discourse," 99–105.

62. Ibid.

63. Deterding, "Eschatological and Eucharistic Motifs," 35–94; although this article focuses on a pericope in Luke, it seems that this pericope resonates with the parables of the ten young women probably coming from an earlier stage in the transmission of the gospel tradition.

64. Rev 19:7 RSV.

65. Walvoord, "Christ's Olivet Discourse," 99–105.

apocalyptic genre. In other words, related to the parable of the ten young women, we might challenge ourselves to evaluate our lives in the context of becoming ready to be part of Christ's eternal people.

We may also learn more by considering Revelation 14:1–6. It presents a group that have prepared themselves by becoming pure and chaste as they follow Christ (the Lamb). In terms of biblical symbolism, this means putting Christ before all others and having an ongoing committed relationship with him.[66] Hence the prolepsis of this passage may pose questions something like this, in anticipation of the coming wedding: "Is planning for the eternal wedding day of Christ the most important thing I am focused on?" "Do I share in his love and passion to prepare others as well?" At the heart of this anticipated wedding invitation is another simple question, "Do I really know Christ in such a way that he is everything to me?" Those who do not enter are those he does not "know." It may be suggested they do not enter because they really did not want to know him. This is of course a contextualization and theologization of a parable that may not have had this background meaning to it.

Three Investors

According to Matthew 25:14–30, three persons were given the wealth of their master to invest. They were advised to invest it wisely through active participation in pursuing their master's business. When the master returns, he rewards each according to their work. The servant who is rebuked for not investing is also not retained in the master's affairs. This is because he did not trust his master's reputation, by actively investing on his behalf in his name. In other words, the main point of this parable is one of lack of trust and commitment to the master, as well as a lack of trust in the master's reputation.[67] However, what is the investment that each of them make?

Chenoweth argues that it does not have to do with how believers use their abilities for the Lord, but rather it is how they invest the secrets of the kingdom of heaven.[68] It has to do with them faithfully increasing the knowledge of the open secret of the reign of God to all those who will listen and accept it. In this sense, it may be argued that the investment has to do with the degree of conscious personal investment by being faithful to God and by putting the values of his love for the world into active missional practices, among those who do not as yet know the secret. In a sense, as I have sug-

66. Ibid.

67. Chenoweth, "Identifying the Talents," 61–72.

68. Ibid.

gested in the case of all three of the proleptic parables of Matthew 25, the fundamental issue is, do disciples follow the Lord based on a passionate love for him, as well as a passionate love for those that he cares for? The parables are calling for us to assess ourselves in the light of our love for God and our love for those he loves.

In the case of the parable of the sheep and the goats, do we really love the marginalized enough to sacrifice our need for comfort and an easy life to rather be where the Lord is by his Spirit among them? In the case of the parable of the ten young women, do we love Christ the Groom and his bride, i.e., his people, including lost and found alike? In the case of the parable of the talents, do we love the open secret of the reign of God enough to faithfully share it with the world? None of these are meant to be moral judgments, but rather to act as ways to evaluate what we value. This is the value of proleptic prophecy of this type. It helps us to keep sharp and focused in our love and faithful service to the Lord, one another, and the world he has called us to make other missional disciples within.

A disciple is called to invest, not based on their own reputation or ability to obtain results,[69] but rather to trust the master's unseen, but real, power to obtain the results he wants through his servants.[70] In terms of the prolepsis of the parable of the three investors, the question we may want to ask ourselves is, "Do I really trust what the Lord has called me to do for him by the way I focus on my life's work?" We may also query, "How am I investing my life's resources, talents, and gifts to serve the Lord?" "In what ways are they focused on Christ's mission rather than on other agendas not related to the matters of God's kingdom?" Once more, this parable is one that calls for us to evaluate ourselves in the light of the anticipated future.

Are we really in love with the Lord so much that we trust his ability to help us to participate in his mission? Are we intentionally focused on getting results that he will recognize as a real desire on our part to be part of his household and its business? This is not as such a theology of works, but rather an ontological assessment of what we really believe and value. Actually it is an ontological assessment of the love we have for Christ and his interests. This is the most important point. God's household and business affairs are based on valuing and loving God first, and our neighbors as ourselves.[71] Valuing the business of God will be evident to us as much as it will to the Lord.[72]

69. Brisson, "Matthew 25:14–30," 307–10.

70. Ibid.

71. Luke 10:27.

72. Ibid.

The Missional Prophetic Voice

The Old Testament people of God found the earliest expression of their theological formation and identity in the stories of the patriarchs.[73] Indeed specific reference begins with Abraham.[74] It is interesting that God's call to Abraham was one that required a journey to a land prophetically promised to his ancestors,[75] which required that he follow the guidance of the Lord to reach it.[76] In an important way Abraham's life story of trust and active response to the Lord's prophetically delivered vision for his people, is informative to how we might discern the pre-ecclesial work of the Spirit ahead of the church in broader society. He is a kind of prototype disciple, who Paul quite rightly calls attention to in Romans 4 to model Christian life on.[77] His kind of faith is to be similar to the faith of those who faithfully seek to follow God.[78]

Abraham does not himself possess the so-called promised land he is directed to by the Lord. His journey is one based on a prolepsis of the prophetic future promise. He lives in anticipation of that future.[79] It is not Abraham but rather his offspring who will inhabit it. This future land is now in the process of forming, as we seek to join with the Spirit in reclaiming secular space for the reign of God in the present. Reclaiming secular space does not imply that God is not sovereign. He is even Lord there, if we are to take the Old Testament prophetic focus of the Lord's sovereign rule over nations seriously.[80] However, in the in-between-times period, between the arrival of the eschaton and now, Newbigin reminds us that we are to seek to participate with the Spirt, at work ahead of the church, in bringing about the reign of God.[81] Temporary that secular structures might be, God seeks to transform them in participation with his people.[82] The ultimate goal is

---

73. Cohn, "Negotiating (with) the Natives," 147–66.

74. Gen 12:1–3.

75. Ben-Gurion, "Bible," 213–20.

76. Gen 12:1–3.

77. Rom 4:9–16.

78. Ibid.

79. Rom 4:16–25.

80. Dan 2:40–45; there is a clear theology in the book of Daniel, as is also found in Isaiah, Jeremiah, etc., that the Lord is sovereign of history and that he raises up kings and kingdoms and overthrows them. This is important to consider, as any claim that we, missional Christians and our churches, can reclaim secular space from the powers opposed to God must realize that God in Christ is Lord of history and he already reigns.

81. Newbigin, Open Secret, 54–58.

82. Heb 12:18–28.

for heaven to be on earth.[83] Missional disciples need to inform themselves that despite appearances that might indicate something different, the Lord is sovereign and he reigns even in secular society. The proleptic nature of missional prophecy here reminds us, as the book of Daniel does (2:40–45), that the Lord ultimately will remove all other contenders to power and he will instead reign. However the Lord does not simply act in judgment, he is patient, wishing to give all a chance to repent.[84]

God's way is to win hearts and minds by his love and mercy, lived out by those of us who seek to prophetically discern what the Spirit of Christ is doing ahead of the church among the people of secular society. Missional disciples are called to be prophets of mercy, who will need to live with the hope of the proleptically revealed future age of the kingdom of God, as the vision that inspires them to action.

It is part of our cone of plausibility that needs to inform our present participation in God's mission, to reclaim all spaces, places, and peoples to live under that reign.[85] Inge discusses the great importance of place and space to the missional work of the Lord.[86] God called his people to live with the consciousness that they have a special eternal destiny. He has a place, a space, his coming kingdom, which will mean his visible reign over the whole earth at the eschaton.[87] This is the basic triangulation of God's tripartite mission which underpins all of Scripture and the whole mission of God.

We are called to remind secular society that the Creator owns all places and spaces, and that mankind has been called to steward it and to serve it, rather than to abuse it and to oppress it and its peoples and creatures. Abraham's story informs us that we need to trust and be obedient as faithful disciples awaiting the arrival of the promised but not yet realized future. This future will include the transformation of all unjust structures and domination systems.[88]

It required Abraham to leave the comfortable inheritance of his earthly father's homeland, so that he might receive an inheritance that is ultimately to be for all of God's people.[89] This also meant leaving behind old ways of doing things, and rather embracing a God who did things in fresh creative new ways in order to restore his creation. Of course there is provision on

83. Rev 21:1–5.

84. 2 Pet 3:9.

85. Col 1:15–21; Eph 1:9–10; Rom 8:30–38.

86. Inge, *Christian Theology of Place*.

87. Ibid.

88. Rev 21:1–9.

89. Gen 12:1–3.

the way, but the inheritance is always calling Christ's followers to keep on seeking the reign of God, in each new place where they participate with his Spirit in reclaiming it for God. This so that it might be based on God's values system, love, and power to recreate and renew it.[90] We are called by the proleptic future kingdom forward, already anticipated in the life of Christ, to participate with the Spirit to call it forth in each place and space we incarnate in, as the mobile missional body of Christ the liberator. Christ is a liberator and so are his followers, as they call yet others to embrace the Spirit of Christ the liberator at work among them. The world is heading toward the goal of the mission of God. The local missional church and its disciples are the hermeneutic of the gospel as Newbigin claimed.[91]

In terms of Jesus' disciples, they followed the incarnate Lord, who was physically present to guide them on their journey. In the case of Abraham, there was a revelation and manifestation of God's prophetic guidance as a direct communication with Abraham at important junctures in his journey.[92] In the case of the disciples, they had the incredible privilege of regularized contact with the incarnate Lord. He was present in a physical way, which compared to Abraham, God was not. In the case of contemporary disciples, we need to prophetically and proleptically discern where God is calling us to participate in mission alongside him. Newbigin suggested that we need to prophetically and proleptically gesture through our communities, a foretaste of the future life of love, grace, forgiveness, and mutual service to those around us.[93] Missional communities like this will inevitably be countercultural and subversive, as we cannot live with the same kind of values that drive late modern individualistic human society in the West. This indeed calls for a radical reassessment of our values as missional disciples after Christendom.

90. 2 Cor 5:16–21.

91. Newbigin, *Gospel in a Pluralist Society*, ch. 18.

92. Gen 15:1–8.

93. Goheen, "Missional Calling," in Foust et al., *Scandalous Prophet*, 37–54.

Section 3

The Qualities, Values, and Convictions of Missional Communities of Praxis

This section focuses on the qualities, values, and convictions of missional communities that shape disciples based on the shared life of the people of God by participation in the Triune life and mission.

Chapter 6

Exploring the Values of Discipleship After Christendom

By Andrew R. Hardy

Introduction

In a postmodern, postcolonial, post-Christendom, pluralistic, and multicultural Western context, it is far harder to represent Christian values, where the barriers of cultural difference, caused by ethnic and racial differences, can cause Christian groups that are dissimilar to misunderstand each others' faith communities. This is as much true between Christians from different races and cultures as it is with other world religious groups represented in the West. Paul declared that Christ had broken down the dividing wall between God and humanity,[1] to provide a new state of affairs where there is no longer slave nor free, Jew nor Greek, male nor female.[2] Nevertheless, in the contemporary context, there is a tendency for different Christian cultural groups, in a variety of denominations and networks, to remain largely separate in their particular ecclesial monocultures, too often with few efforts made to fellowship with others different from their own culture.

---

1. Eph 2:14.
2. Gal 3:28.

Power, its use and abuse, are hot potatoes we all need to be aware of in this multicultural context. The power structures of our churches and their traditions play a significant part in keeping Christian groups separated or united, although Christ is their single Lord and his kingdom embraces all despite differences in culture.[3]

A primary value of being part of God's multicultural family is that all believers are one united people by virtue of Christ the Lord.[4] This chapter focuses on the shared heritage that all peoples and cultures have as part of God's family. The Trinity's family is one new united people. Indeed Trinitarian theology is also being explored in terms of the theology of religions and interfaith mission and dialogue.[5] We need to find fresh ways of sharing our diverse gifts with one another, based on our common bond in Christ.[6] This will inevitably mean sharing in interfaith dialogue. Moltmann focuses on the value of a communitarian faith, where people can creatively and freely choose how to live in the light of their shared identity, in light of a relational doctrine of the Trinity.[7] The Trinity by nature is missionary and seeks to reconcile all peoples to their family. Hastings comments:

> Some churches, perhaps most in the West, are so focused on
> their gathered life that there is little intentionality in equipping
> God's people for the dispersed life of the church.[8]

The book of Acts highlights the challenge in the early church where Jewish and Gentile believers were in conflict.[9] There was an attempt to alienate the new Gentile believers from the emerging Christian community. The so-called Jerusalem Council settled the matter. However, this demonstrates the tendency of the kind of issues that can inhibit the "dispersed life of the church."

The New Testament documents also highlight what it was like for Jews and Gentiles who were challenged by the forces of Roman governance to coexist under the reign of another emperor other than Christ. This, later in the century, meant that believers literally went underground in the catacombs of Rome and worshiped in secret to avoid being persecuted for their allegiance to Jesus.

---

3. Hardy and Yarnell, *Forming Multicultural Partnerships*, ch. 3.

4. Gal 3:28.

5. Karkkainen, *Trinity and Religious Pluralism*.

6. 1 Cor 12.

7. Moltmann et al., *Passion for God's Reign*, 35.

8. Hastings, *Missional God*, 49.

9. Acts 15.

Moreover, in the melting pot of the diverse peoples and social classes who were part of the early church, theoretically united by the one Christ, claims of abuse of one group of Christians over another was an issue. For instance, the original apostles had to appoint deacons to care for the Hellenist Jews' poor and widows.[10] Some Jewish believers looked down on the Gentiles for not keeping all the Jewish traditions, customs, and laws.[11] Wealthy members at the Corinthian church refused to share in eucharistic meals with the poor or slaves.[12] Educated Greek Christians looked down on uneducated believers.[13] Peter refused to eat with Gentile Christians, when Jewish believers came from Jerusalem to meet with him.[14] Some professing Christian faith tried to syncretize their pagan beliefs with Christian beliefs.[15] Women were expected to be subordinate to men.[16] Intercultural conflict occurred in the early church. The one new people of Christ were to become one body, united in the one Christ.[17] However, it was not a simple task to unite because of significant cultural differences.

The world of the first century was similar to the postmodern world in some ways, in the sense that the Romans had displaced people groups around the empire, meaning it had become somewhat multicultural and certainly pluralistic in its various provinces. There was a hunger for spiritual experiences, such as we find with those influenced by late modern postsecular consciousness, along with a plurality of religious practices. The mystery religions of Serapis and Isis and the Oracular faith focused in the Oracle of Delphi were renowned as part of this ancient mysticism. The *Pax Romana* offered a degree of peace and security to the empire which was unprecedented compared to that offered by earlier ancient Near Eastern kingdoms.

Late modern democracies seek to provide equal rights for everyone as part of their humanitarian ideology, which is different from the first century and its divisions between Roman citizen, slave and free. In this sense secular society encourages the tolerance of difference in others as much as it can. However, we must not forget Roman law was progressive and it permitted nations to retain worship of their deities as long as they paid homage to the divine emperor cult begun by Augustus Caesar. However, Christians could

10. Acts 6.
11. Col 3.
12. 1 Cor 11.
13. 1 Cor 1.
14. Gal 2.
15. Col 2.
16. 1 Cor 11.
17. Eph 2:14.

not worship Caesar as their lord. This made it hard to live as equal citizens much of the time in the empire after the Jews lost favor with Rome after 70 CE. It was hard to live the value of love and forgiveness when persecution meant martyrdom and death, especially in the second and third centuries. Are not our Christian values meant to be of a kind that promote preferring one another in love?[18] As hard as it is to be servants toward others who often may despise a belief in an all-loving God, there is a great need for the multicultural family of Christ to model the values of Jesus, who was sent to serve rather than to be "served."[19]

What are some of the important values that might cause God's multi-culturally diverse people to partner together to win hearts and minds for the Lord? In this chapter we will consider eight themes: risky compassion, trust and trustworthiness, vulnerability, transparency, and nonjudgmental regard, humility, love, and service, forgiveness as normative, generosity and hospitality, unity and acceptance of otherness, and openness to the reign of God.

Values Defined

How are each of these category descriptors values? Perhaps it will help to define what we mean by values. As a noun, the word "value" could be said to include two important definitive qualities. First, it can mean to consider something to be deserving of consideration because it is important, useful and something of worth. Second, it can represent the principles or standards of behavior that enable a group to evaluate and make judgments of what is important in life. Both definitions may be said to lead to behaviors that are motivated by values. Convictional communities are also communities that are intentionally defined by their beliefs and values.

In this sense human behaviors take on actions motivated by values and convictions. They could be called an important dimension of convictional disciple-making communities of praxis. The first action, often missed, is the mental process of considering someone, or something, to be of significant worth. If we consider something to be of high value, it will inevitably lead us to action that puts a high priority on behaving in a way that is beneficial and positive toward that thing or person. Each of the values categories to be considered are intrinsic to the life of discipleship after Christendom.

Jesus set out the primary qualities that underpin all the values that might be said to motivate our behaviors. These qualities are the basis to

18. Rom 12:10.
19. Matt 20:28.

abundant Christian living (the so-called blessed life) according to Matthew's account of Jesus' ethical teaching.[20]

These qualities are foundational to the worldview, beliefs, expectations, values, and practices of disciples after Christendom. They are part of the convictional architecture of our communities in terms of the qualities that will define how people's convictions motivate them to behave. The Greek term used for the blessed abundant life (Greek, *makarios*) is expressive of an active state of positive spiritual and relational thriving in the Christian life of praxis. The beatitudes begin with "Blessed are the poor in spirit."[21] In other words, knowing that one is in need of help from God is the basis to seeking it and receiving it. Chan suggests that this blessed state is nothing less than the communities' actual inclusion in the kingdom of heaven, as recipients of the benefits of the new age that is being inaugurated.[22]

The "blessed" life, is one that will bring about peace and wholeness in relationship with God and others. It means a life that is whole and optimally functional. Even the suffering and persecution of a community can be part of the healthy Christian life. The beatitudes are intrinsic to the all-time honored tradition of the historic Christian faith. We cannot but let our present outlooks and horizons be challenged by these highest of kingdom qualities. Out of them come some important values which we have tried to capture.

Risky Compassion

> When Jesus had spoken these words, he lifted up his eyes to heaven and said, "Father, the hour has come, glorify thy Son that the Son may glorify thee, since thou hast given him power over all flesh, to give eternal life to all whom thou hast given him. And this is eternal life, that they know thee the only true God, and Jesus Christ whom thou hast sent. I glorified thee on earth, having accomplished the work which thou gavest me to do, and now, Father, glorify thou me in thy own presence with the glory which I had with thee before the world was made.[23]

> If you were of the world, the world would love its own; but because you are not of the world, but I chose you out of the world, therefore the world hates you. Remember the word that I said to

20. Matt 6:3–12 RSV.
21. Matt 6:3, 4.
22. Chan, *Ten Commandments*, 282–83.
23. John 17:1–5 RSV.

you, "A servant is not greater than his master." If they persecuted me, they will persecute you; if they kept my word, they will keep yours also.[24]

RISK TAKING

ACCEPTED

CONFIRMED

DISCONFIRMED

REJECTED

SELF REVELATION

We learn from John 17:1–5 that Christ was sent by the Father to convey the message of God's love among humanity. Not only did the infinite God choose to create mankind with the capacity to accept or reject their Creator, but Moltmann suggests that from the days of eternity the cross of Christ was a defining value of God's sacrificial love for the cosmos.[25] In other words, to create real beings made in God's image took risk and compassion. To be real, humans need to be able to determine their destinies, which includes the ability to shape their lives. God's love for those he created can be confirmed, or disconfirmed, by those who accept or reject God. John's gospel does not present God as an unmoved mover,[26] without emotion or the ability to have deep empathy with creation.

Father, Son, and Holy Spirit are moved. The language of deep passion for their creation is intrinsic to the picture of God to be found in Jesus' relationships with his disciples. Schweitzer suggests that God may, in one sense, be termed transcendent, but in Christ he has passion and love for people, meaning his transcendence does not entail loss of love for his creation.[27] The

24. John 15:19–20 RSV.
25. Moltmann, *Crucified God*.
26. Such as Thomas Aquinas and Aristotle present.
27. Schweitzer, "Passionate God," 34–45.

passion story is the most oft repeated narrative in the New Testament. God's love is presented as risky compassion.

According to Thomsen, God's love is noncoercive.[28] For Tupper, God takes the risk of self-limitation to his omnipotence, by taking on humanity in the incarnation.[29] The aim is to give humanity the freedom to respond to his love. This makes humanity able to choose whether or not to participate in a meaningful relationship with God.

Humans are made in God's image (*imago Dei*).[30] They can choose to embrace a life of deep communion with God. According to Zizioulas, God is defined by the personal and relational nature of the persons of the Trinity, as they interact in deep interrelations in their life as the imminent Trinity. This also is what humanity has been created to participate in to some degree.[31] Scripture speaks of the great passion and oft-reported pain and grief of God,[32] when his creatures choose to reject the overtures of the divine love toward them. We find this grief often expressed in the Hebrew Bible by the prophets.[33] Disciples after Christendom do not serve a God who lacks feeling or empathy, like the unmoved God posited by the Enlightenment's philosophical theology.[34] They serve a God who calls them to deny themselves, to take up their own crosses of risky compassion to follow in Christ's footsteps after him.[35] It is costly to invest our lives as followers of Jesus. Like him we are called to seek out the lost. We too, at times, face rejection and grief because people turn away, just as the Lord does.

Relational psychologists point out that in order to form meaningful relationships with people, we need to take the risk of revealing who we are to them.[36] This opens up the possibility of being hurt or psychologically injured.[37] Our overtures of friendship may be rejected. People may abuse our love and use it against us. It is costly to love in this way. In a hyper-individualistic Western context, where a belief in an omnibenevolent God

28. Thomsen, "Expanding the Scope," 85–94.

29. Tupper, "Self-Limitation of God," 161–91.

30. Gen 1:26–27.

31. Zizioulas, *Eucharistic Communion and the World.*

32. Jer 8:18—9:3.

33. Hosea 1–3; in this profound book God demonstrates his love through the parable of Hosea's love for his prostitute wife, Gomer.

34. McGrath, *Historical Theology*, 12.

35. Luke 9:23.

36. Watson and Moran, *Trust, Risk and Uncertainty*, 31.

37. Winch, *Emotional First Aid.*

no longer defines public perceptions, people seek to protect themselves by fighting for their rights to get things their own way.

In the church of Christ, the risky compassion of a more open, loving way of being a Christian community of friends, brothers, and sisters can be resisted and avoided even by Christians. Is Hastings right, that we have retreated from God's mission and proactive participation with the Spirit in the work of reconciliation?[38] He offers an alternative view,

> I believe we can feel positive about mission in this era insofar as we can see evidence of windows that the Spirit has created within postmodernity for receptivity to the gospel.[39]

He qualifies his optimism usefully,

> As Tom Smail notes, "In our own day, the deconstructing scepticism that Feuerbach applied to religion has in much post-modern thinking been extended to all claims to know the truth about any reality that is objective to us." Postmodernity has therefore exposed the gods of modernity as unreliable, and this can only be good for Christian mission.[40]

Christians can point to a God that can be present to help all who seek such an experience. However, skepticism and hyper-individualism is not unknown as a pervasive egotistic virus that can effect believers as much as unbelievers. No one is free from the selfish gene of a niche market consumerist individualistic society, where people compete for personal gain. Christians can too often be driven to seek late modernity's materialistic benefits, even if others are pushed aside to obtain them.

Moreover, no one, not even believers, are unaffected by the loss of faith in objective truths. Can anyone be trusted? It may be just too risky and costly to let down our guard, then only to be hurt or harmed by those who profess the same faith in God, let alone those who do not.

By way of contrast, John's gospel calls for the deep, intimate fellowship of oneness and togetherness between the followers of Christ,[41] somewhat like the oneness of love and intimacy that the Father, Son, and Spirit enjoy. This is on offer to all who would take the risk of approaching the Lord.[42] This puts a high value on the quality of love as service and openness to risk, because of Christ's risky compassion.

38. Hastings, *Missional God*, 49.
39. Ibid., 57.
40. Ibid., 54.
41. John 17:21–26.
42. Matt 11:28–30.

Christian faith communities need to be safe places to engage in risky relationships with those close to them.[43] They need to be carefully cultivated environments that help people to exercise risky love and compassion toward each other. A strong Christian family that supports and loves its members well can be a powerhouse that supports efforts to participate in the Spirit's work of risky compassion. Disciples after Christendom are called to be role models of risk and compassion, as activist proactive love that seeks to help others find their highest sense of meaning as sons and daughters of God.

We can choose to take the risk of revealing something about ourselves to others. They may prove receptive. They may confirm our efforts to build meaningful friendships with them. Alternatively, we may risk revealing something about ourselves to others, and they may disconfirm our risk-taking behavior. Hence a meaningful relationship will not be possible. Given that all human beings, Christian or not, can only effectively relate to each other based on relationships that are affirming and reciprocal, it will not be possible for them to work unless this happens.

Success inevitably depends on how safe people feel it is to take risks of revealing their deeper selves to others. The diagram below models how risk-taking can succeed or fail, in terms of building trusting relationships, where people feel mutually accepted and affirmed or disconfirmed and rejected.

Risky compassion and empathy requires risk-taking to build meaningful lasting friendships with people, as we seek to disciple them. It needs to become a primary Christ-like value we aver.

43. Holmes and Williams, *Church as a Safe Place.*

Trust and Trustworthiness

The diagram below illustrates something from a module which one of the writers designed for a course in cross-cultural mission.

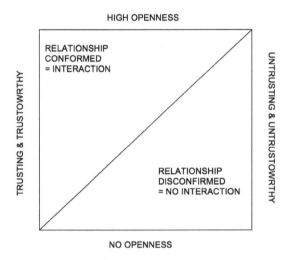

It is adapted from Johnson's psychosocial work.[44] The diagram illustrates how trust can be formed and developed between people. Essentially the diagram demonstrates that for optimum relationships to be developed, there needs to be a reciprocity of trust given to another, who experiences this to imply that a person is trustworthy. The other also needs to respond in a trusting manner, by being willing to risk revealing things about themselves in what is communicated between two or more people. A trust-based relationship needs to be built on mutuality, where each person involved in a friendship of trust toward the other, as well as the other proving themselves worthy of that trust placed in them.

Trust and trustworthiness are high values for human relationships. Trust and trustworthiness are key values for missional disciples to celebrate and exercise well. Drane has adequately demonstrated that late modern people are not turning to churches, because they intrinsically distrust them because of perceived misuse or abuse of power.[45] Do churches have relevance, given that their authority structures and motives are too often discredited due to abuses revealed in the media.[46] Youth and young adults

44. Johnson, *Reaching Out*.

45. Drane, *Do Christians Know*, ch. 1.

46. This is just one news media report among many. It takes little effort to proliferate them in Google searches and their like. The goal here is not to vilify the Catholic

seem not to perceive the church to be an environment where they can feel comfortable to be open about their life challenges and questions. Generations Y and Z make up the 40 percent who have never gone to church.[47]

We are not saying that no one is seeking to engage with Christian people. However, it is notable that the majority of the population do not seek to do so in churches. The diagram above illustrates the value of openness and sharing, that has to be founded on high trust between people when they are seeking to get to know each other better. This means we need to build trust with people in their own contexts outside the church.

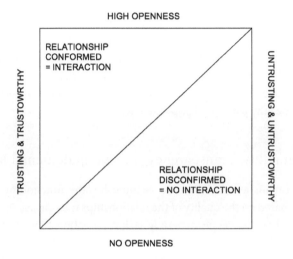

According to Johnson, it takes a risk to put our trust in another. It is foundational to all relationship formation.[48] Openness can be optimized by developing relationship-building approaches and skills, that are based on an authentic reciprocal conveyance of trust and trustworthiness. It has to be genuine in its expression and intentions or people will not respond positively. The key question to ask ourselves is, "Do we share in the love of God for people in such a way that we are not seeking to get something out of it for ourselves?" Inevitably love is a costly gift to exercise well. It takes time and investment in order to care for others properly. We need to prove ourselves trustworthy.

The discussion of risky compassion and empathy raises the importance of effective relationship formation, as a primary catalyst for a Christian missional community to develop, in order to disciple people well. Risk-taking,

church either. Holpuch, "Ongoing Child Sex Abuse."

47. Stoddard and Cuthbert, *Church on the Edge*, 30.

48. Johnson, *Reaching Out.*

where we share deeper, riskier weaknesses and needs with others, in order to offer support and insight, is built on trust and the trustworthiness of others in our faith communities.

Even before we consider shaping new disciples to become like Christ, we need to have healthy-functioning relationships between people in our Christian groups. This chapter is discussing values vital for missional communities that disciple people properly. It is not possible in this chapter to do more than express the need for churches to obtain resources to help Christian communities to function in healthy ways, as trustworthy environments for people to participate within. There is much need for the development of the relational and social capital that people in our faith communities need to exercise and possess, in order to be effective in making new disciples. We probably need to strategically consider ways to help less healthily functioning Christian groups to become safe places to disciple people within.[49] Perhaps further work needs to be encouraged on how to shape and form faith communities to become optimally healthy places to disciple people.

Vulnerability, Transparency, and Nonjudgmental Regard

At best humans are socialized to become healthy-functioning relational creatures, based on the quality of the relationships they engage in from birth to the day they die. People generally seek out relationships where it is safe to be vulnerable with those closest to them. There are of course pathological psychological conditions whereby people seek out those who are not safe to be vulnerable around. This kind of pathology occurs when people seek to work on deep psychological wounds that come from abuse or suffering from the past, by reliving them again with those who abuse them in similar ways to past experiences in present unhealthy relationships.[50] Churches can have people who, to one degree or another, fit this latter pathological typology. Some people may seek to appease an angry or abusive inner image of an abusive parent, which in some way they project onto God as the ultimate parent in need of placation. The church, like any other socially constructed group, is not immune from human intra-psychic and extra-psychic injury among its participants.

49. Holmes and Williams, *Becoming More Like Christ*; at the heart of this work is the recognition that becoming more Christ-like as a disciple is to become more human and more whole.

50. Nouwen, *Wounded Healer*.

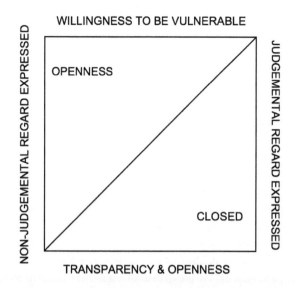

Having briefly noted the complexity of human psychosocial functioning, it is important to consider relational values at their best, based on the primary value of grace and God's nonjudgmental regard, toward a fallen humanity through Jesus Christ. In the case of healthy-functioning relationships, there will inevitably be a high degree of willingness to make oneself vulnerable to trusted others, which in turn leads to a higher degree of openness and transparency about the darker sides of our own human natures, with those we trust.[51] A healthy-functioning community, that can help shape and form Christ likeness among its members, will be one where we feel safe to talk about our darker sides without fear of judgment or reprisal.

The things we are less proud of, such as our lust, our selfishness, our hurts and how we have hurt, harmed others or ourselves need to be dealt with. There is often a reserve about sharing the shadow side of our natures with others, because we have learned that people can use negative information against us, given the right opportunity.

Having said this, in order for the forgiveness, acceptance, and active grace of God to be experienced among us, so that we can support each other to overcome our temptations, bad habits, and weaknesses, we need to be willing to express nonjudgmental regard toward others.

This is especially important when we express darker things about ourselves with another. The diagram above demonstrates that people can only realistically be expected to become vulnerable and transparent with others,

51. Johnson, *Reaching Out.*

if they can trust others not to judge them. In other words, there is the need for them to feel we have accepted them as valued and loved by God, being deserving of his forgiveness, grace, and power to effectively heal and restore them. And of course, deep wounds take time to heal and scars can remain. We need to foster patience like that of the Lord.[52] He gives us time to grow and change. This fruit of the Spirit is crucial.[53] Hence the primary values of communities that disciple people well need to learn how not to judge others' weaknesses.[54] They need to become communities that are determined to accept weakness and the expression of it as normal. They will need to welcome weakness as a strength. God's grace operates under the rubric of there being no more condemnation in Christ.[55] Communities that shape disciples to become like Christ will have empathy and tolerance for the recognition of human weakness as the starting point where Christ can bring transformation. It is a principle when we are weak then we seek the strength that comes from the Lord and we receive it. The first step to healing is always the step where we let another in to help us. We are to bear one another's burdens in love.[56] Love covers a multitude of sins. Willingness to declare our weaknesses is the means by which we create opportunities to overcome them. This chapter, in many ways, seeks to draw on practical pastoral wisdom in its discussion of values.

52. 2 Pet 3:9.
53. Gal 5:22–26.
54. Matt 7:1.
55. Rom 8:1.
56. Gal 6:2.

Humility, Love, and Service

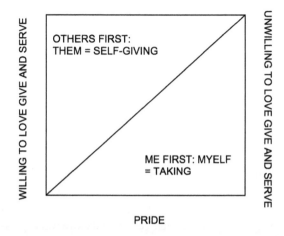

At that time the disciples came to Jesus, saying, "Who is the greatest in the kingdom of heaven?" And calling to him a child, he put him in the midst of them, and said, "Truly, I say to you, unless you turn and become like children, you will never enter the kingdom of heaven. Whoever humbles himself like this child, he is the greatest in the kingdom of heaven."[57]

Pride at its extreme is an anti-God state of mind. That is, of course, if it locks out any influence from the deity, with the alternative being our own ego-driven self-determinism as the key guide to our futures. It can also be the largest cause of strife between people, when one is not willing to admit or accept they were in the wrong. Even if someone is in the right, pride can still fester. Standing for what is right may achieve a good result for the parties concerned, but the downside is that it may feed the pride of the one who takes joy in being seen to be right.

Humility, conversely, creates openness to accept that there is always more to learn. Accepting and admitting that one is wrong is a strength that can aid growth and allow others to have influence on our lives. False humility is sycophantic, with the effect of someone putting themselves down to make another feel better about themselves, in order to keep in with them for personal benefit. It also expresses a lack of love for one's self as a valued person made in God's image.

57. Matt 18:1–4 RSV.

Christ defined greatness as the humility of the child that does not use the sophistry of adult power games to get their own way.[58] In the ancient Near Eastern culture, the child was completely subject to the will of parents and society in general. They had no power to exercise until they came of age.[59] All they could do was to trust themselves to the care of those with the will and power to care for them. Ultimately Jesus called his disciples to put their trust in God as their heavenly Father, whose will was that love and service should define the motivations of those who would be the leaders of his vulnerable children.[60]

Mark records Jesus' words to the Twelve regarding the nature of greatness and leadership in the kingdom, "If anyone would be first, he must be last of all and servant of all."[61] Primary to this view of greatness is that Christ himself is portrayed as the fulfillment of the Servant Songs of Isaiah. According to Phillips, Luke-Acts portrays the disciples to be the same.[62] Christ's ministry was defined by acts of sacrifice, service, love, and forgiveness, so must the disciple define their lives in a similar vein.[63] God's love was expressed through Christ in the kind of genuine love that motivated people to want to love him in return. Disciples after Christendom need to seek to serve others in similar ways to those of Christ. Humility is needed by all of us. It is even more important for those in leadership positions to exercise well.[64]

A leader that seeks to control, manipulate, and pull the strings of those she or he has responsibility for, to get things her or his own way, is indicative that he/she suffers from pride—having the need to be in control and in the right. It can prove very hard to allow oneself to receive constructive critical feedback. One way that we seek to avoid pride is to make ourselves open to accountability to trusted others, who can give us insights into our blind spots and weaknesses.[65]

This is a simple way to help us to develop and maintain humility. More than ever, in a hyper-individualistic society, we need to be humble. Humility and love are closely associated as qualities of divine agape love, which may be defined as sacrificial, self-giving love. In this sense, love and humility define Christian love for each of us. One who is not willing to take the humble

58. Matt 18:13.
59. Clements, "Relation of Children," 133–44; Gal 4:1–5.
60. Matt 18:13.
61. Mark 9:35 RSV.
62. Phillips, review of *Followers of Jesus*, 196.
63. Mark 2:5.
64. Standish, "Whatever Happened to Humility?," 22–26.
65. Frederick et al., "Effect of the Accountability Variables," 302–16.

place of service, is the one that cannot as such really serve in the sense that Christ did. In Philippians, Paul captures the humility of Christ's act of sacrifice by which he emptied himself and became as a servant.[66] Disciples need to practice radical self-emptying.

> Have this mind among yourselves, which you have in Christ Jesus, who, though he was in the form of God, did not count equality with God a thing to be grasped, but emptied himself, taking the form of a servant, being born in the likeness of men. And being found in human form he humbled himself and became obedient unto death, even death on a cross. Therefore God has highly exalted him and bestowed on him the name which is above every name, that at the name of Jesus every knee should bow, in heaven and on earth and under the earth, and every tongue confess that Jesus Christ is Lord, to the glory of God the Father.[67]

Jesus the representative disciple is the one for all of us to model our lives upon.

Forgiveness as Normative

In Christian theology, the belief in the forgiveness of God is normative as a practice that all Christians are called to exercise toward others.[68] There can be no good news if God's gift of forgiveness in Jesus is not both the grounds and active outworking of what all our relationships with God and others are based on. Without forgiveness there will be no new society, and there will be no harmony in an eternal kingdom of peace. The gift of forgiveness must be the basis of a new start for every person. It has to be the primary behavior of all those who are part of the eternal kingdom of grace, both in terms of how they exercise forgiveness toward others, as well as toward themselves. In other words, we need to forgive ourselves because God has forgiven us. If we do not forgive ourselves for things that have troubled our consciences, then we will inevitably be without inner peace.

66. See ch. 4.
67. Phil 2:5–11 RSV.
68. Worthington, *Just Forgiveness.*

The basic glue of God's activist love is the free gift of forgiveness, most often described as justification.[69] God has set us right with himself through the once-for-all-time sacrifice of Christ, who is the new elect humanity, as Barth classically articulated it.[70] All punishment for sin, past, present, and future, is covered and repealed by his death. Christ has the power to transform our lives by virtue of the power contained within his resurrection life. It renews us on a daily basis.[71] It is the basis of the reign of God, that those who receive personal forgiveness also forgive all those who have wronged or harmed them.[72] Nothing is to be held against anyone else, anywhere.[73] Nonjudgmental regard has already been highlighted as a fundamental quality of the kingdom of God. It is arguably the lifeblood of the family of God.

Jesus iterated that it is not possible to have received forgiveness from God, if the one forgiven cannot forgive others.[74] This has often been misunderstood. In terms of the Judeo-Christian worldview of Jesus' first-century culture, the correspondence between receiving forgiveness as an experience that transforms the human inner psyche, and living it out as a new defining behavior, are united realities. The Jewish mind could not separate inner

69. Matson, "Divine Forgiveness in Paul?," 59–83.

70. Hastings, *Missional God, Missional Church*, 45.

71. Spurgeon, "Paid in Full," 66–69.

72. Luke 6:37.

73. Rom 8:1.

74. Jones and Célestin, *Forgiving as We've Been Forgiven*.

states that motivate behavior from outer behaviors that showed the inner fruit of the heart.[75] If God's forgiveness is received, then it will also motivate people in fresh ways to forgive others, in the same way that God in Christ has fully forgiven them.[76]

The parable of the unforgiving servant, who was forgiven a great debt, but who then would not forgive another's lesser liability, illustrates the principle of forgiveness received leads to giving it freely to everyone else.[77] Notice how the parable highlights a direct relationship between behavior and motives. To not act out our personal experience of forgiveness received from God toward others, is not to have received forgiveness as a motivating force in our hearts. There is deep psychology here. Disciples after Christendom need to practice forgiveness as the defining outlook they have toward others.

It is intrinsic, a primary value to be experienced in the missional community. One important way the church models the gospel as the good news is when people experience fellowship in it, as an assumed active participation in a community based on forgiveness. It is an expectation that it be exercised without reservation toward one another. In this sense, the Christian community is a place that seeks to model kingdom society, by the way people live out the grace and forgiveness of God toward each other. Forgiveness is normative to disciples after Christendom.

In a late modern society, where bad news and assignment of blame is good news, too often sought out by a vicious news media, the Christian community is called to model a way of life that seeks to heal and restore those in need of forgiveness. Forgiveness is the normative lifeblood for every follower in Jesus to exercise, without qualification or excuse.[78]

Generosity and Hospitality

> He entered Jericho and was passing through. And there was a man named Zacchaeus; he was a chief tax collector, and rich. And he sought to see who Jesus was, but could not, on account of the crowd, because he was small of stature. So he ran on ahead and climbed up into a sycamore tree to see him, for he was to pass that way. And when Jesus came to the place, he looked up and said to him, "Zacchaeus, make haste and come down; for I must stay at your house today." So he made haste and came down, and

75. Matt 15:18–19.
76. Eph 4:32.
77. Matt 18:23–35 RSV.
78. Eph 4:32.

received him joyfully. And when they saw it they all murmured, "he has gone in to be the guest of a man who is a sinner." And Zacchaeus stood and said to the Lord, "Behold, Lord, the half of my goods I give to the poor; and if I have defrauded any one of anything, I restore it fourfold." And Jesus said to him, "Today salvation has come to this house, since he also is a son of Abraham. For the Son of Man came to seek and to save the lost."[79]

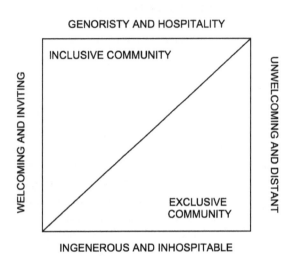

GENORISTY AND HOSPITALITY

INCLUSIVE COMMUNITY

WELCOMING AND INVITING

UNWELCOMING AND DISTANT

EXCLUSIVE COMMUNITY

INGENEROUS AND INHOSPITABLE

In a strange quirk of reverse logic, Jesus was generous and hospitable to Zacchaeus, the hated collector of taxes. Though small in stature, Zacchaeus's reputation cast a bigger shadow, that caused the crowd that accompanied Jesus to critique the Lord's generosity in accepting his hospitality.[80] Accepting it meant that Christ extended the generosity and hospitality of God's grace to Zacchaeus. The messiah chose to accept the hospitality of one that the Pharisees would have treated as unclean and unworthy to associate with. Their reputations rested on distancing themselves from the impure and outcasts. They saw it as their job to keep the faith of Israel pure. Jesus' presence in Zacchaeus's home brought the generosity of God into his heart, home, and life practices as a consequence of it.[81]

Home is after all where the heart is. The Lord of Israel showed the grace of God to embrace and forgive those that polite religious society would not entertain. Jesus subverted the values of Jewish polite society, by

79. Luke 19:1–10 RSV.
80. Luke 19:7.
81. Luke 19:8.

modeling the key value of God's generous love to those considered to be beyond redemption, in the estimation of popular religious belief.[82] A key value of discipleship after Christendom is to seek to rehumanize and to re-integrate those who are on the margins, reinstating them as valued citizens of the kingdom of God. This is particularly to be emphasized among those who are treated as beyond society's acceptance.[83]

It is as we give and receive hospitality from people on the margins that we invite them into friendships with us. Sharing food and participation in the social activities of the home is an invitation to enter into a person's private world. It is an invitation to take part in the intimacy of the host in their territory. Christ as host and guest, in Zacchaeus's home, on the one hand receives Zacchaeus's household into the banquet hall of the heavenly Father. On the other hand, Zacchaeus's view of himself is transformed. He now considered himself to have been generously welcomed, forgiven, and taken into the household of God.

So powerful was the transformation, that he actively sought to pay back all those he had defrauded. His view of himself was transformed. The one seen as outcast now puts himself alongside the outcast. He gives his wealth to care for the poor, powerless, and disadvantaged. His words and actions provide a window into his heart, that is now being transformed and softened. He could from then on seek to empower victims and outcasts, us-ing his resources to help them find a place of welcome and acceptance with the God who had shown him hospitality and generosity.

In terms of how disciples are shaped, it is important that life is shared more deeply than at a superficial level in our missional communities. Gen-erosity and hospitality need to be given to strangers. It expands our capacity to love, not only those we like or those that society values, but also those we find it hard to accept. This is costly love, love that takes outsiders into the in-timacy and hospitality of the home.[84] The difference between an inclusive or exclusive community can be understood in answer to a question, "In what ways does this faith community exercise hospitality to outsiders and those disowned by society?"

82. Pippert, "Faith Should Rewrite," 28–30.

83. Heuertz and Pohl, *Friendship at the Margins*.

84. This article discusses some critical challenges more recently made by scholars suggesting that social justice to widows, orphans, and strangers was not such a high val-ue as some Old Testament scholars have argued. Sneed, "Israelite Concern," 498–507.

Unity and Acceptance of Otherness

Now there are varieties of gifts, but the same Spirit; and there are varieties of service, but the same Lord; and there are varieties of working, but it is the same God who inspires them all in everyone.[85]

God has so adjusted the body, giving the greater honor to the inferior part, that there may be no discord in the body, but that the members may have the same care for one another. If one member suffers, all suffer together; if one member is honored, all rejoice together.[86]

Otherness is hard to accept when someone is very different from ourselves. It is much easier to accept people who are similar in temperament to ourselves, who do things in similar ways or those who have similar expectations and values compared to our own. Moreover, it is much easier to relate to people of the same culture as our own, because we tend to interpret things in similar ways compared to those who come from a culture very different from our own. In other words, there are degrees of ease or uneasiness that are experienced when we relate to people. The degree of perceived difference can cause misunderstandings and conflicts between people, because

85. 1 Cor 12:4–6 RSV.
86. 1 Cor 12:24a–26 RSV.

we misinterpret the behaviors and motives of others. Conversely, we may feel attracted to those who are very different from ourselves, if we perceive them to be the kind of people we would like to become.[87] The acceptance of otherness and difference is a complex reality we all face to differing degrees every day of our lives.

In the Western multicultural context, many different subcultures are present. It is hard to understand this complex homage of human cultural difference.[88] In a recent publication, we have sought to deal with the complex issues of multiculturalism and partnership between different ethnic and cultural Christian groups.[89] What we learned from our research in ministry practice, is that in order for cross-cultural unity to be possible, in what might be termed multicultural churches, there must be a strong drive for participants to seek to understand each others' cultural differences and outlooks, and to accept them as normal. Conflict caused by differences in outlook is a high risk in multiethnic churches, where significant differences exist between people groups culturally.[90]

Disciples who seek to share their faith and lives with different subcultural groups need to have strong intentional drive, where they intentionally choose to learn to understand differences in others—which requires accepting difference as normative.[91] If late modern churches wish to model the power of the Spirit of Christ to unite diverse cultural groups, then we will need to develop cultural intelligence that equips us to read and understand our own cultures and those of others.[92]

It will inevitably feel uncomfortable, but what an exciting opportunity we face. We have the chance to model the unifying love of Christ, whose Spirit seeks to draw all peoples together as part of his multicultural kingdom. Disciples after Christendom need to have the drive of God's all-embracing grace to accept otherness and difference as normal. It is normative to accept otherness. It is part of belonging to God's universal kingdom that welcomes all people, tongues, nations, cultures, and races.[93]

87. Baron, *Opposites Attract.*

88. Hardy and Yarnell, *Forming Multicultural Partnerships*, chs. 2, 3.

89. Ibid.

90. Ibid.

91. Ibid., ch. 7.

92. Ibid.

93. Matt 28:16–20; Rev 7.

Openness to the Reign of God

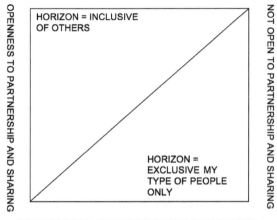

It may sound strange to raise the question of openness to the reign of God. Surely everyone who is properly a Christian should be open to it. Well, in theory, whether Christians like it or not, Jesus declared the basis to his mission to be the arrival of the kingdom of God, which we define as God's reign over all aspects of our daily lives without exception.[94] It includes the final establishment of the government of God and the keeping of his will on earth as it is in heaven.[95] It would be hard to read the gospels without drawing this conclusion. We readily enough accept that we need to abide by the laws of the land in order to not harm ourselves, others, or things. What we want to draw attention to here, is the importance to understand ourselves as belonging to the *one* kingdom of God, despite our cultural or theological differences. It is quite possible to limit the horizon of our view of the kingdom to the particular Christian tradition we belong to.[96]

In other words, there can be a tendency to conceive of discipleship as being what our tradition does. Its beliefs and practices are the best ones, or at times the only way of being a follower of Christ in the views of some. However, the kingdom teaching of Jesus did not set out a theological textbook of what all the beliefs and practices of the kingdom of God might include. Rather, we would argue that the beliefs of Jesus were informed by

94. Mark 1:13–14.

95. Matt 6:10.

96. Peers, "Problem Trap," 19–22.

qualities of heart that informed personally held values, that in turn motivated his disciples to think, feel, and behave in certain ways toward God and
others, based on God's grace and love.

Christ's incarnation implies that he interpreted his beliefs and values
to suit the horizon of first-century Jewish culture in Palestine. However, the
gospels portray Jesus' view of the kingdom to include more than members of
the Jewish race.[97] It was to include all nations, peoples, and their cultures.[98]
In other words, it did not have a limited horizon made up of Jews alone,
where peoples would be called to become Jewish in their beliefs, practices,
customs, and culture, if they were to be acceptable in the kingdom of God.

The kingdom of God is bigger than any one tradition, culture, race, or
hermeneutical horizon. The horizon of the kingdom is to love and value all
peoples as those who are called to join together in the one new cosmos that Jesus' life, death, resurrection, ascension, and coming again will finally establish
upon earth. In other words, we need to be open to join together as disciples of
Christ, based on the values of God's unifying love, which beckons all followers
to share together as the one new people of God, despite their denominational
differences.[99] This one new people needs to welcome difference as normal.

It will provide opportunities for people to grow beyond and to transcend their own limited theological horizons—to thus embrace Christ in
the other. In other words, the great opportunity facing disciples after Christendom, is that we are all one new humanity in God's kingdom.[100] But being
one new humanity does not mean we throw the richness of our cultures
away. We can all be enriched by each others' cultural heritages. We need to
readjust our lenses to seek to transcend our own ecclesiastical horizons, and
thus to embrace otherness in the rich tapestry of our multicultural society.

The secular world is looking for evidence that there is a way to overcome
barriers that cause different people groups who resist each other, making them
enemies or in conflict. This is important to model through our churches, that
live based on the refreshing influence of the love and grace of God. Christians
of different racial, cultural, and class boundaries, who seek to participate together in creating a new culture of unity, inspired, led, and empowered by the
Spirit of the Trinity, can provide prophetic gestures of what the grace of God
can do to unite diverse peoples in multiethnic churches.

97. John 10:16.

98. Matt 28:16–20.

99. Gal 3:28.

100. Hardy and Yarnell, *Forming Multicultural Partnerships*, ch. 3.

Chapter 7

Shaping Effective Disciple-Makers within Communities of Missional Praxis

By Andrew R. Hardy

Introduction

The Judeo-Christian God is a located God. He does not exist as a non-embodied unmoved mover, as Aristotle articulated. He is not the distant nonmaterial deity of Plato or later Gnosticism. He does not disdain the corporeal world he has made. Spiritual life, in terms of the biblical texts, is one made up of the seen physical world and the unseen spiritual presence of God's Spirit. Spirit and matter are not disconnected but related. The tri-personal God, Father, Son, and Holy Spirit, are not only interpersonally united in the perichoresis,[1] as a relational dance of intimacy, but God also reaches out and invites God's creatures to join in the dance. In other words, the Trinity is a relational, personal God. John's gospel calls each believer a son or daughter of this tri-personal divine family.[2] The God who reveals God's self in the physical world of space, time, and place inhabits not just the believer's human spirit, but also the places and spaces of the world God upholds by his mighty power.[3]

---

1. Karkainen, *Trinity*, 35, 39, 41, 47, 60, 111–12, 115, 135, 207, 218, 220, 222–23, 341.

2. Hastings, *Missional God, Missional Church*, 80–117.

3. Parler, *Things Hold Together*.

The life, beliefs, convictions, values, and practices of Christian communities are vivified by his presence. The foundation to what it means to be part of the kingdom of God is that God is in the process of renewing the spaces and places of the earth, as the final goal of his mission.[4]

Hence we need to seek to enter into secular space and to participate with God's Spirit in it as partakers in the Triune life and mission, in order to help prepare for its new society. We are sent to reclaim and rename secular spaces in the name of the God who is in Christ. We are also sent to participate with the Spirit in reaching into the newly recognized postsecular consciousness of generations Y and Z (see chapters 8 and 9). This requires followers of Jesus to engage in some serious theological and sociological reflection.

Part of that reflection must recognize that post-Christendom society does not disciple people into faith, and we would include many churches in this assessment. It has lost its Christendom culture, which we argue did not effectively disciple people anyway. Its influences are diverse. Its places and spaces may include sacred buildings like churches, but the majority of people no longer go to them to get shaped. There is not just a crisis of discipleship formation of people in the church, but even more so in a society that does not have a culture that shapes any kind of Christian sense of what it means to follow Jesus. Clearly the people of late modernity do not factor in to their thinking that churches are places to spiritually seek for the deep need they feel, to find meaning to life in a postsecular world.[5]

We now live in an emerging postsecular state of consciousness, where the forces of secularism are also coming undone in the consciousness of many, meaning people are spiritually seeking once more.[6] Secular power still governs society, but not all the minds of its peoples. We need to theologically reflect on how to incarnate in the places and spaces where late modern people gather, in order to find ways to disciple them there. It will not happen overnight. Yet the missional church after Christendom is called by Christ to seek to engage in the whole life discipleship formation of people within the church, as well as those outside its sacred canopy. This will require us to seek to invest new places and spaces with fresh sacred stories in order to encounter God in Christ in them.

4. Kerr, "Come Holy Spirit," 98–103.

5. Altemeyer, "Decline of Organized Religion," 77–89.

6. Mobsby, *God Unknown*. Mobsby demonstrates how ancient ways of being a Christian community are becoming increasingly attractive in a postsecular world, where people look to the genuine and desire smaller more intimate relational communities in order to be shaped.

Theology of Place

Brueggemann, the distinguished Old Testament scholar, makes a vital observation about the importance of God's self-revelation in spaces and places. Places are tangible locations to position the God story within. God's people were met by the self-revealing God in the places of the ancient Near East. If God had not met them there, then those places would not have attained sacred auras as places to go on pilgrimage. God's appearance in a place creates an identity that is from then on expressed as part of the biblical story. Brueggemann comments:

> In the Old Testament there is no timeless space, but there is also no spaceless time. There is rather storied place, that is a place which has meaning because of the history lodged there. There are stories which have authority because they are located in a place. This means that biblical faith cannot be presented simply as an historical movement indifferent to place which could have happened in one setting as well as another, because it is undeniably fixed in this place with this meaning. And for all its apparent "spiritualising," the New Testament does not escape this rootage.[7]

To begin this chapter, it is important to consider the importance of God's revelation as it occurred not just in history, such as in the life of Jesus, but also in particular places such as Judea and Galilee. It even happens in our stories as parts of his ongoing story in our places and spaces. Those places are invested with meaning even today, people go on pilgrimage to the (so-called) Holy Land. God in Christ incarnated, lived, died, and rose again in this space-time world of places. So too is the missional disciple-maker to seek to meet people in the proximity of their places and spaces. The church building may rightly be said to be a "storied place," and its stories are largely only known to the few who attend these sacred places. This means in our post-Christendom context that the majority of society needs to meet God in their own places ad to have new sacred stories of God's presence and work among them invested in their particular environments. This will require missional disciple-makers to incarnate among them as the hands, feet, and face of Jesus. We quite literally may think of ourselves as a sacramental people sent out to serve the eucharistic communion to the world. We need to share the bread and wine of the Lord's sacrifice with all who will partake. According to Paul in 1 Corinthians 12 the body of Christ is a people. This body of people need to become the mobile missional incarnational body of Christ, that seeks to incarnate in secular spaces, to reinvest secular spaces

7. Brueggemann, *Land*, 187.

as sacred "storied places"; where people discover Christ and the presence of his Spirit. We likely need to participate in the creation of new sacred spaces in places other than church buildings.

Lane comments:

> One necessarily reads the scriptures with map in hand. Yahweh is disclosed, not just anywhere, but on the slopes of Mt Sinai, at Bethel and Shiloh, at the Temple in Jerusalem. The God of Old and New Testaments is one who "tabernacles" with God's people, always made known in particular locales. When Paul celebrates the "scandal of the gospel," this is a reality geographically rooted in Jesus, a crucified Jew from Nazareth, of all places. The offence, the particularity of place, becomes intrinsic to the incarnational character of Christian faith.[8]

The "character of Christian faith" is based on the "incarnational" reality of God continuing to reveal his presence by the Spirit of Christ in particular places. Those who seek to mentor fresh disciples, after Christendom, need to recognize the importance of the incarnation to the message they bring into the life contexts, made up of the places secular people inhabit. These secular spaces need reclaiming to become the new sacred ground of a fresh kind of new Jerusalem, or Mount of Olives.

Yet they may be named after pubs, clubs, and playgrounds where adults, parents, and children meet. This means we need to turn our attention to the importance of understanding some of the psychology and sociology that defines spaces and places. We will start by considering how the communities people belong to, whether at work, at home, or in churches (for some), provide storied places invested with meaning. In other words, these places are invested with the particular convictions that cause people to identify themselves as part of a group. Moreover, almost all communities are defined by their common beliefs and practices that they share together. Then we will move on to consider the sociology of proxemics and the encoded human psychology of distance and proximity to our missional discipleship discussion.

Convictional Communities

An important question raised by the late Anabaptist theologian James Mc-Clendon (1924–2000) was how do contemporary disciples get shaped suited to the contexts of their cultures and historical locations. He suggested in an

---

8. Lane, "Landscape and Spirituality," 5.

important work entitled "Biography as Theology" (1974)[9] that contemporary disciples are formed within what he termed "Convictional Communities."[10] For McClendon, a "convictional community" was one that shaped its adherents based on the operations of "mind," "feeling/affectation" and "will/action." The three dimensions iterated are the components that make up his understanding of a conviction. "Conviction" was not a singular attribute of convictional communities to McClendon. In his view conviction, as a means to define any Christian community, Baptist (in his case), Catholic, or Protestant was a plural concept.[11] In other words, communities construct their identities based on more than one, two, or more convictions.[12] This is important to recognize as any convictional community constructs its identity based on several convictions that its people (i.e., a particular Christian faith community) adhere to as basic to their identity.

McClendon's view of convictions can be diagrammed as possessing three dimensions. These three dimensions are not separable but intrinsic to McClendon's concept as a holism of what convictions are based upon.

The "affective" level[13] is where Christian convictions, or any convictions, start. People are often unaware of the convictions that their religious conversion has invested in them. The "new heart" spoken of in Ezekiel[14] and Hebrews[15] may be rewirings of the brain's neural architecture.

The affective dimension of convictions, McClendon argued, are, at a base level, driven by the things we are the most passionate about. In other words, the beliefs and values we would die for, in other words, or if we were to break them we would feel deeply guilty for doing so. Disciples after Christendom need to gather in convictional communities of discipleship, where people share affective level convictions similar to their own, or the ones they aspire to develop in their own lives. However, people will probably most often be unaware of why they hold certain convictions as strongly as they do. Alternatively, they may come to a conscious self-awareness, when for the first time they consciously recognize a conviction that up to that point has not been part of their conscious life.

Affective level convictions that come to consciousness, as "my convictions," naturally lead to a discussion of the cognitive dimension. The

9. McClendon, *Biography as Theology*.

10. Ibid., 32.

11. Ibid., 36–38.

12. Ibid., 32.

13. Ibid., 194.

14. Ezek 36:26–28.

15. Heb 8.

Christian faith is a revealed faith, and Christian conversion and transformation into the likeness of Christ come about as an inner revelation, which transforms us on an affective, as well as a cognitive, level. The cognitive dimension is how we reason and think about our beliefs and the practices of our faith. They are not principles but rather our way of thinking through why we are convicted by some beliefs and values more than others. Convictions, by their very nature, entail things we feel convinced about, even if we have some doubts about the actual reality of them. For example, we feel convicted that we should submit our lives in trust to Christ, and not to put others before him in our life choices. Hence Christians, as people of the "book," the Holy Scriptures, have their life stories shaped by the biblical stories. McClendon thought of the biography of Christ's story, and indeed every Christian's story, including contemporary Christian stories, as a powerful way of doing theology as biography.

Our life stories, in the Christian community, help us to shape each others' stories as our stories are invested with the Christian story. These life narratives need to be contextualized to our life situations and by our convictions, which we understand cognitively and seek to adhere to passionately.

Adherence to our convictions iterates the third dimension of convictions. We are talking about a volitional dimension. If we passionately seek to live by our convictions, then it will give us will to act on them. The volitional dimension of convictions is that they are those passionate beliefs we will act on. They are the motivating forces of our lives. They too form the architecture of our convictional communities of missional discipleship. McClendon argued that every believer's life represented a kind of biographical theology, which was based on their interpretation of the Christian story and how that motivated them to act. In other words, convicted missional disciples need to be motivated by their convictional communities to live as Christ lived, where their life stories are contextualized to make it possible to live as Christ lived.

According to McClendon, each believer's life is a biographical theology, but also at times key missional leaders are born who embody an ethical movement that can embody and incarnate what people gather around and become part of as a movement:

> Now consider this fact. In or near the community there appear from time to time singular or striking lives, the lives of persons who embody the convictions of the community, but with a new way; who share the vision of the community, but with new scope or power; who exhibit the style of the community, but with significant differences. It is patent that the example of these lives may serve to disclose and perhaps to correct or enlarge the community's moral vision, at the same time arousing impotent

wills within the community to a better fulfilment of the vision already acquired.[16]

This kind of person or persons (McClendon included individuals like Martin Luther King Jr.) can act in a prophetic way in a community, bringing into missional focus what God is calling for it to become, in order for it to be prepared for what is to become next in its life of mission.

Communities of Missional Discipleship and Praxis

Related to a discussion of communities we must also turn to the work of the social learning theorist Wenger, who discusses the importance of communities of practice, in which learning meaning and identity are constructed in an ongoing process of participation and reification, as a negotiated set of meanings owned by a community.[17] Reification has to do with the human tendency to try to encode meaning into ideas, concepts and convictions (and other forms), that seek to define the boundaries of a community's practices. Reification entails some kind of objectified representation of core meaningful beliefs and values for a community. Given that convictions of a community can be both reified and developed by individuals as they participate in constructing a community's convictions, it is these convictions of communities which are part of what Wenger calls "communities of practice."

In terms of faith groups, their convictions lead them to prefer some interpretations for their existence over others and they engage in Christian practices motivated by them.

McClendon noted those convictions which are passionately held tend to be the ones that help to define a community. Wenger notes that meaning is always negotiated in communities of practice, as people participate in the life of the community together, as they seek to contextualize reified concepts (including their convictions), etc., in the context of the circumstances faced by a community.

In Wenger's theory, whether it be in business, government, factories, offices, organizations, or churches, people learn by what they are doing in social, cognitive, and computational environments. Given that this book focuses on discipleship and communities that shape them, we use the phrase convictional communities of missional discipleship and practice, to define faith groups that intelligently and consciously seek to shape disciples. This

---

16. McClendon, *Biography as Theology*, 37.
17. Wenger, *Communities of Practice*.

headline concept takes into account that convictions shape the practices of formation that are undertaken in any discipleship community.

Meaning making involves an ongoing process of negotiation, coming from social participation between community members, that seek to keep on defining formalized meanings, concepts, and convictions (objectified reifications), as well as what they might mean in the various contexts they face. In other words, in terms of missional communities that shape disciples, each new disciple brings their fresh participation into an established community of reified meanings, which then need reinterpreting to some extent to help the newcomer and community to be able to interact mutually together (i.e., contextualization is required). Wenger suggests that learning is a lifelong process that always faces communities with the fresh opportunity to negotiate the meanings of what they are doing. Surprisingly, we are most often not even aware we are engaged in doing this. He comments:

> Communities of practice are an integral part of our daily lives. They are so informal and so pervasive that they rarely come into explicit focus, but for the same reasons they are also quite familiar. . . . Most communities of practice do not have a name and do not issue membership cards. . . . We can probably distinguish a few communities of practice in which we are core members from a larger number of communities in which we have a more peripheral kind of membership.[18]

Wenger's work is useful to bring into dialogue with McClendon's, as both focus on the dynamics of community life and the practices which our communities cause us to intentionally take part in and therefore to reflect on together.

Wenger sets out what he considers to be the primary components of a social theory of learning. This includes the learning and bringing to consciousness of those convictions that we hold passionately. He considers that every community of practice has four primary components, that are necessary in order for social learning to occur. They are based on the explicit focuses and practices of a community, including the negotiation of meaning by community members as they participate in social learning, seeking to keep on defining who they are faced by the challenges of life as part of their shared communal practices. These components are important for us to consider alongside McClendon's three dimensions of a convictional community, as the Christian faith has historically (during Christendom, and still today in many cases) placed a high value on a "taught" faith rather than a "caught" faith.

18. Ibid., 7.

Wenger sees communities of practice as a primary arena of learning that takes place through the reification of key ideas and concepts that a community has constructed. Hence learning occurs in four overlapping ways.

First, communities of practice themselves lead to a process of learning based on the belonging of the people who participate in them. Because people feel they belong, they learn together based on each member of the community taking some ownership of what they have learned together as a kind of common property, which is then taken to be a property of the community that is passed on as normative practice. Second, people form identities as a shared part of what they do together. Wenger terms this component "learning as becoming." Third, being a part of a community of practice also leads to a shared set of meanings among the group, which Wenger terms "learning as experience." People learn together based on commonly shared experiences which are also passed on as reified learned practices a community adopts as its practices. Last, Wenger focuses on the practices of the community together, which he terms "learning as doing." We all learn together based on shared learning that becomes the property of our community of practice. All four aspects describe what communities of practice engage in doing together as learning communities.[19]

McClendon's three dimensions of conviction can be considered to be applicable to each of the four components of Wenger's social learning theory. Our convictions will influence each aspect of these four components when people learn together in a community. Just as convictions are caught rather than taught, so is much of the type of learning Wenger details. We need to distinguish between a "caught" and "taught" faith as well here. We believe it is important to understand how post-Christendom has changed the need toward a "caught" rather than "taught" faith.

It is important to grasp this change, as it will be important for the effective discipling of late modern people. A "caught" faith is one that comes from participation in a community, where social learning occurs and reified meanings are continuously reapplied and negotiated, suiting them to fresh contexts. A "taught" faith assumes that things like reified doctrinal beliefs of a community cannot be so readily recontextualized, because they remain the received deposit of community truth. In actual fact, most Christian communities continuously negotiate meanings of reified doctrinal truths, as community members participate together in negotiating their meaning suited to fresh contexts.

For example, the issue of women using head coverings, found in 1 Corinthians 11, was once taken literally, requiring women in many evangelical

19. Ibid., 5.

churches in the UK to literally wear a hat to church. It is also to be noted that this is still the case in some black majority churches. Today this has been reinterpreted culturally, with an understanding that means most churches in the UK do not interpret this passage literally. Another example would be the practice of homosexual marriage, and the participation of practicing homosexual couples in some churches as active members. Although this is not an issue we seek to make a pronouncement on in this book, we note that some churches now take the view that the New Testament does not address the question of monogamous homosexual marriage, and hence it cannot be used to make judgments on relationships of this type. Both examples provide evidence of the negotiation of meaning of received biblical texts to form community opinion, as reifications of truth, and how participants in faith communities may come to negotiate fresh meanings. Often this does not happen through a process of teaching, but rather new contextual meanings are caught on a less conscious level. Once they have been caught they slowly become part of a communities' convictions.

It may be argued that McClendon's and Wenger's understandings more directly relate to a caught or learned faith.[20] In other words, both relate to a coming to consciousness (in Christian conversion terms for McClendon) of what we believe and value passionately, which motivates us to engage in an ongoing process of transformation into Christ's likeness, as we negotiate the meaning of our faith by participation in our communities.

Wenger's work focuses on what we learn. It relates much more to a "caught" learning rather than a formally "taught" kind. Learning for Wenger, in the context of communities of practice, is not so much formally taught, but it naturally happens as participants negotiate meaning together, because as social creatures we seek meaning in everything we do, which causes us to engage in ongoing lifelong learning. Most learning throughout life is caught rather than taught in other words. Hence the practices we take part in are mined for meaning, and we learn from engaging in community social practices—learning from doing them together—whatever they might be. In other words, both scholars recognize that in a late modern context people learn by participation and negotiation of meaning in a community context, rather than by the former modernity paradigm's approach, where expert teachers taught a fixed truth to those who were nonexperts—expecting them to conform to them. This seeming evangelical preoccupation with teaching needs to be transformed somewhat, to become more focused on helping people to learn by participation and negotiation to arrive at shared

20. Although Wenger is not talking about religious communities, but his ideas apply.

meanings together, or it will prove less possible to see new disciples formed among generations Y and Z to the degree that they could be.

Those communities where we see ourselves as core members, such as our churches or small discipleship groups, are the places we learn in, because we feel we belong to them. Hence we invest in seeking meaning in shared learning together as a group. It is vital that small discipleship groups, which are the focus of this chapter, promote a sense of belonging and participation—so that every believer may invest by meaningfully participating in them. These communities of belonging often develop their own traditions, or might we say "customs," which we would term "praxis customs." Disciples after Christendom will be best shaped to take on the praxis they have learned in their communities together. In other words, Christian faith communities might be said to define the practices of their members as praxis, based on their "customs," or traditions, which participants continuously creatively help to meaningfully negotiate and shape together. They will do this with reference to the reified deposit of God's revelation to be found in Scripture, and the ecclesial traditions they participate in, in dialogue with their cultural contexts.

However, belonging is just one of four components detailed by Wenger. Communities of practice also are the environments in which people form an identity. Social group identity is something Hardy has discussed at more length in *Pictures of God: Shaping Missional Church Life*. People gather in communities to which they feel they belong, as well as identify with, sharing similar convictions to their own. In this sense, people learn as they become more deeply invested and integrated into a social identity group. Hence it is vital that communities of praxis create opportunities for people to participate, and therefore invest in more deeply, as they learn about the community's convictions, beliefs, and values.

The third component of Wenger's social theory of learning draws attention to communities of practice that live by a shared set of meanings, that group members invest in. In this sense, community members learn through their experiences in the shared practices of other community members, who find similar meaning to them by being part of a given community. Meaning is also clearly connected to McClendon's view of convictional communities, in the sense that each community member's life biography, or "life story narrative," brings meaning to others in the group; as it is shared as part of a group's experience. Hence it is vital that disciples after Christendom get shaped in smaller and larger group environments, where they can share their experiences and hear those of others. This participation will require the negotiation of how to meaningfully apply the gospel of Christ to the contexts of each new disciple's life situation.

Fourth, Wenger details that groups that are shaped by the other three dimensions also learn by doing. In this sense, we are talking about the practices, products and intentional actions of a community, as they work together. All four dimensions are vital to convictional communities of discipleship, because missional churches and missional communities, properly understood, should, in my view, become convictional communities of missional discipleship and praxis.

Wenger's work is vital, as it sets out a process theory of social learning, rather than a programmatic approach. The church of Christendom was well known, at one phase, for its programs and the claims that each new program paved the way to transform a church. We know from bitter experience that this never really worked, as the late modern context demanded a more fluid, or liquid, approach that does not set out a predetermined programed approach to change. This may also be a critique applied to church planting programs. Those who consider that planting churches in a programmatic manner is the answer to bringing Christian faith back to the attention of Westerners probably delude themselves. The reason for this is because the far more basic need is to develop communities that can disciple people, rather than simply assuming a church plant will do this. Too often church planters are so overstretched in the planting of new churches that they soon lose the energy to disciple people.

Wenger's work provides insights into what a missional community needs to understand about learning processes that occur in contexts like convictional communities of missional discipleship and praxis. These processes are what really need to occur in order to empower new converts to learn their faith, rather than simply planting churches. Convictional missional communities of praxis are required rather than simply a new church in order to shape new believers to be disciples and disciple-makers.

It is important to understand the assumptions Wenger makes that contribute to an appreciation of what he terms the components of his social theory of learning. In theological terms,[21] a recourse to a relational and participatory view of the life of the missional church, and missional disciples, may be best articulated related to a relational Trinitarianism. Following theologians like Zizioulas, Moltmann, and Karkainen,[22] each of us can be called to participate in the life of the mission of God, as we seek to discern what he is calling each ordinary disciple in the church to do, by sharing their faith with those they live alongside in their everyday lives. Moreover, by the guidance of the Spirit and the received deposit of the revealed Word of God,

21. Wenger is of course not a theologian but a secular social theorist.
22. I discuss their work more fully in Hardy, *Pictures of God*, ch. 7.

each discipleship community may be guided to negotiate the meaning of its faith suited to its context and local culture.

This includes the work places of each believer, which are one of their communities of practice, as much as their families. How might they share something of their convictions to transform the meaning of the work practices their colleagues engage in, as they live and participate in work practices together. This is where Wenger's theory might help the missional church that seeks to form convictional communities of missional discipleship and praxis—to think through how to do this in each learning context the people of God incarnate within.

In terms of our argument for this book, God's people are called to incarnate as Christ's hands, feet, and voice of welcome in their everyday life contexts, in everything they do. As participants in contexts, such as their work places, ordinary disciples may seek to negotiate the meaning of what they can offer to their work communities of practice, thus making it possible to offer fresh ways of defining meaningful interaction among their colleagues. For example, an important Christian conviction is honesty; this simple conviction may be part of a negotiated meaning that could help a company or work colleagues to become more transparent in the way they negotiate a deal or claim for expenses.

Wenger's approach has the dexterity to represent various functions a community of practice might iterate. Some within the missional church might seek to incorporate people into the community of disciples through learning processes that help them to understand what belonging to a particular faith group might mean. This may entail learning about the convictions of a convictional community of missional discipleship and praxis, including a negotiation of the meaning and recontextualization of reified beliefs and values suited to a new disciple's life situation.

Another group may engage in a meaningful missional initiative, such as in one church, where a coffee shop has been started that local people can enjoy inexpensive food and quality drinks. It has become a kind of missional community, whose members and customers are actually learning about each other through conversations and sharing of their daily life experiences, as they attend this intentional missional enterprise. It is becoming a kind of coffee shop missional community of faith. People of faith and no Christian faith are constructively negotiating what the meaning of this community of practice exists to do—in their shared local community. These are but two ways of thinking about the usefulness of Wenger's social learning theory, and how it relates to the creation of communities that at first create a sense of meaning around doing things together, which in turn then can become places of belonging and shared activities and convictions.

However, the discussion of convictional communities of missional discipleship and praxis are only one dimension of a complex missional challenge, that missional discipleship practitioners need to consider. Another significant missional challenge has to do with how to meaningfully incarnate in secular spaces, among those who may have an emergent postsecular consciousness, which means they are seeking for spiritual input into their lives, but not in the sacred canopy of the church and its buildings.

Proxemics

In order to effectively incarnate alongside people, we need to move on to a consideration of what is known as proxemics. In order to incarnate alongside people, we need to come into proximity to them. Proxemics theory was developed to describe and analyze the distances people feel comfortable to be from each other in the places they inhabit together. The sociologist Hall developed this theory and its nomenclature (i.e., "proxemics").[23] In the diagram below, the basic theory is articulated in a simple fashion. The distances indicated in the diagram are measured in feet and inches. The distances represent the degree of engagement that people have with each other in the spaces they interact with each other within. These distances vary between cultures, but those articulated in the diagram are generally correct in the context of Western culture. This is an oversimplification, given that we live in a multicultural society with people groups that have differing proximities, which have been socialized into them from birth. The distances people have between each other symbolize the degree of comfort they have to relate to each other. The diagram below is suggestive of a feature of social place as religious space. It is important for us to reflect on the significance of the church as a place where people meet, which must include a discussion of its fitness to engage in making disciples among those who no longer feel comfortable to enter church spaces.

The diagram below explains roughly what each of the distances between people psychologically symbolize to them.

23. Hall, *Hidden Dimension*.

Proxemics: Distances Interpreted as Relational Zones			
Intimate Distance	Personal Distance	Social Distance	Public Distance
Often experienced by lovers, life partners, and siblings. People share a unique level of comfort with one another. Those who are not comfortable with someone who approaches them in the intimate zone will experience a great deal of social discomfort or awkwardness.	For talking with family and close friends. It is still very close in proximity to that of intimacy, and may involve touching. If a stranger approaches someone in this zone, he/she is likely to feel uncomfortable.	In meeting new people and interacting with groups. People do not engage physically. People may be particular about the amount of social distance that is needed to avoid any physical contact.	An example of this is where a person is more than 12" from an other.

It is vital to understand proxemics theory and how it can help us to think about the way we interact with peers in the church, or broader society. In traditional church seating formations, the focus of the congregants is most often orientated with them facing forwards toward the platform or lectern. This is symbolic of power and authority that comes from gathering around the worship leader as a representative of God.

People are most regularly seated in close proximity to each other in traditional churches, meaning they are in the personal zones of others. Those most closely seated to us will be those to our left or right. Often those to our left and right will be family members or friends, who we feel some degree of comfort with. We may feel less comfortable to sit close to someone we do not know, or that we feel discomfort about. Interestingly, in formal seating arrangements like these, our choices for where to sit can be limited in packed churches. This can be off-putting even to regular visitors to the church, let alone those who come for the first time.

Close proximity seating arrangements in traditional worship environments are a potential barrier, they can create a sense of a less safe environment for new people who visit, if they feel forced to sit close to those they do not know. The fundamental seating architecture of churches is debated from time to time by churches. What is vital to note is that the traditional placement of pews, or chairs, is not designed as an environment suitable for people to build relationships with each other.

If the major task of missional church is the formation of lifelong followers of Christ, then we will need to do more than simply consider how we design the largest spaces in our churches dedicated to worship. Can they be designed to feel more like a café with tables, such as in so-called café churches. This may help solve some problems so that people can relate to each other better. However, whatever we do with the architecture in our church buildings, there are those who will never enter the church to worship or fellowship there.

People are caused to gather together with a shared faith, representing a united effort to worship God, as one crowd of believers facing the front following the instructions of the leader(s). This view of engaging in the life of the church will often most regularly be the mental image that people possess, as their icon of what going to church or belonging to it might imply.

This iconography is a deliberately engineered environment, most often used in worship areas throughout the churches of the land. The default position, even in rooms where seating is not fixed, is to have everyone facing the front, although at times people sit in a circle or crescent moon configuration (which can create a different feel). This seating architecture is an artifact of the Christendom era, where the gathered people of God united around the authority structures that dominated their culture. Authority was held by the church and its leaders. The role of the laity was to conform to the norms and values of gathered, controlled worship structures. This is deeply threatening from a proxemics point of view to late modern youth and young adults, who do not want to be told what to do.

If we stick with this iconographic typology, then it is argued that this way of gathering as disciples of Christ is not as such an effective way of developing interpersonal fellowship, even between committed members of the Christian community. Yet relationships that happen in a communal environment are vital to foster as we are helped in our journey as followers of Christ.

Having said this, different sized congregations have different relational dynamics at work within them. In congregations consisting of up to sixty members, termed by Croft a dynastic or family church,[24] the sense of togetherness and social cohesion between people will be higher, despite a traditional seating pattern. This is in part due to there not being too many people to get to know on a personal level. Larger churches of 70 to 130 members, termed pastors' churches by Croft,[25] will tend toward less contact being made between people due to increased numbers.[26] Groups of twelve to fifteen members seem to be optimally sized and suited for people to get to

24. Croft, *Transforming Communities*, 50–52.
25. Ibid., 52.
26. Ibid.

know each other more deeply and meaningfully.[27] From a proxemics point of view we can more effectively be in others' personal and social zones.

The larger the membership group, the more likely it is for people to have a larger array of distances existing between them and others, which will put quite a few people outside others' personal or social zones. Some people will be less well known to us than others, especially if people tend to sit with the same people each week. It takes time for people to develop relationships in a busy late modern world. Maintaining some kind of relationship with more than 150 people is the limit that we all have in terms of effectively sustaining them.[28] This is due to the constraints placed on us by work, family life, and travel. So what is it that is important for us to learn from proxemics?

Optimal Group Sizes for Effective Discipleship

A trait of late modern young adults (generation Y) and youth (generation Z) (see further chapter 8) is that they tend not to put trust in larger formally structured religious and civil institutions such as the church. The perception of being spectators in a formally structured seating arrangement, among a crowd of others, is viewed with suspicion. The exception to this will be that these generations value large concerts with their favorite bands, as well as large crowds that meet at sports events. In these events there is a sense of being able to choose the kind of music they like and the message it conveys, or the entertainment of watching something like a football match, where the sense of mystery experienced is the uncertainty of whether their preferred team will win. But winning rather than being told what to think is quite a different perceptive category. The feeling of being passive recipients being told what to think or believe is symbolic of a past age.

Late modern youth and young adults do not want to be told what to do, how to live or what to believe. In the bygone age of Christendom, the expert clergy delivered a message that was to be the basis to maintain religious conformity to the prevailing domination system of Christendom society. It is known that postmodern people do not respond well to power structures and figures of authority as once was the case.[29]

Late modern people seem not to feel comfortable with being part of captive audiences in the institutionalized iconographic church building.[30] Generations Y and Z largely represent the 40 percent of people who have

27. Zempel, *Community Is Messy*.
28. Abell, *Inside Out*, ch. 4.
29. Larkin, "Approaches to and Images of Biblical Authority," 129–38.
30. Schweitzer, *Postmodern Life Cycle*, ch. 1.

never gone to church or heard the Christian story.[31] They mostly never enter church buildings of their own volition, except in occasional rites of passage such as funerals or weddings. The missional church after Christendom needs to engage in a fresh kind of iconoclasm, which seeks to deconstruct the public/private divide between the majority of secular persons and Christians. Fresh ways of being missional communities is required in the emerging church environment.[32] We need to find fresh ways of entering into the social and personal zones of late modern people.

Public space is not the place where it is possible to build meaningful friendships, that lead to the possibility of eventually seeing new believers accept Christ. It will often begin there, but it is not the kind of environment that people feel comfortable to develop closer social bonds with people. The effective missional community needs to incarnate in meaningful ways in the social and personal zones of late modern people, in the places where they feel most comfortable. One student in a course we were teaching planted a missional community in a pub, and those who attended were gay and lesbian young people interested in exploring the gospel. This kind of missional church innovation requires new ways of engaging with communities, or tribes (see chapter 9) like gays and lesbians. It may be that to begin with, we need to join in social action initiatives with people to help them improve their general living environments, where we seek to bring about change for the common good. In other words, we need to meet people where they are struggling to cope with life's challenges, in order to help in improving things by participating with them, seeking to transform theirs and our circumstances together.

A New Language of the Common Good

Organizations such as Citizens UK, not a faith-based organization but that welcomes partnerships with faith and secular organizations alike, has found one very important way that all sorts of people can work together.[33] It has to do with community organizing.[34] Citizens UK fosters partnerships with groups, rather than with individuals, in order to help them to become aware of how to address and fight for the rights of their groups. The question of social justice is a live issue within many urban and suburban areas, particularly among those who do not have connections with the right kinds of activists, who have the skills to obtain a hearing for change with the right

31. Stoddard and Cuthbert, *Church on the Edge*, 42.
32. Stuvland, "Emerging Church," 203–31.
33. See their website, http://www.citizensuk.org/birmingham_survey.
34. Ibid.

authorities. Specialist activists are needed who can bring social issues to the right kinds of public forums to get them addressed.[35] Citizens UK seeks to make this possible for disempowered groups.

It is interesting that many of those engaged in social organizing and community development report that many of the projects that are commonly taken on are those closest to the hearts of a group. For example, there might be the need for a proper footpath to be constructed alongside a busy road, so that children can walk safely to school. Although these kinds of projects are practical, rather than representing higher level kinds of engagement, such as those aimed at transforming social policy, political will, or law, they prove to be the most frequent kinds of activism that people of all persuasions most commonly work on together. The language of the common good is used to create a narrative that different people can participate in together. Indeed, the language of the common good is an important part of public theological debate.[36] In other words, people may share a common identity that is based on a project requiring group activism to achieve it.[37]

When the project is achieved, the people who did it together may no longer relate to each other socially. This is because it was the project that gave them their common identity. Its end means they no longer have a shared identity to gather around to give their group meaning. Hence they split up. Sometimes one successful project seen through to the end can cause some to find other things to do together.

In terms of the people of God engaging incarnationally in community development projects, it can mean that the commonly shared project in that place can be invested with something of the sacred story of God. Community organizing is one important way for people to collaborate together for the common good. God's Spirit can and will be present, and the presence of people of faith can prove to be a catalyst to help people recognize remarkable and providential evidences of God's liberating presence. The God who liberates may provide new storied places that people from then on might consider to be invested with new meanings.

It is an excellent way for Christians to share in the development of social capital and the formation of relationships with others, in these new kinds of social zones that can be brought to reality by community organizers.

Castells speaks of this phenomenon in terms of network society.[38] People associate through networking with others, using multiple social

---

35. Ibid.

36. Sagovsky and McGrail, *Together for the Common Good*.

37. Ledwith, *Community Development*; Lishman, *Handbook for Practice Learning*.

38. Castells, *Networks of Outrage and Hope*.

channels to interact with others, rather than established institutions like the church, which the people of Christendom culture once looked to as their purveyors of empowerment and identity. It was more typical during Christendom for people to assume that fixed religious, social, and government institutions were the bodies to approach to get things done.

Of course in the case of Wilberforce's work to end the slave trade, his activism involved strong political will and constant lobbying to see slavery ended. Finally, the act was passed that ended the trade, on the same day that Wilberforce finally died. There is the need for Christian social and political activists to seek to change the spaces, places, and laws through social capital and community development projects. This calls for a new kind of discipleship formation process where followers of Christ seek to apprentice new believers in the heart of their local communities, in work places, in schools and universities, etc.

It is quite common nowadays for young adults and youth to form multiple networks with all kinds of groups,[39] including social media and the internet. They are linked with people who share common interests. They may live on the other side of the world but be in communication with each other in seconds. These new virtual networks also have their own proxemics, where someone a thousand miles away can share face-to-face intimacy with another, using media like Skype or Zoom. The internet can therefore become a virtual world that can also provide space for the sacred. In other words, it is possible to seek to disciple people in meaningful interpersonal ways outside of our normal physical locations and spaces.

People on the other side of the world, or even next door, can find people of faith who seek to bring them to know the story of Christ. One student known to us has created his own internet based game, which involves players in building their own dwellings, towns, and cities. Some of the two hundred gamers who take part go to the designer's virtual church, hosted in his game every Sunday, to hear him preach. This student literally preaches a sermon at home into this virtual church in his game environment. God is incarnated in this cyber game world.

Whether we form close discipleship formation friendships with people in our neighborhood, work place, in India via Skype or through a game we design, the insights of proxemics help to inform the need for us to inhabit the social and personal spaces of those we want to share our faith with. If we want to invest cyber or literal physical spaces with the story of God in fresh ways, then we need to enter the social and personal zones where people may lower their psychological barriers, in order to relate to us.

39. Rainie and Wellman, *Networked*.

Discipleship formation strategy has to focus its attention on the incarnation of the disciple-maker in the social and personal zones, with those they are called by God to disciple. Small groups, whether made up of three people, ten people, or fifteen will be optimal for the forming and mentoring of missional disciples of Christ.[40] One-to-one joint mentoring or triplets (made up of three people) can also be effective as ways that allow people to reveal more of themselves without feeling exposed. In one-to-one relationships like this they can then hold each other mutually accountable to grow, which avoids power games, where a mentor can be seen as superior to a mentee. Whether larger groups or pairs or triplets, new sacred spaces need to be invested with the stories of how God transformed those places and the people who meet in them. This requires us to incarnate in these social zones in fresh, interesting, and imaginative ways.

Proxemics theory is not enough to help us to effectively engage in group dynamics. Effective theories of how to succeed in running healthy groups or mentoring schemes are not enough to form disciples of Christ. It requires a Trinitarian vision of God at work in the community, through the ongoing work of the missional Spirit of Christ. We need to invite the Spirit to be present to actually provide the energy and motivation that is needed to transform our lives. A Trinitarian vision of God makes Father, Son, and Holy Spirit the baseline community that all communities will be transformed by, by being part of the Trinity's family. A Trinitarian vision can provide a useful means to theologically reflect on what Christ is shaping small discipleship groups to become, in the light of the intimate life of trust, love, and openness that defines the Trinity's being. What we need to do as part of our exploration of how to enter into the social and personal zones of late modern people, will be to consider what kinds of groups we will need to form.

Small Group Dynamics

Small groups that give people the opportunity to discern their God-given calling, by the exploration and reflection on the challenges they face together, can empower them to take greater responsibility for their engagement in God's mission in their everyday life contexts. However, these groups need not feel that they are isolated from a larger worshipping community. Cell group or life group leaders also need to be shaped and mentored by leaders of larger worshipping communities. Moreover, when smaller discipleship groups meet as part of larger worshipping communities, there needs to be opportunity for them to give feedback to the larger body. This in turn

---

40. Gorman, "Search to Belong," 479–83.

can create an atmosphere of celebration, because stories are shared which makes the larger missional church body feel empathy with what each of their groups are experiencing and celebrating together. Larger gatherings remind small groups of the one kingdom they belong to, which God is shaping and forming in the present space-time world. God wishes to transform all places and spaces to come under his reign of love and grace. This requires the complete transformation of all places to become the arenas of the sacred presence of the Trinity. Astin notes:

> It is more important for a church member to be at the cell group than to be at the Sunday service. The Sunday service is still important for teaching and for celebration, but the fundamental life of the church is not found there. Rather, it is found at the cutting edge of personal relationships within the cells.[41]

Of course Astin's voice offers one way of describing a small discipleship group as a cell, with the implication that numerous cells together make up a body. And moreover, cells as part of one body, made up of numerous cells, provides a picture of a unity of purpose as participants in one organism, i.e., the body of Christ. Readers will have numerous terms they use to define smaller groups they connect with.

So whether we use the term cell, life group, discipleship group, etc., some basic principles are worth considering. Sticking with the term cell, it seems that cell groups need to also have their identity enhanced by being part of something bigger that they can feel part of. Cell group leaders need to find the strength that comes from a larger leadership group they are part of. This is equally true of other kinds of group that call themselves by other names. There is a need for small group facilitators (leaders) to have access to other leaders who can support them and help them to be resourced to continue. A team of cell group leaders is one common approach adopted in some networks. These teams can help small groups to keep healthy. Consider the following principles:

- The leadership team needs to actively train, inform, and shape the leaders of smaller groups so that they do not become isolated without accountability;

- The small group leaders need to be part of a larger church body's leadership team so that they buy into being part of God's broader and bigger kingdom family;

---

41. Astin, *Body & Cell*, 17.

- Small group leaders need to cultivate an atmosphere where people focus on their own lives and what God is doing in them beyond the church so that they can participate in his mission in the world;

- The small group members need to feel valued in terms of their experiences as group members and in terms of their value to the broader church to which they belong.

It seems like a healthy thing for small groups to be integrated into larger congregations they belong to, if they are to find sufficient support to sustain their micro-communities. Small discipleship formation groups need to be excellent at encouraging their members to participate in each others' ongoing faith journeys. It would also seem prudent for them to have the opportunity to meet with other groups so that they can celebrate their lives together and be challenged to explore new ideas that come from broader fellowship.

Effective Group Participation

Johnson and Johnson somewhat classically provide nine dimensions of a healthy small group that functions well. It is suggested that these dimensions should be present in a group's normative behaviors, attitudes, values, and communication systems. They are:

- "Group goals must be clearly understood, be relevant to the needs of group members, [and] highlight positive interdependence of members;

- Group members must communicate their ideas and feelings accurately and clearly;

- Participation and leadership must be distributed among members;

- Appropriate decision-making procedures must be used flexibly if they are to be matched with the needs of the situation;

- Power and influence need to be approximately equal throughout the group;

- Conflicts arising from opposing ideas and opinions (controversy) are to be encouraged. Controversies promote involvement in the group's work, quality and creativity in decision-making, and commitment to implementing the group's decisions;

- Group cohesion needs to be high. Cohesion is based on members liking each other;

- Problem-solving adequacy should be high. Problems must be resolved with minimal energy and in a way that eliminates them permanently;

- The interpersonal effectiveness of members needs to be high. Interpersonal effectiveness is a measure of how well consequences of your behavior match your intentions."[42]

Johnson and Johnson's work remains basic to the field of group dynamic theory, coming to a large extent out of the insights of Rogerian therapy and its like.[43] There is a need for groups to be able to treat group members with nonjudgmental regard, while at the same time being able to point out behaviors that might need addressing, especially if they cause a group member to dysfunction as a participant in the community.[44] The basic formula for such interpersonal unconditional positive regard is that it is important to accept the person but not necessarily to accept all of their behaviors. This separating of acceptance of the person from their behaviors is important, as it creates the chance for a person to not feel excluded or judged, as well as providing the freedom for them to reflect on constructive feedback that may help them to grow.

This means that group members need to be effective mediators, or bridge builders, that help each other feel safe to participate in group life and group sharing.

A group that practices nonjudgmental regard does not disregard the authority of the Lord and his claims on their lives.[45] However, it must be noted that in the First Epistle of John it is said that God's love means there is no fear of punishment or judgment in the Christian community that practices forgiveness and grace.[46] It is worth noting that the church of Ephesus in Revelation was said to have lost its first love.[47] It seems that they had become so good at rooting out possible heretics that in the process they had lost sight of the defining architecture of God's forgiveness and grace.[48]

We need to be able to confront people nonjudgmentally if issues need to be addressed, but in order to do this well, the relational capital of love and acceptance needs to be experienced as the glue that bonds people together.

---

42. Adapted from Johnson and Johnson, *Joining Together*, 8–9.

43. Ibid.

44. Johnson, *Reaching Out*, chs. 1–5.

45. Ibid.

46. 1 John 4:1–16.

47. Rev 2:1–7.

48. Rev 2:1–7.

Groups That Mediate Participation

Optimal discipleship formation groups function well in terms of the basic dimensions articulated above. It is in the context of these groups that two vital processes take place. The first of these is that small groups enable and empower their members to fully participate in their life cycle. The second has to do with what occurs when participation is high. It leads to the mediation of fresh ideas and insights to group members. Participation and mediation are fundamental to missional ecclesiology.[49] Research into how missional communities mediate a *missio Dei* ethos to their members demonstrates the importance of well-functioning group dynamics.[50] The mediation of a view of a God who wants his people to participate with him in his mission is best caught rather than taught. This does not imply that teaching is to be neglected, but it needs to find appropriate expression.

How it is caught is down to how groups function when they do it in a healthy manner. Healthy groups welcome participation and exploration of matters of the life of faith. In other words, a group that can communicate about the intimate things of their faith is enabled to be a reflective group, where group members can theologically reflect on the activities of God in their life situations. Ward comments:

> Reflection is a participation or sharing in the Trinitarian life. It is therefore also a participation or sharing in the mission of God. The minister [or group] who seeks to reflect theologically does so from an embodied commitment. Commitment for the minister is not simply a task, or a professional role. Neither is it simply a sense of self or communal identity, it is a vocation, a calling. So the theological task forms a part of an active and vocational participation in the mission of God. Mission finds its origins and its energy in God.
>
> . . . This means that the mission of the church is an expression of the divine sending forth of the self, the sending of the Son and the Holy Spirit to the world. . . . This kind of reflection is not passive, it is energized and animated by the life of God itself, and this life is the missio Dei. Attention therefore finds its origin in this mission and it is stirred as it is taken up into the life of God. Reflection therefore is a participation in God who is mission in the world. Sharing in the mission of God through the intentional practice of practical theology and theological

49. Ward, *Participation and Mediation*.
50. Ibid.

reflection is both cultural practice and participation in the divine life. It is lived in and indwelt.[51]

Ward demonstrates how mediation of a missional participation in the life of the missionary God is communicated. It occurs through the lifeblood of the faith community's spiritual practices and as a kind of reflexivity.[52]

The important point to consider, at this stage, is that reflection takes place when a small group welcomes the Holy Spirit's presence into their midst. It needs to be based on the group's openness to hear each others' thoughts and feelings empathically, as much as helping them remain open to the Spirit's presence and communication through each group member. Reflexivity implies that as we reflect on others' stories, they cause us to reflect on our own. The image projected by these kinds of communities to outsiders can be that they are worthy of exploration, in order to discover what it is that makes them healthy relational environments.

In the context of missional communities that seek to incarnate in the social and personal zones of late modern people, there will inevitably be times when new seekers will be attracted to a group by the way it welcomes them, and by the way it treats people. In the case of the pub church mentioned earlier, gay and lesbian people felt they were safe to be vulnerable with each other, as they explored the gospel.

The Image of God Portrayed to the World

The local church may be said to be an environment where people obtain a picture of God that shapes their identities, as those made in the image of God. The Holy Spirit guides the church to engage in God's mission to reconcile people to his family.[53] We need to discern where the Spirit is calling us to participate in God's mission. The question is, what sort of vision of the Trinity might help us to theologically reflect on what God is doing in the missional groups we belong to. The Greek Orthodox theologian Zizioulas highlights that God can only be meaningfully said to exist based on the perichoresis of the divine dance between the persons of the Trinity.[54] Karkainen summarizes the implications of Zizioulas's communion theology related to the being of the church:

51. Ibid., 102–3.
52. Ibid.
53. Acts 16:6–10.
54. Zizioulas, *Being as Communion*, 2004.

> By being a member of the church, a human being becomes an "image of God," existing as God Himself exists; he or she takes on God's "way of being." "This way of being . . . is a way of relationship with the world, with other people and with God, an event of communion, and that is why it cannot be realized as the achievement of an individual, but only as an ecclesial fact."[55]

What Zizioulas and Karkainen recognize to be the nature of the power of the Christian faith community, intentionally lived out in groups who gather in Christ's name, is that God reveals himself as a relational deity. The Spirit mediates participation in the divine life based on a group's intimate participation as life shared together. Believers who share in this life also seek to share it with those who as yet do not know the Lord. The relationships that exist between believers and those exploring Christian faith can become an opportunity to display what it means to be in the image of a God. God is defined by his desire to have meaningful relationships as a tri-personal deity with people. God's image is reflected by his relational nature as an intimate communion between Father, Son, and Holy Spirit. All those who engage in relationships are making themselves open to be shaped into God's image. This can be in convictional communities of missional discipleship and praxis, as well as in the social and personal zones of late modern people, in their territory. What seems vital is that a process begins by which new spaces and places are invested with a fresh identity, as zones of spiritual conversation where spiritual formation can take place.

---

55. Karkainen, *Trinity*, 90–91.

Section 4

The Pragmatic Life of Contextual Participation in the Mission of God among the New Generations

This section focuses on how the emergent generations of secular people after Christendom need to be, first of all, reached by missional disciple-makers who understand their context. Second, the focus will be on the pragmatic question of evidence for how congregations are being shaped to practically participate in the Triune mission.

Chapter 8

Discipleship of the New Tribes

By Andrew R. Hardy

Introduction

Who are the new tribes? They do not exist in some distant nomadic culture but on our own doorsteps. They consist of indigenous Westerners. They are aged somewhere between eight to thirty-seven years old. Mostly they know nothing of a past Christendom era. They are open to explore all kinds of postmodern fantasies, genres, and fashions. No one truth defines their worldviews. They may even be best termed to have a postsecular consciousness, which factors in spirituality and interest in the supernatural. They are innocent, as they do not know what it means to be shaped by Christ and his life. They do not belong to one single tribe but can happily travel and network between many. Their tribes exist in the millions. Some sociologists and market researchers speak of them as generations Y and Z. We also like to call them the "new tribes." Generation Y have also been termed the Millennial generation. They are many and no one of them is the same. *Britannica* provides an anthropological definition of a tribe:

> Tribe . . . , a notional form of human social organization based
> on a set of smaller groups (known as bands), having temporary

or permanent political integration, and defined by traditions of common descent, language, culture, and ideology.[1]

The definition suggests that a tribe is made up of smaller "bands" of people who all identify as their tribe. This is the case with Bedouins who live in the hard, arid regions of the world, such as in Arabia or the sub-Sahara, etc. Though they be made up of many bands, they associate their origins to a tribe and a common ancestral stock. In the late modern context, indigenous Western youth and young adults value gathering in smaller groups of peers based on common interests. These groups may not be called "bands" because they do not consider that they belong to one defining larger tribe, even though sociologists may use terms like generation Y or Z. These neo-tribes do not consider such terms to be the basis of their identity. Generation Y did have a proclivity to associate with labels like Goth, Boy Racer, Emo, etc. From this perspective, a kind of tribal identity was averred. We would argue that the small groups generations Y and Z value being part of are tribes that are based on their common social identity, of which, in the case of generation Z, the language of Goth or Emo no longer has meaning.

For generation Z, one group is not necessarily associated with another, thus making them a kind of tribe in their own right. Sociologically and anthropologically speaking, we cannot as such call generations Y and Z tribes. An exception to this might be young people who are part of migrant diaspora cultures that have come to the West to find a better life.

In their case youth may gather in what we might call "bands," to the extent that they might consider their diaspora communities in the West to be their tribes. Hence a band of Chinese youth may consider their tribe to be the Chinese diaspora in Britain. Indeed, we know strong cultural links exist in these communities in the UK, from work with our students from this diaspora and others.

A profile of generations Y and Z is nevertheless a useful general exercise, as it provides some broad brushstrokes of characteristics that may be shared in common by indigenous Western youth, or at times by diaspora communities of youth, who have been Westernized. However, late modern people defy being defined by reductionist categories. The contents of this chapter will hopefully prove informative to help thinking into how to disciple these generations.

Generally speaking, we are discussing native indigenous Western youth and young adults in this chapter, although there may be applications that apply to diasporas. In a previous publication,[2] we discussed the

1. *Britannica.com*, s.v. "tribe," https://www.britannica.com/topic/tribe-anthropology.
2. Hardy and Yarnell, *Forming Multicultural Partnerships*.

issue of third-culture children and adults, which may be useful to consider alongside this chapter. It discusses diaspora youth and young adults and the challenges they face.[3]

Generation Y are those young adults born between 1980 to 1994. The members of this generation are currently twenty-three to thirty-seven years old. Those that make up generation Z are those born between 1995 and 2009, currently making them eight to twenty-two years old. Sociologists generally consider a generation to last fourteen years. The aim of building a profile of both generations is to provide suggestions how to disciple them. Any profile is at best suggestive and limited. Just as in many ways modernity's flirtation with absolute claims about the power of science proved to be seriously flawed. We use the language of "tribes" to designate members of both generations, in terms of the smaller social groups they identify with, rather than their generations as such. The aim is to identify some of the characteristics of both generations that may help us to understand something about them.

The journalist Ethan Watters terms the groups that young people and young adults belong to, "tribes."[4] The language of "Chav," "Geek," "Smoothy," etc., may not be as common now, but it certainly is a representation of a language used by members of generation Y. The language of "tribes" represents the preference for belonging to smaller groups that gather around a common identity that they own. Ownership is a high value for both generations, influenced as they are by consumerism and the age of gadgets. Brand identities, such as Nike, can be a status symbol, as well as a means to identify members of a tribe. So fashion can also play an important part in tribe identities for some but not all.

"Tribes" is a useful nomenclature to designate the social bubbles that generations Y and Z inhabit. It may be claimed that they belong to these identity groups to insulate themselves from the demands of late modern society, and its uncertainties, as Nydam understands it.[5]

He argues that youth culture in North America is defined by the deliberate attempts by teenagers to create a bubble around themselves, so that they do not need to make themselves vulnerable to the world outside these bubbles. For example, wearing head phones while listening to personal music is a way to shut others out.

Whether we use terms like "bubble" or "tribe," they represent the goal of some members of generations Y and Z to protect themselves from the

3. Ibid., ch. 3.
4. Watters, *Urban Tribes.*
5. Nydam, "Relational Theology of Generation Y," 321–30.

impinging influences of those forces they do not understand, or want to model their lives on. Nydam comments:

> How do I describe this so-called bubble that I am suggesting many youth live in today? It is a way to live, to survive, where lots of things do not get to you. It is first of all protective in that it keeps things out. In this bubble, judgments, commitments, ethical imperatives, as well as the expectations of others, especially parents, are to some degree filtered out. What does get through this permeable membrane are the connections with others and society that have relational value. Attachments to others are primary for Generation Y. They are a relational generation. . . . They know how to "hang," how to be with friends. The bubble I am describing is also insular. It keeps things in. It keeps something inside safe, safe from fragmentation, safe from parental expectations, safe from the encroachments of what everyone else thinks, and safe from "being sold out" to society. The bubble, as I call it, insulates the very genuine, authentic self of youth—the most precious part of a human being—the soul, if you will. This has its price though. For one thing, young people know how to be alone.[6]

Jason Gardner speaks of this "bubble" reality as "connected cocooning," by which he means the way young people use the internet and personal devices to form their own safe worlds, made up of friends they select to be part of them.[7]

Generations Y and Z have been brought up in the world of postmodernity, or Bauman's liquid modernity.[8] Relativity reigns, and each person has the right to construct their own identities.[9] In this constructivist world, reality is whatever you want to make it.[10] The individual can construct their own virtual world, where they have their own norms, beliefs, values, practices, and rights to be who they want to be. The bubble reality that protects both generations from conforming to authority structures has a small circle of friends in a shared tribe (alongside others they too aver), which they have access to through social media like Facebook, Twitter, Snapchat, smart phones, web groups, as well as gaming groups, et al.

They do not need to be physically present to interact, which has the advantage of them being able to select who they interact with.

6. Ibid., 323.

7. Gardner, *Mend the Gap*, 56–57.

8. Bauman, *Liquid Modernity*.

9. Cray, *Disciples and Citizens*, 84–85.

10. Ibid.

It means they can choose those things and people that conform to their individual tastes.[11] They may live much of their lives in these virtual social worlds.[12] Castells suggests this may be termed a network reality, where people network across the global web in a way that is unprecedented in recorded human history.[13]

It is possible for new tribes to have members from different parts of the world, gathered as virtual groups together in cyberspace. Cyberspace is transforming human consciousness. It is now possible to grasp a far bigger picture of the world that we live in, compared to the average person of even ten years ago.[14]

Nydam makes a profound observation about the loneliness of the virtual world,[15] where young people can construct their own fantasy realities, isolating them from their immediate material communities. They quite literally construct their own plausibility structures in these cyber simulation zones. Are we witnessing the deconstruction of human community that was once lived out as being physically present to others? Perhaps we need to consider how we might disciple this generation, in fresh ways, using the cyberspace they value.

Can they be discipled in this virtual world? Do they need enticing to reexplore the physical world, as an exciting arena of meaningful encounter that transcends the imaginative simulated realities of cyberspace? Perhaps it will be realistic to adopt a both/and approach. Some of the most recent technologies are implanting equipment into spectacles, ear pieces, and the human body itself.

The imaginative cyberspace games that can be played online can now be played virtually anywhere. The imaginative simulated realities of these games is enticing and far more engaging than real-life experience. New experiences cannot be generated like those found in these gaming worlds. Is it possible that both generations have begun a retreat of human consciousness into these fantasy realities? It could be that we are witnessing a new kind of spiritual warfare that is seeking to deconstruct the material encounter of people with the real world.

11. Rainie and Wellman, *Networked*.

12. Ibid., 3–20, 117–46; Castells, *Networks of Outrage and Hope*.

13. Castells, *Power of Identity*, xvii–xviii.

14. Ibid. Castells, *Networks of Outrage and Hope*.

15. Nydam, "Relational Theology of Generation Y."

Profiling Generation Y: The Post-Metanarrative Culture and the Happy Midi-Narrative

Members of both generations are arguably the most affected by postmodernism and pluralism. They may suggestively be claimed to no longer accept overarching metanarratives, such as Christendom culture educed for its time.[16] Missional churches need to make themselves contextually relevant to young people, if they want to disciple them.[17] The whole Christian story fits into a broadly assumed overarching framework (worldview), moving through narrative iterations of creation, fall, redemption, election, and final consummation.[18] The Christian metanarrative[19] locates humanity as a creation of God.[20] God has a purpose to restore humanity through Christ to a state of peace with God and others.[21] This restoration will entail people living in community and communion with each other. Generation Z may become even less communally present, so it would seem important for missiological strategies to be considered that seek to incarnate with them in their cyber worlds. Might we be able to begin the process of discipling them there?

Simpkins's unpublished MA research demonstrates the limitations of the influence of Christian belief on generation Y.[22] The days of the Christendom metanarrative that put Christianity at the center of Western life has ended. Hence it is much harder for generation Y to have ready access to a Christian worldview.

Simpkins iterates the challenge to be one of innocence. The members of generations Y and Z simply do not know the Christian story. They cannot be held accountable for this deficit. They cannot be influenced by it, unless they obtain realistic access to it.[23] Their identity is not formed by a Christian faith, but by a late modern relativistic constructivism.[24] The immediacy of popular culture focuses on present proximate experiences. There is very limited access to meaningful connections with sources to inform them of

---

16. Savage et al., *Making Sense of Generation Y*, 35–54.

17. Moynagh, *Church for Every Context*, 57.

18. This is at least quite an evangelistic account of what is included in so-called metanarratives.

19. And I do not make the fundamental error of suggesting there is just one, but I deliberately select the evangelical version for now mentioned above.

20. Gen 1:26–27.

21. Rom 3:23; 6:23.

22. Simpkins, "Generation Y and the Gospel."

23. Ibid.

24. Ibid.

the Christian story. A diagram from Simpkins's work illustrates their situation, note how there is a reinforcing cycle.

Key Findings on the Four Themes

Innocence
Failure of religious transmission
Absence of Christian community
Social change and Sundays
Unattractive church culture
Pluralist views of spirituality

contributing to

leads to

Intentionality
Personal happiness sought via family, friends and leisure
Aim to be good and feel good
Short term choices, not commitments
Lack of a 'formative spirituality'
But 'something is missing'

Identity
Consumerism – brands and logos
Lifestyle and leisure choices
The 'narcissistic self'
Search for the 'authentic self'
Individual freedom of choice
No consensus on what is good to choose

which results in a lack of

reinforced by

Immediacy
Influence of popular culture
Electronic media shape communication
Life as immediate experience
No need for a transcendent reality
'Eternity' not within the attention span

> An *innocence* about the gospel means that Generation Y's *identity* is shaped by their present world, which is reinforced by a culture of consumerism, and the *immediacy* offered by today's digital media and communications. This results in a lack of *intentionality* in pursuing any longer term purpose or transcendent truth which in turn contributes to a lack of interest in, and *innocence* about, the gospel.

25

Savage, Collins-Mayo, and Mayo's 2006 research into generation Y suggests something similar to Simpkins's findings.[26] Cray also suggests generation Y are not interested in the bigger questions of life, such as their eternal destiny, due to the sociocultural constructivism of late moder-

25. Ibid., 53.
26. Savage et al., *Making Sense of Generation Y*, 35–54.

nity and the loss of a Christendom culture.[27] Cray discusses the impact of constructivism and how it has undermined the concept of a stable theological truth. Such claims to absolute truth were assumed during Christendom, but are now replaced by multiple truths being considered equally possible.[28] The Fresh Expressions website has this to comment in response to the 2006 research of Savage et al.:

> Youth workers and others report that if you scratch the surface, most youngsters still want to be loved, to feel their life is worthwhile and to be part of something bigger than themselves. Though not expressed in spiritual terms, these longings speak of a God-shaped gap in their lives.[29]

What Simpkins's research has highlighted, is that there are potential successful socio-spiritual movements, like that of Soul Survivor, which possibly offer a way to address the deficits of the loss of a Christian worldview for a few. His positive findings have an increased relevance to members of generation Z, where the work of Soul Survivor, and other missional organizations like it, are having an important impact on a significant minority of them. We might also include Hillsong, Youth for Christ, and the Hope Projects. In the diagram below, Simpkins's findings are articulated. The work of Soul Survivor, and other youth mission movements like it, are seeking to create a new kind of faith-reinforcing cycle for postmodern youth tribes to explore.

The diagrams above and below iterate findings from Simpkins's research based on interviews with those who went to Soul Survivor. It is noted that the so-called innocence of generation Y is positively informed by good Bible teaching at Soul Survivor. Simpkins reports that there is good evidence that it positively informs their identity and the self-worth of participants.[30] It also seems evident that some young people were overall intentionally seeking to serve God in future careers and in their churches.[31] Their need for an immediacy of experience with God was met and facilitated through the worship music and other visual media at the Soul Survivor events.[32] What proved very important was the relational environment of Soul Survivor.[33] Generations Y and Z find it important to feel part of a shared journey with

---

27. Cray, *Disciples and Citizens*.

28. Ibid., 84–85.

29. http://freshexpressions.org.uk.

30. Simpkins, *Generation Y and the Gospel*.

31. Ibid.

32. Ibid.

33. Ibid.

peers, who are having a similar experience as they explore the Christian faith.[34] One important conclusion to Simpkins's research is suggestive of the kind of training needed for youth workers:

> It is common in Christian leadership training to address the functional skills required in ministry—teaching, evangelism, leading worship and prayer, pastoral care, and the various organizational and administrative skills required. Yet all of this will be of little avail if the youth worker does not have a sound grasp of the drivers, beliefs and attitudes that are actually shaping the world of those amongst whom they serve. Chris Folmsbee gives a personal account of how a period of immersion in understanding the culture of postmodern young people transformed his own approach to youth ministry. He realized he needed to understand the real issues young people were facing, and the questions they were asking, if he was to be truly effective in relating the gospel to them. Only with such an understanding could he give them the spiritual direction they needed.[35]

Important to this "immersion" to understand "young people," is the need for there to be strong relational capital developed between the youth worker and the tribes they seek to incarnate among. Discipleship will not happen if the youth worker is ineffective in how she, or he, relates to young people. It requires the use of popular language, using meaningful idioms of their culture, as part of the forging of an effective discipleship formation strategy. It will be impossible to mediate the Christian faith to them, unless it is communicated in terms that they can resonate with and find interesting, suited to the real challenges of their lives.

34. Ibid.

35. Ibid., 94. It is important to note that Simpkins's research is based on a model which we have not sought to analyze in this chapter due to the constraints to do with word count. However, we thoroughly recommend reading a copy of the dissertation as it provides some really important insights into how we might go about seeking to understand generation Y. Understanding from within their frame of reference is recommended by Simpkins, and we thoroughly recommend this approach as fundamental to contextual ministry and discipleship formation approaches and processes.

Soul Survivor and Interviewees Responses to the Themes

Innocence	Identity	Intentionality
Tell the Christian story	Base self-worth on God's love	Ask God for dreams/adventures
Explain key Bible passages	Show the value being a Christian	Pursue a purposeful career
Address apologetic issues	Seek to heal inner hurts	Serve the local church
Share personal 'faith stories'	Affirm young women	Serve the community
Give guidance on practical Christian living	Teach Christian sexual identity	Be concerned for social justice

Immediacy	The Relational Environment
Share the gospel through music	Worship together
Be 'visual' not just 'literary'	Serve with one another
Beware of Internet/Facebook dangers but utilise the digital media	Provide safe places to foster intergenerational relationships
	Take young people on adventures
	Show authentic love to young people

36

Simpkins has provided a model (see above) by which we might seek to understand how to authentically and genuinely disciple generations Y and Z. The writer found it useful to note Simpkins's findings when he was working with youth of generation Z at Soul Survivor Week B in 2016.

It struck him that there were strong correspondences to Simpkins's research findings exhibited by the fifty-eight young people that made up the group he went to the event with. It was useful to be a participant observer, working among these young people. The five-part cycle Simpkins discusses

36. Ibid., 78.

above as a way to effectively engage with youth, by informing their innocent ignorance of the Christian gospel with the narrative of it, was powerfully reinforced by the impact of the spiritual and relational capital of the event on them. They responded positively to the challenge to explore Christian faith for themselves.

Before we turn to the research of Savage et al., it is important to add further comments about the Christian young adults of generation Y. It is broadly correct to suggest that there are mixed views on spirituality among churched and unchurched youth alike, in generations Y and Z.

In a youth church that one of the writers worked with, some of the youth found it hard to reconcile what they were learning at school, in philosophy and religion classes, with the Christian story. They found it hard to see it as an authoritative worldview for them to have confidence in, given the secular narrative they were learning. This is not to say that the youth concerned were not open to try to make sense of their world by the Christian story. It was one story among others they were open to explore.

Some of the young people in this group held the view that their Christian faith was the only form of belief that mattered to them. Was this an instance of their tribal identity being defined by parental ties to a Christian community? The bigger question was, had they really embraced Christ as their Lord, on their own terms? Others in the group did not have a personal faith but were open to explore if it made sense to them.

For a number of this group, if pushed, they said they were looking for answers and did not think that any one given brand of Christianity had all the answers. Moreover, some who were doing philosophy at "A" level, found it hard to accept that any one version of religious belief could be termed authoritative, whether it was Christian, Muslim, Buddhist, or Hindu, etc.

A conclusion may be drawn, suggesting that there will be a need for youth and young adults to be encouraged to make a commitment to faith in Christ based on an experience of his real presence, alongside them in their lives. This is certainly a challenge that many of the neo-Pentecostal and Charismatic churches seek to achieve among their youth and young adults. In the case of one community church known to us, young people intentionally seek to learn how to hear God's voice as a means to feel meaningfully connected to the living God of self-revelation.

The Happy Midi-Narrative World

A profile of generations Y and Z needs to recognize the priority of the individual's demand to be free to make up their own mind about their beliefs.

Savage et al. term the story that late modern youth and adults use to define themselves by, "the happy midi-narrative." It is important to understand the difference between a midi- and metanarrative:

> We have coined the phrase "Happy midi-narrative" to describe the storyline of our young people's [i.e., generation Y] world view. We use the term "midi-narrative" to distinguish it from the concept of a "meta-narrative." A meta-narrative is a story on a grand scale about how the world works. Meta-narratives are often stories with an end goal. For example, in the Enlightenment meta-narrative the goal is "progress" and the improvement of the human condition. In the Judeo-Christian meta-narrative, we could say that the goal is the "end times," the return of the Messiah. In contrast, the world view of our young people operates on a more modest scale of the here and now, rather than something beyond. Yet it is not an individualistic, midi-narrative. It is communal on a small scale (me, my friends, and my family): a midi-narrative.[37]

The youth house church referred to earlier is interesting from a certain point of view, in light of the values inferred to be part of a midi-narrative. The youth group itself met in both a home and in a church. The young people who attended it did not all go to the same church, indeed some did not go to a church at all. There were a range of youth from different churches and churchmanships. The group concerned, treated this particular youth church very much like a tribe, that they belonged to among other tribes. It is enough to comment that although these young people were interested in seeking to have an experience with God (seeking experiences is a generation Y trait),[38] it was not the only kind of tribe they belonged to. For instance, some of them had other groups who they did sports with, went to parties with, or they connected with on Facebook. They were open to explore and experience other alternatives that might offer them an even happier life. Happiness is the key phrase of the so-called happy midi-narrative.

Savage et al. go on to describe the nature of this midi-narrative. There are three main sequences recognized in the happy midi-narrative. First, there is what they term the "initial sequence of the main storyline":[39]

> My aim to be happy will be realized through me being myself, and connecting to others and the universe (without harming them).[40]

---

37. Ibid., 37, 38.
38. Gardner, *Mend the Gap*, 56–57.
39. Savage et al., *Making Sense of Generation Y*, 39.
40. Ibid.

The importance of a person being themselves is so that a person is not forced to be other than what they perceive themselves to be. Being "myself," means not being the projection of another person's desires for me. Being "myself," means being given permission by my tribe to be myself, without judgment from others. Being "myself" means I can really be me, and the things that make me real and valuable to others who affirm me. Affirming "me" is a high priority. This does not imply that there is no room for constructive feedback to help a person grow. Indeed, the willingness to receive support from friends implies a willingness to be open to receiving help from others. The difference is that the happy midi-narrative does not allow for a big overarching story to make sense of the world.

Indeed, happiness is confined to more immediate wins that bring happiness. Death, heaven, and hell are not factored into the happy midi-narrative with an expectation for future eternal happiness. The immediacy of now is much more important. The nirvana of a purposeful future might include "me" achieving the ideal life of celebrity culture. The consciousness of now overpowers and consumes any fantasy of an unknown other future life. "Now" is life in this world and no other world beyond it meaningfully impacts me "now."

Second, there is what Savage et al. term the "topical sequence: the obstacle and the help"[41] that a person who is not happy needs to receive in order to get back on track to being happy:

> Bad things can happen in real life that prevent us from attaining this happiness: broken relationships, suffering, loneliness, depression, self-rejection, addiction, injustice, ageing.[42]

Although these bad things happen, they can be part of the movement toward the ideal life of being happy, even if real-life situations prevent happiness at times on the journey toward it. Help can come from family, friends, or the arts—such as music that can point the way toward ideal happiness.

Third, there is the "final sequence: The resolution"[43] of the "happy midi-narrative," which goes something like this:

> Having received help, having "grown" as a result of the meaningful microcosm of family, friends and the popular arts, the happy ideal that once eluded us is now possible.[44]

41. Ibid.
42. Ibid.
43. Ibid.
44. Ibid.

It could be all too easy to find weaknesses in the happy midi-narrative. However, this would be to do some of its key parts a disservice. The midi-narrative does not claim to provide the ultimate ideal happiness that generation Y seeks. It offers a limited scalable kind of happiness, suited to the human context, in terms of perceptions of what the real world is all about. This "real world" is not interpreted using theological language. At best the ideal material world can be "glimpsed through the popular arts since they" provide "the tools of imagination and a taste of experience."[45] Hence parties, night clubs, music, dancing, and sexual release provide the architecture to be happy, and to experience an embodied joy.

Being genuinely happy with a life partner is sought after, but if a couple outgrow the ability to be happy together, then it is time to move on. These are rather modest aims of the narrative, which does not seek to make overall sense of the world and a person's place in it. It provides a source that might construct a rather humble attitude toward a world with its uncertainties, which generation Y favors compared to a worldview that calls them to take on broader concerns regarding their destiny, or that of the world.

God-consciousness is not factored in. Indeed Savage et al. suggest that in their findings, "the young people's actual world was perceived as largely benign, if sometimes a little dull."[46]

Theirs is a world divested of the divine, angels, demons and spiritual forces, and a higher appreciation of the infinite possibilities of life with an infinitely imaginative God.

Wink spoke of this perspective as the "materialist worldview."[47] It is a world that is much as it appears, and which is subject to chance occurrences that at times impact human thriving and well-being. However, the popularity of films like *Lord of the Rings* and *Harry Potter* and TV series like *Fringe*, *Shannara*, and *Grimm* speak to an inner craving for the supernatural at some level. I think this is possibly underplayed by the church, but it has not been missed by scholars such as Drane.[48]

Drane speaks of the spiritual seeking of youth and young adults alike, which finds them looking to other sources than the Christian religion to inspire their postsecular emerging spiritual consciousness. I would suggest this consciousness will be increasingly evident, especially among generation Z, as the years pass and as they mature. We have written elsewhere of the

45. Ibid.
46. Ibid., 40.
47. Wink, *Powers That Be*, 17.
48. Drane, *Do Christians Know*.

reemergence of interest in paganism, Wicca, and Gnosticism.[49] It is worth noting that each of these renewed spheres of interest do not necessarily mean that their adherents believe in a deity or divine beings.

Voices from within the Millennial Generation

An important voice comes from a North American member of generation Y, who has done much missional work among the millennials. It is important to hear her voice in order to appreciate insights that come from those engaging in reflection on their missional ministries, while still being part of this generation themselves. Sarah Guldalian comments:

> This self-expressive, self-aware group appreciates that which is experiential and "real." Although turned off by institutions, they may not, however, be opposed to hearing about Jesus. And so, as Christians, we should focus on introducing them to Jesus Christ first and the church second. Most appealing to them would be hearing your personal experience with Jesus Christ (i.e., what has He done to change your life?). Remember, they are open to change—and your experience.
>
> Although the Millennials are a breed different from previous generations, spiritual truth does not change. Jesus is the same yesterday, today, and forever. There is a heaven, and the only way to get to our Father in heaven is through Jesus, who is the way, the truth, and the life. Eternity looms in the balance for every person. So, the question is not, "Should we reach the Millennials?" As Christ's ambassadors, the resounding answer to that question must be "Yes!" But, instead, we ask, "How do we as the church reach Millennials with the Gospel of Jesus Christ in a manner that will lead them to listen?"[50]

Guldalian has significant relevant media expertise in working with the existing emerging generations, which helps her to understand their challenges and contextualize Christian media to them. Although her work is focused in North America, the insights she offers seem to articulate well with the situation of generations Y and Z in the UK.

---

49. Hardy et al., *Power and the Powers.*
50. Guldalian, "Millennials," 43.

Profiling Generation Z

It was important for the research for this chapter to seek insights into generation Z from sources that do not seek to theologically reflect on them. The reason for this is that there is very limited literature that seeks to understand this generation from a theological reflective perspective. Some of the characteristics highlighted by market researchers for this generation were careful not to assume that what they disclosed is always true of all of its so-called members.[51] Moreover, in the context of discipleship formation research concerning the new tribes, a wide range of contextual approaches are needed to address the broader needs of peoples from different world cultures in Western multicultural society. Generation Z is needing to increasingly be multiculturally savvy and have many friends across cultures.

A multivalent approach needs to be used in order to learn about generation Z, which is highlighted in Chilcote's simple and practical ethnographic accounts of the views of generation Z, among others.[52] Having noted this, the table below seeks to pick out some of the key findings that profile generation Z. The data in the table was constructed from a broad trail through available marketing literature focused on key characteristics of this generation.[53]

51. Hecht et al., *Religion and Culture*, 57, 103, 107–8, 114, 118–19, 124, 126–28, 289, 301–2. Chilcote, *Making Disciples*.

52. Chilcote, *Making Disciples*.

53. Combi, *Generation Z*; Seemiller and Grace, *Generation Z Goes to College*; Palfrey and Gasser, *Understanding the First Generation*; Wagner, "7 Skills"; Savitt, "Gen Z"; Renfro, "Z Future Is Here!"; Stone, "Children of Cyberspace"; Renfro, "Generation Z."

Characteristics of Generation Z

Overview	Social Media	Gadgets	Commerce	Socialisation and enculturation	Future Life	Enhanced Learners	Future Challenges
Born 1995-2010	Always connected to games, friends through social media	Creative using Apps and tools	Pick and mix culture not brand loyal	They are almost always connected using social media	Their largest concern is will they have a job	They are multi-taskers who love to have access to all kinds of random sources	Health problems which may come from more sedentary desk related work
Lives shaped by: war, internet, technology, terrorism, recession & social media	Electronic devices and instant access vitally important	Most data and media consumed using mobile devices	Huge impact on large companies – who seek to understand this emergent technological generation	Highly aware of global news and have a high sense of ethical and social responsibility	They are entrepreneurs – they sell their music and games etc. online	They are self-learners and do not respond well to stand up and deliver lecture styles of communication	Other generations need to communicate using technology on Gen Z's terms
Highly proficient in use of technology	Take up new social causes more readily due to social media	Prefer interactive media rather than static media like TV	They spend more than any other generation on gadgets, iTunes etc.	They want work and school to be fun	They want things to work quickly and lose interest when they do not	They learn best and fastest through multiple technology avenues	Vulnerable to cyber bullying and internet crime
Global technological connection to peers and knowledge	Seek careers that will help the world and others	High preference for multifunctional mobile devices	Desire to buy environmentally friendly products more than any other generation	They are closer to their parents and siblings than previous generations	They will be loyal to bosses but bosses only win this if they are loyal to them	Educators are brining gaming design and theory to them as they value these media highly	Recession, war and terrorism mean they are highly aware of uncertainties
Highly flexible and expect flexibility from others – they accept and value diversity	Social justice / conscience comes from media images of suffering – this includes concerns for climate change	Prefer multiple feature sites and social media which allow upload of videos, blogs, tweets, pictures	Seek alternative ways to get educated for work than expensive educational courses	Obtain high self-esteem from parents and ability to use gadgets means they are very confident	They are not looking for lifetime careers but flexible options – freelance work will suite them well		

Moreover, Giselle Abramovich, senior and strategic editor of CMO. com (writing from the North American context) offers some important insights found in market research concerning generation Z. They relate well to the table above.[54] She comments:[55]

> While many marketers still struggle to figure out the Millennials, a new generation Generation Z is growing up behind the scenes. Members of Gen Z, born after 1995, are quite different than their Millennial counterparts, with their own set of expectations when interacting with companies. They are the first truly mobile-first generation, so they place a big emphasis on personalization and relevance. In addition, Gen Zers are entrepreneurial and resourceful, courtesy of growing up during a recession. Marketers will need to take all of this into account when shaping their strategies for this group.[56]

Those who make up this category have important characteristics that market researchers need to take into consideration, in order to brand their products so they can sell things to them. Although we must be very careful not to consider anyone as a product, as all humanity (in our view) is made in the image of God, we can at least allow ourselves to learn some things of importance from what is notable about this category in marketing terms.

First of all, those from the age of nineteen years old and younger communicate most readily using social networks. They prefer that communication with them is through media like Snapchat, Secret, and Whisper. In the United States, a quarter of thirteen- to seventeen-year-olds have left off using Facebook in the year 2016. It is important to note this preference. It is suggested that new ways of communicating with young people to disciple them will require creative use of these resources. Next, it is important to recognize the ability of generation Z to self-educate themselves, by accessing and finding information quickly and efficiently using the new web-based technologies. Abramovich speaks of them as "adept researchers." In the United States, 33 percent watch lessons on line, 20 percent read textbook tablets, and 32 percent work with classmates online. If we wish to disciple

---

54. Abramovich, "15 Mind-Blowing Stats."

55. Obviously as an empirical researcher I recognize the very real cultural differences between young people of this so-called generation Z between North America and the UK. However, the data shared by Abramovich may be at the very least considered as suggestive of what is true of this group in Western society more broadly.

56. Abramovich, "15 Mind-Blowing Stats."

this generation, then we need to seek to enhance online resources that capture their interests.[57]

It is also interesting that generation Y tends to use three screens to access cyberspace-related sources, whereas generation Z use five screens or more, consisting of smartphones, TVs, laptops, desktops, and iPods. It is notable that 79 percent of generation Z show symptoms of emotional distress when not able to have access to their personal electronic devices. This is of concern, as it speaks to a growing dependence on these devices in order for them to feel connected to others. Moreover, isolation from these resources means they do not have access to the protection of their mobile virtual-bubble realities.

It is important to realize that their bubble realities are constantly active, protecting them while on the move. It is quite possible that mobile devices represent a kind of sanctuary, where generation Z can escape to be themselves in their simulated plausibility structures.[58] How might we disciple this generation in light of this? Could it be that they could conceive of somewhere in their cyber-worlds as a kind of virtual chapel, where they can commune with God and their virtual Christian friends?

Moreover, the average attention span of those who belong to generation Z is an amazing 8 seconds.[59] This is not to say that they cannot concentrate for longer periods of time, but the rapid fire of information coming to their senses from web-based sources has potentially conditioned them to be less interested for more sustained periods on topics that require reflection and time to understand.

Teachers are having to be far more creative in helping their students to learn in the light of deficits in attention spans. It is also quite possible they are becoming abler to assess a broader range of information at higher speeds, which makes it important for communication with them to be delivered in sound-bite-sized pieces of data.

Generation Z also share the entrepreneurial spirit of generation Y. Seventy-two percent want to own their own businesses, or even have started small ventures already. A further 76 percent aspire to want to turn their hobbies into full-time jobs.[60] It is likely that generation Z will effectively make a living for themselves from the comfort of their living rooms, based on the hobbies and interests that they can sell as products on the World Wide Web. How might we inspire such a generation to engage in community-

57. All the above data can be found at Abramovich, "15 Mind-Blowing Stats."
58. Ibid.
59. Ibid.
60. Ibid.

focused businesses that benefit others? It is quite possible, given a surprising up-turn of interest among generation Z in helping others by joining causes, that their interest in voluntary engagement in social action projects might lead them to work with Christian activists.

Sixty percent of sixteen- to nineteen-year-olds in the United States want their jobs to make an impact on the world, 26 percent currently volunteer in charities and other organizations to help others, and 76 percent are deeply concerned about humanity's impact on the environment. We have noticed similar activist interests in the UK. Added to these ideological instincts, 58 percent are somewhat to very worried about their futures. There is a sense of a positive do-gooder mentality to be found among generation Z, which may prove to be an opening created by the Spirit of God.

Some critical challenges are faced by generation Z, just as any other generation that does not know Christ that has not been positively influenced by the Christian message. Combi, an experienced teacher of pupils of generation Z, in the UK context, has published case-related findings about this generation. She comments:

> One question I have been asked a lot, . . . is how, based on my experience, I would label this generation. Are they the internet Generation, the Sex-Mad Generation, the Social-Media Generation, the Celebrity-Obsessed Generation or the Not-Much-to-See-Here Generation? Technology, the media, sex, celebrity and apathy are certainly features of this generation. But there is so much more to Generation Z. . . . There hasn't been a subject that I've discussed with them about which they haven't been interested and interesting.[61]

Combi notes that this generation feel that they are the most misunderstood generation. Her work provides numerous interviews with this age group. These interviews provide invaluable ethnographic lenses into the kinds of matters that obsess this emergent generation. However, her comment that this generation's members are "interested and interesting" comes from the recognition that they have the inquisitiveness, empathy, and capacity to transcend the weaknesses of their generation, as she and others have highlighted them. Seemiller and Grace also resonate with Combi's findings.

They have obtained interesting results related to research on the personality characteristics of generation Z, in the context of their entry into higher education. Interestingly, and importantly, this generation is being brought up to value family, responsibility for others, and independence:

---

61. Combi, *Generation Z*, see preface.

> How Generation Z students describe themselves is influenced
> not just by the nature of the world they were raised in but the
> nurture of the families they were raised by: mostly Generation
> Xers. As parents, they are using an involved parenting style
> similar to that of the Boomers, but they're also instilling values
> of individual responsibility and independence.[62]

It is worth noting what things Seemiller and Grace pick out as some
of the personality traits that seem to be evident among members of generation Z. They include loyalty, compassion, thoughtfulness, open-mindedness,
and determination. These are the kinds of qualities that may prove to be the
contextual clues of the Spirit's work among this generation. These personality
qualities are the kinds of traits that the Spirit of Christ can shape and form in
a new generation, that could become highly effective followers of the Lord.

It seems that there is evidence that generation Z are even more open to
empathize with the world around them. The plight of the poor, a revulsion
to injustice, a strong dislike for the abuse or misuse of power. These characteristics may also be enhanced by their compassion and determination to
make a difference to their lives and the lives of others.

Certainly the political will of the British government places value on
education that provides students with life skills and social and relational
capital.[63] The focus here is on the younger generations, who will become
tomorrow's citizens, as well as tomorrow's potential followers of Christ.
Cray calls for Christian's to not only be disciples of Christ, but also citizens
who seek to transform the structures of society, so that God's reign might
influence people. However, it will be crucial to help to develop generation
Z's critical capacities regarding the weaknesses of a disintegrating individualistic public sphere:

> Despite the inadequacy of their midi narrative, Generation
> Y [and Z, our words] thrives on uncertainty and risk. It has
> known only this society and has not been equipped with the
> analytical tools to critique it. But with good national policies
> and effective local communities, it can be helped towards new
> forms of social capital.
>   Nevertheless, the challenge is great. How do we grow Chris-
> tians who can be public disciples, living the life of the future in
> advance, in this culture which, as we have seen, has the capacity

62. Seemiller and Grace, *Generation Z Goes to College*, ch. 1.

63. In our work in higher education, in the programs we have helped to design for
undergraduate students we have been required by universities and quality assurance
agencies to enhance college programs to meet national government requirements to
provide practical skills to students.

to corrode both the public or civic sphere and public discipleship? Where do you grow both "involved distinctiveness" and
"subversive engagement"? God has only one answer. It is called
the church.[64]

Cray suggests generation Y need to develop their critical skills, and we
would include generation Z, who are even more ready to critique the selfish
DNA of the me-first culture of late modern hyper-individualism.

Ward points out that late modern people are addicted to the gratifica-
tion of their wants being met by a consumer culture that keeps on feeding
its cravings.[65] This feeds a self-centered "me-first nature" rather than the development of a "second nature" concerned for others. Indirectly it discour-
ages thoughtful reflection about the needs of others.[66] Cray recognizes that
a character needs to be formed based on a different type of social capital that
thinks of the other first, rather than me-first. Ward reflects on his work with
youth in Oxford in the 1980s and 90s.[67] He speaks of the power that comes
when young people are helped to form their own language and imagination
of what it means to be a Christian.

He suggests the power that comes from them writing their own music and performing it with the Christian story influencing it. It can be a
powerful medium of transmission that helps them to positively engage with
society.[68] This is where there is particular hope with the emergent generation Z, who have been sensitized to the needs of others. The world recession
that their parents lived through has made them much more aware that they
need to do good for others. Their entrepreneurial spirits have seemingly
been stimulated by a more frugal upbringing. They may be encouraged to
positively critique the consumerism of late modernity, with an attendant
development of seeking the common good for others.

Cray suggests that the church is the answer. However, it will only provide an answer if it is able to transcend its own hermeneutical horizon and
self-imposed privatized status on the margins. It must seek to translate its
message into a contextually relevant idiom for generations Y and Z.[69]

Cray follows Walker in calling for a new kind of sectarianism, in order
to shape those from generations Y and Z. This new kind of sectarianism will
need to grow both "involved distinctiveness" and "subversive engagement":

64. Cray, *Disciples & Citizens*, 93.
65. Ward, *Politics of Discipleship*, 22, 218.
66. Cray, *Disciples & Citizens*, 101.
67. Ward, *Participation and Mediation*, 1–29.
68. Ibid.
69. Rogers, *Congregational Hermeneutics*.

> As Andrew Walker says, "If the world staggers onwards with more consumption, wrapped up in mass culture yet splitting at the seams, we will need to create sectarian plausibility structures in order for our story to take hold of our congregations and root them in the gospel." By "sectarian" he does not mean separate from society, he means involved distinctiveness: salt that remains salty.
>
> Christian character is formed by the making of consistent choices, within a community of faith, where there is mutual encouragement to live a distinctively Christian life.[70]

As discussed in chapter 5, this kind of "sectarian plausibility" structure requires at least a qualitative prophetic vision of the eschatological future. It can be provided in the prophetic prolepsis of the future kingdom, where God's reign is based on loving those on the margins, as well as welcoming and serving the weak.

God is not just on the margins but in many places in the cities that Christians do not frequent. The projection of the anticipated future age into the present casts a qualitative vision of what generations Y and Z can build their identities on as followers of Christ.

Globalization and Life beyond the Generations: The Gen Z Effect

Koulopoulos and Keldsen discuss the exponential developments which seemingly may follow what they term the "Gen Z effect."[71] This effect is that unlike any other generation, generation Z has grown up in a time when cyber-based technologies make them link into a global network of interconnectivity. This interconnectivity is seemingly changing the way all of the generations are communicating together.

It means that it is possible to relate to all of the generations on the same level, in cyber networks, theoretically, whether they be the boomer generation, or generations X, Y, or Z. At the very least, they argue, this will be increasingly the case, as globalization and the global web, with cheaper and more powerful communication technologies, link people across the globe together. Koulopoulos and Keldsen suggest that generation Z represent a sea-change generation, where it will become less meaningful for businesses, governments, and societies to treat each generation distinctly and differently.

70. Cray, *Disciples and Citizens*, 104.

71. Koulopoulos and Keldsen, *Gen Z Effect*, introduction.

The reason for this is because these technologies increase communication and interconnectivity of human consciousness between all age groups. It means that all age groups will buy into new products, new ways of thinking and new ways of relating to each other, as a kind of intergenerational cross-fertilization takes place, between the generations. Therefore, intergenerational understanding will increase, including the interests they share. Although their futurist view is highly optimistic, it seems that many companies are starting to think in fresh terms of how to relate to all generations, on more even and equal terms, because it is becoming ever easier to use new technologies that give access to globalized knowledge, which most of the generations can increasingly and effectively access and use cheaply.

This represents a new kind of social capital.

They suggest six forces that are transforming the way generation Z and other generations will impact each other. These six forces are already affecting the way we interact, in their view. They include:

1. Breaking Generations: Generation Z will be strong competitors with older generations: their even greater skills with new technologies outsmart older generations including some members of Generation Y giving them advantages over them in terms of competition for work and business success;

2. Hyper-connecting: hyper-connectivity among peoples through computers and social media increases the ability of generations and peoples to interrelate from the comfort of a mobile device anywhere any time;

3. Sling-shotting: New technologies becoming more affordable quickly means people catch up (almost overnight) on former disruptive changes of technologies. In the past because it took much longer to release new technologies which meant it took longer to catch up and be competitive. Now rapid change takes place faster as each year passes hence new technologies are more affordable in a market a-flood with economic resources because of mass purchasing of new products, and ever increasing speeds in accessibility to faster and better technologies. The speed of change will get even faster;

4. Shifting from affluence to influence: to cut across old barriers to influence others by cheap web-based technologies—power comes to those who influence others on the web—affluent rich business people become a thing of the past in terms of their power to influence the world simply because they are rich and could afford expensive marketing campaigns;

5. Adopting the world as my classroom—learning beyond higher education is a new way to self-educate for all generations—getting a university certificate becomes less valuable because everyone can have access to learning beyond these institutions;

6. Life-hacking: breaking through barriers, taking short cuts and outsmarting the system and its structures may follow, so that meaningful change can happen more quickly with less stoppage happening because power will no longer be held by a rich and powerful elite.[72]

The fact that these new technologies anonymize the age, generation, and profile of those who communicate across generations means that communication can occur on a basis of greater equality, where prejudices and judgments will not be made with ageism playing such a large role for how we learn and make judgments.[73] How might the so-called "Gen Z effect" help us to disciple fresh followers of Jesus in the future? It is hard to say. However, it will be vital that future missional disciples from these new tribes are related to in contextually relevant ways, which are spiritually discerned to be the keys to bring them into a meaningful relationship with Christ.

72. Koulopoulos and Keldsen, *Gen Z Effect*, introduction.

73. Ibid.

Chapter 9

Missional Leaders That Equip Disciples to Discern God's Mission

A Congregational Case Study

By Andrew R. Hardy

Introduction

This chapter focuses attention on research carried out by Andy, with a congregation that has been going through a transformation from what might be called a traditional evangelical attractional church model, toward becoming a missional incarnational one. The identity of the church, and the real names of participants in this research, have all been changed and anonymized in order to maintain confidentiality. However, other names are used rather than codes to make the chapter more readable. The research focuses on the importance of an approach to missional leadership exercised by college graduates that serve in this church as mediators of change.

The fundamental hypothesis is that in order for the church to effectively respond to a secular society, with an increasing postsecular consciousness, as Habermas suggests,[1] believers need to come to see themselves as participants in God's mission. This is not to argue that people do not participate in

---

1. Mendieta, "Postsecular World Society?," 3.

it, if they are not conscious of it, but rather Andy argues being conscious of it helps us to more intentionally seek to participate in it.

It is important to find out if missional leaders who have a *missio Dei* theological vision are successfully mediating it to equip ordinary missional disciples—in their so-called missional churches. Are ordinary followers of Christ being motivated to participate in the Triune mission in their everyday lives? As missional educators, we believe it is essential to discover if graduates who leave courses, like those we teach on in missional and contextual theology, are being effectively equipped to bring about this kind of missional church transformation, among the members they seek to influence. This research demonstrates that some graduate missional leaders seem to be effectively mediating this vision of a missional God to ordinary believers in their churches. Hence in terms of churches that effectively equip ordinary followers of Christ to be missional disciple-makers, this research will indicate some very interesting results, limited that they are to one congregation.

It cannot make universal claims to be applicable to every situation, but it does provide encouraging evidence that missional leadership programs of some colleges can enable graduates to be effective mediators of missional change management. This change process needs to equip contemporary disciples to seek to participate in God's mission in their everyday lives. The critique that the reader may make of this chapter is that it could be seen as rather prescriptive, if believers feel forced to change.

However, the goal is not to force change but rather to offer an opportunity for each ecclesial tradition to explore how it might interpret the way it seeks to shape disciples of Christ, in the light of a vision of God as a missionary being in essence and purpose, who calls believers to participate in it alongside his Spirit.

A Fresh Postsecular Spiritual Consciousness

Before attention is focused on the research, it is important to briefly comment on the emergence, in the sociology of religions literature, of the suggestion that the West is becoming postsecular and more open to spiritual and religious matters. Habermas suggests that Europe has a strong postsecular religious consciousness.[2] In his view this does not mean that European society has become a postsecular society. It clearly still has secular governments and ways of maintaining its political structures as it was noted

2. Ibid.

earlier in this book.[3] It is a change to the consciousness of some people in society which Habermas considers to be postsecular.

There is an obvious strong interest in the religious and spiritual spheres, as they impact late modern society, post 9/11, post the Manchester bombing and the attack by gunmen in London in 2017. This challenges the older thesis that secularization would end religion and its influence on society. Radicalization of the type that motivated these attacks comes from a form of religious fundamentalism which it would be impossible to associate with more rounded and grounded expressions of faith communities as part of their beliefs and practices.

Habermas argues that multiculturalism, pluralism, and the rise of charismatic and New Age spirituality means that Western secular society is highly conscious of religion.[4] He argues these forces play themselves out as influences on Western Europeans in three important ways: first, the media continuously emphasizes the continuing role of religion in fostering both conflict and reconciliation; second, there is the ever-increasing way that religious opinion shapes and determines public opinion through their interventions in civil society; and third, there is the way that "European societies" have not yet made the "painful transition to [become] post-colonial immigrant societies."[5] In this latter case they have not embraced the changes in their culture which this will require, including their attitudes toward a variety of world religions found now in their societies. In other words, this may well be evidence of a resurgence of the work of the Spirit in the West. A larger question still is, are leaders of churches equipping their congregations to hear God's voice so as to be able to discern and participate in God's mission among those with a postsecular spiritual interest?

Moreover, is there evidence that graduate missional leaders, who are passionate about transforming society by equipping their congregations to participate in God's mission to disciple new believers are actually achieving meaningful outcomes? And these outcomes need to be meaningful to their congregations, or they will not make an impact on disciple-making practices of ordinary believers like you and I.

---

3. Habermas, "Notes on a Post-Secular Society"; Habermas, "Secularism's Crisis of Faith," 17–29; Habermas, "What Is Meant by 'Post-Secular Society'?," in *Europe*, 59–77.

4. Massimo, "Longing for a Postsecular Condition."

5. Habermas, "What Is Meant by 'Post-Secular Society'?," in *Europe*, 65.

The Research

The research account that follows demonstrates how it seems missional leaders are making a meaningful impact in a church that was once more like closed brethren (see below), but is now potentially being transformed by five graduate missional leaders. Ordinary members seem to be increasingly seeing themselves as participants in God's mission. Not everyone is coming to see themselves in these terms, that would be a pipe dream, but there is encouraging evidence that some are starting to see themselves as missional ministers in their ordinary life contexts.

Research Explored

The research account begins with a discussion of the conscious adoption of *missio Dei* theology during the twentieth century, as a new horizon to orientate the church to see itself as a participant in the sovereign God's mission. It integrates its theological reflexive methodology with a sociological field-work methodology with the congregation that is the focus of this research account. It draws on important research conducted by the South African scholar Niemandt. It considers a case study piece of research that was first written by Andy as an article to be published in a journal.

The missional church scholar Van Gelder maintains that *missio Dei* theology is intrinsic to an understanding of Christian mission.[6] It is essential to believe it to properly establish missional churches that seek to practice participation in God's mission to make disciples, and to see the kingdom of God come. It was developed as a concept following the Willingen World Mission Conference in Germany in 1952.[7]

Vicedom subsequently developed the concept in terms of a Trinitarian theology,[8] as did others including Newbigin.[9] It has existed as a theological concept used by academics, and in some ministry training programs, since then. It seems that little research evidence exists that it has gone deeper into the everyday beliefs of lay people in the church. *Missio Dei* theology may have existed largely as an academic concept used among missiologists and seminary students, rather than at a popular level among ordinary church people.

Missio Dei theology has done much to create a theological vision of the Triune God, as one that beckons believers to participate in God's mission

6. Van Gelder, *Missional Church in Context*, 30–35.

7. Engelsviken, *Missio Dei*, 367; Flett, *Witness of God*.

8. Haapiainen, "Development and Outlines of Missio Dei," 45–64.

9. Newbign, *Open Secret*.

through the guidance of the Spirit of Jesus.[10] What is much less obvious from the scholarly research is to what extent leaders, educated in missional theology, have effectively mediated this outlook to their faith communities. Sixty-five years of existence for the more defined concept of *missio Dei* is a fraction in time in terms of Christian church history, compared to the two millennia of theological history before its appearance. How has this more recent theological idea actually penetrated to the ordinary, everyday church members, at a grassroots level, among different faith traditions?[11]

How has the idea that God has a mission for each follower of Christ to participate in actually become part of the grassroots ordinary theology of believers? Can it transform churches that have historically not resonated with a type of discipleship formation that encourages members to share their faith more generally outside their faith communities? The church discussed in this case study began with what was described as a more reformed mindset, where people brought people to church to hear the gospel, to become one where people are beginning to see themselves as missional disciples in their everyday lives taking the gospel themselves to those they work among.

This reported case study will seek to determine to what extent has a *missio Dei* theology been mediated, communicated, and understood at a grassroots level through the instrumentality of graduate leaders from a college program to an evangelical missional church termed MLC? Three of the leaders (one being the pastor) of MLC interviewed for this research graduated from this college's ministry education programs, at BA and MA level. One is currently still doing the college's MA program. Four others who were also interviewed have not done the college's programs. It is one of the college's goals to enable leaders to transform their churches to obtain a view of God as one who is a missionary in purpose and action, who calls believers to participate in mission with God.

No research has been conducted focused on leaders as mediators of missional theology from graduate ministry programs among independent Reformed churches in the UK. Research in a related field has been conducted by Professor Nelus Niemandt among evangelical churches of a different theological evangelical (charismatic) tradition.[12] He expresses the view held by other scholars that God may be thought of as a missionary.[13] He comments:

10. Hardy, *Pictures of God*; Roxburgh, *Missional*; Ross and Bevans, *Mission on the Road to Emmaus*.

11. Astley, *Ordinary Theology*.

12. Niemandt, "Five Years"; Niemandt, "Trends."

13. Laing and Weston, *Theology in Missionary Perspective*; Kim, *Joining In with the Spirit*; Barrett, *Treasure in Clay Jars*; Hunsberger, *Bearing the Witness of the Spirit*; Van Gelder, *Missional Church in Context*; Flett, *Witness of God*.

> Mission begins in the heart of the Triune God. . . . Mission is
> an extension and amplification of God's very being. Missional
> theology builds on the understanding that God is Trinity and
> missional. Mission is participation in the life of God. It is to be
> caught up within the dynamic sending and being sent that God
> the Holy Trinity has done and continues to do.[14]

Missional theology may be termed deeply relational, in that it motivates missional praxis for those who perceive God to be calling them to personally participate in God's mission. Ordinary disciples may see themselves
as those called to participate in the mission of the Trinity. It may also be
termed theology in action, with an emphasis being put on mission-focused
orthopraxis.[15] *Missio Dei*[16] theology may also be claimed to be intrinsic to
the spiritual life of churches that may see themselves as participants in God's
actions toward the world.[17]

Niemandt's Contribution to My Research

Niemandt's, like Hiebert's, theology seems to have a "way of doing theology—
a way of thinking biblically about God's universal mission in the context of
the world here and now,"[18] that Niemandt[19] and Hiebert term "missional
theology."[20] Niemandt details research outcomes that have been derived from
empirical field work that he carried out in a longitudinal study (over a five-
year period), with the founding churches of the South African Partnership for
Missional Churches (SAPMC).[21] This partnership has over 170 churches in
it.[22] Marais sets out the missional theology of these churches:

> To listen to God's specific call to us, to let God send us and,
> through the Holy Spirit, empower us to participate in God's mis-
> sion in the world, so that both our outreach and our life together
> as a church are a witness to Jesus Christ.[23]

14. Niemandt, "Trends."
15. Graham et al., *Theological Reflection*, 170–71.
16. Kim, *Joining In with the Spirit*, 34–36; Mellow and Yates, *Mission and Spirituality*.
17. Niemandt, "Trends," 1.
18. Hiebert, *Gospel in Human Contexts*, 44.
19. Niemandt, "Trends."
20. Hiebert, *Gospel in Human Contexts*, 44.
21. Niemandt, "Five Years."
22. Ibid.
23. Ibid.

Niemandt's research focuses on the difference in outlook that a missional theological focus can have, that might lead to the transformation of a church's identity.[24] He demonstrates the correlation between *missio Dei* theology and the way this redefines the *"missiones ecclesiae"*:[25]

> The *missio Dei* institutes the *missiones ecclesiae*. . . . The church has come into being as a result of mission and mission characterizes the whole of Christian existence. . . . The church is mission and participates in God's mission because it cannot do otherwise. This is the very reason why the church exists.[26]

Niemandt details how SAPMC congregations demonstrate characteristics of participation in missional activity based on a missional theology.[27] Niemandt's research focused on SAPMC churches, concerning the defining characteristics of what makes them missional in nature. Andy's research is focused on the mediation process of how college graduates have helped MLC members to understand a mission of God theology, which represents a different research focus compared to Niemandt's. Niemandt highlights the difference between a church-centric (ecclesia-centric) view of a faith community that aims to maintain the church's traditions and way of life, compared to a theocentric view[28]—focused on discerning what God is calling the church to actively engage in next.

In the diagrams below the ecclesia-centric church has got a generalized inward focus, whereas a theocentric church has an inward and outward focus on its community, and the broader society beyond its horizon, which it also considers to be part of God's mission to reach out to. According to Niemandt, a theocentric focus can propel a church to participate in God's reconciliatory movements toward the world (see on illustrations below).[29]

---

24. Ibid.
25. Latin phrase meaning "the mission of the church."
26. Niemandt, "Trends," 3.
27. Ibid., 2.
28. Ibid.
29. Niemandt, "Five Years"; Niemandt, "Trends."

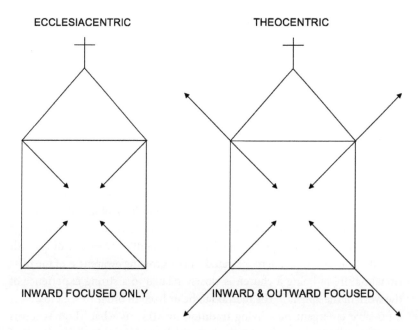

Missional congregations can recognize God's actions directly around them, as well as in the wider world. They are learning more about God's mission of redeeming, restoring, and reconciling the world through Jesus Christ. They can give answers to the question: What is God doing?[30]

The missional church actively seeks to discern revelation from God, which helps to guide it toward transcending its present horizon, toward new horizons of engagement with the God of mission in the world.[31]

Niemandt's research has helped to determine if a new living tradition is evident at a grassroots level in MLC. It is this theocentric, rather than ecclesia-centric focus, that will help to determine if MLC's members are being transformed from an inward focus, toward becoming those who seek to participate in God's mission outside their own faith community.[32]

30. Niemandt, "Five Years," 398.

31. Ibid., 398–99.

32. Branson, "Missional Church Process."

Methodology

Niemandt utilized ethnographic action research to conduct his investigations, among the twelve SAPMC congregations. Andy's research was also ethnographic,[33] qualitative,[34] and interpretivist[35] in nature. It used semi-structured interviews with MLC's leaders. Rhetorical artifacts[36] were considered taken from the interviews conducted with a view to show how they provided insights into how the MLC congregation viewed themselves. Roger's research into congregations,[37] demonstrated the importance of understanding a congregation's hermeneutical horizons in order to obtain insights into how they interpret their faith and practices in relation to God and the ecclesial tradition they inhabit. Niemandt's theology of *missio Dei* provides the means to theologically reflect on the thematic coded findings from the interviews with MLC's leaders.[38] Niemandt's research findings with SAPMC congregations, demonstrated "that a growing awareness of the missional nature of being a church is closely related to a strong experience of the work of the Spirit."[39] The method to be utilized in order to seek to detect a possible emergent new living tradition in MLC, is what Thomas terms the "Constant Comparative Method,"[40] which has helped in the coding[41] of recurring themes that have been identified from consideration of interview artifacts with MLC's leaders.

Do these findings provide an indicator of a view of God as a missionary, who is perceived to motivate members in MLC to participate in the triune mission? It will be MLC's leaders' perceptions of this deeper experiential side of *missio Dei* theology, and its presence at grassroots level, that will provide evidence of whether some of its members are being impacted by it. Is it leading to a new and living tradition arising, that has stimulated their ordinary theological imagination to see themselves as participants in God's mission?[42]

Niemandt demonstrates specific outcomes from his research, which provided evidence that an incarnational participative *missio Dei* theology

---

33. Bryman, *Social Research Methods*, 400–434.

34. Ibid., 539–41.

35. Thomas, *How to Do Your Research Project*, 155.

36. Foss, *Rhetorical Criticism*, 244–45.

37. Rogers, *Congregational Hermeneutics*, 128–35.

38. Niemandt, "Five Years"; Niemandt, "Trends."

39. Niemandt, "Five Years," 408.

40. Thomas, *How to Do Your Research Project*, 234–39, 242.

41. Bryman, *Social Research Methods*, 550–51, 553–54.

42. Astley, *Ordinary Theology*.

caused SAPMC congregations to become more open and ready to live incarnationally among people in their neighborhoods. He comments:

> The movement towards a more incarnational understanding of the church is clearly visible in the congregational narratives. For respondents, doing God's work in their daily lives played an important role. The following observations illustrate this incarnational emphasis:
>
> - a shift in focus from church to community;
> - a shift from life in the church—to doing God's work in everyday life; and
> - a shift from church programs to living and participating in God's mission.[43]

These three critical qualitative measures will also act in this research as indicators of evidence of an emerging *missio Dei* tradition coming to life at a grassroots level in MLC. The diagram below illustrates what coded artifacts from interviews in this research look to determine, from the expressed theological outlooks of MLC's leaders about members.[44]

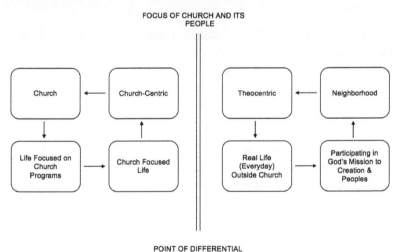

FOCUS OF CHURCH AND ITS
PEOPLE

POINT OF DIFFERENTIAL
SEPARATION

---

43. Niemandt suggested a fourth measure but it was so close to two and three as above that I redacted it for critical reasons to do with clarity, to help to better distinguish what was different between each category (this is the redacted measure, a shift from church life to real life—doing God's work in everyday life). Niemandt, "Five Years," 408.

44. Foss, *Rhetorical Criticism.*

The Participants in the Research

The participants in this research are eight members of MLC's leadership team. Four of the leaders (one is the pastor) have done (or is doing) a college's programs in missional leadership and four have not. The four who did not undertake the courses provide a control group.[45] The goal was to obtain the views of these two different categories of leaders, regarding the impact of a mission of God theological vision on MLC's members. What did these leaders agree on in common? What did they disagree about, or not share the same views about? Their views provide much needed critical comparisons between possible alternative hermeneutical horizons present among members of MLC.[46] Each participant was interviewed for thirty minutes. The semi-structured interviews were recorded and then transcribed.

Following Niemandt,[47] the three are:

- a shift in focus from church to community;

- a shift from life in the church to doing God's work in everyday life;

- a shift from church programs to living and participating in God's mission.

He suggests these three shifts represent whether a church is more theocentric in outlook compared to ecclesia-centric in outlook. The question is, are these shifts evident at MLC?

Limitations and Bias

MLC is an independent evangelical church found in a city in the UK. It belongs to the Fellowship of Independent Evangelical Churches (FIEC),[48] which has a mixture of Reformed Calvinistic evangelical and less Reformed congregations within its 665-strong network of affiliated churches. It also has evangelical churches like MLC, that are far less Reformed and much more open to be challenged to grow beyond their theological horizons; although in the past MLC may have been somewhat like closed Brethren according to one of MLC's leaders (Sophie).

---

45. Thomas, *How to Do Your Research Project*.

46. Rogers, *Congregational Hermeneutics*, 43, 60–65, 68, 91, 177–78, 191.

47. Niemandt, "Five Years."

48. www.fiec.org.uk.

Ecclesia-centric to Theocentric Shifts
in Mission Life Church (MLC)

Coded thematic findings from interviews with participants suggest a change in perspective at MLC, from an ecclesia-centric toward becoming a theocentric focused faith community. A critique made by participant Tamsin of the more recent missional emphasis in MLC (beginning in 2009) was revealing, in terms of some potential tensions that this outward focus has caused in the views of some members. Tamsin commented that MLC needs to improve in the care of its existing members so as not to neglect their need of pastoral support. The pastor addressed this concern somewhat, commenting on the most recent preaching series called "An In-Out Missional People."

It aims to help MLC's members to consider their deeper inward spiritual lives and faith, as much as how they are motivated by this inner life to be missional in their everyday life contexts. Another goal is to help them to become more responsible for each others' pastoral needs, as well as to be supportive to those they live and work with outside the church on an everyday basis; so as to make them less reliant on the professional pastor. Tamsin's view demonstrated a deeper critical challenge to MLC of the mediation process of a missional focus among members, if people feel less cared for then they may resist change toward becoming more missional and outwardly focused.

The interviews with MLC's leaders, overall, provided positive evidence that there is a shift of outlook in terms of how the church perceives itself as a faith community. It seems to be slowly transitioning from a more inward-focused traditional church, to a more outward-focused missional church, which correlates positively to Niemandt's research: with a move from a focus on church programs to the broader needs of the community outside of the church.[49]

The pastor suggested that MLC has embraced a strapline they used for a preaching series to define themselves. It is, "God's People on God's mission in the Spirit's power with the message of his Son." He also mentioned that at a recent leader's weekend (November 2016), it was decided that MLC needs to more fully view itself as a mission-equipping agency, which seeks to enable members to engage in God's mission in their everyday lives. There is a perception of a theocentric horizon emerging.[50] But the pastor commented that some members still see the pastor as their personal "chaplain," which means that professional pastoral support is still expected by some members.

49. Niemandt, "Five Years of Missional Church."

50. Rogers, *Congregational Hermeneutics.*

Contradistinctively, other members consider that they have a "ministry" to care for others in and outside the church (i.e., evidence is here indicative of both ecclesia-centric and theocentric outlooks being evident among church members in MLC). The thematically coded findings, taken from these interviews, expressed the difference between the church of "then" and "now." "Then" was the way the church was about eight to ten years ago, compared to "now" 2016.

According to Peter, one major catalyst that seemed to lead to MLC's shift from an ecclesia-centric horizon, toward more of a theocentric one, "was the burning down of the old church." The church burned down in 2008. The church subsequently moved into a nearby working-man's club to meet and worship, at which it has since remained. Sophie suggested that the fire "challenged" members to start to become more "outwardly focused" as they no longer had "that comfy old building" available. Sophie also commented on the move to the new venue,

> Wasn't it interesting . . . the bar staff were listening to the sermon, . . . people [members] started getting . . . interested in what was going on locally"

Sophie suggested that this has increasingly led to the church focusing on its work in the neighborhood, as well as in broader communities members engage with. According to Niemandt, this shift from what happens in the church to what is happening in the community is one of the measures of a church that is becoming missional and participatory in the *missio Dei*.[51]

Peter commented, "I think God burnt the building because they were so inward looking." Sophie and Lucinda consider that the church fire was an important catalyst to a change in perspective, toward an increasing theocentric focus on God's work in everyday life, which fits with Niemandt's second criteria coded for: "a shift from life in the church—to doing God's work in everyday life."[52] Indeed, Caspian commented, "I've always considered God to be . . . a missionary God." Caspian shared a number of examples from his working life, going back over a period of twenty years, where he engaged in what he considered to have been his participation in God's mission in his work place. It seems that the influence of the graduate leaders on the congregation has given Caspian an opportunity to share his outlook more expansively than in previous years.

This shift in focus has seemingly led to the church slowly becoming more outward looking, compared to back "then." Sophie commented on

51. Niemandt, "Five Years."
52. Ibid.

MLC's earlier outlook, saying it was (then) "still quite closed." James commented on back "then":

> Before that change [the fire] we would find ways of inviting people to church, so we invited people to meals at church, and people came and we saw people saved. . . . the role of the congregation was perceived to be to bring people to church.

Lucinda commented that "about ten years ago it was felt that you had to come into church to hear about God." The congregation was ancillary to this primary role of the "pastor" as the professional gospel evangelist. James commented,

> So the perception was that in order for that to happen you bring someone to hear gospel preaching to the church. So the focus was on regular guest services, the goal was to prepare for them to get people ready to come to them.

The focus of the faith community's theological horizon was mediated[53] and communicated through the professional gospel preacher. This was well expressed as a difference between "then" and "now" by Caspian, who commented,

> In the past [former ministers] have been wonderful in terms of Biblical exposition, but they haven't been the kind of people that have delivered a kind of down to earth in the streets kind of ministry, that can be relevant to you and me, it can be relevant to somebody who is not a believer as well.

The new pastor (a missional college graduate) seems to be viewed by leaders as a catalyst of the mediation process of something new, which has led to an ongoing process of transformation in MLC. A mediator[54] is a go-between, or a bridge-builder that helps to connect theological horizons together, in the context of the integration of new beliefs into a group. Tamsin commented on the new pastor, who "has ignited something in quite a lot of us that we'd been waiting for." The new pastor started in the church in 2009, just after the church fire. Tamsin expressed a sense of readiness for change subsequent to the church fire that some church members had become prepared to embrace when the new pastor arrived.

---

53. Ward, *Participation and Mediation*, 106–20; Rogers, *Congregational Hermeneutics*, 143, 144.

54. Ward, *Participation and Mediation*, 106–20; Rogers, *Congregational Hermeneutics*, 141–44.

So the logical question is to ask what is the outlook "now" (2016) at MLC, compared to "then" (2008)? One outcome is that some members of MLC have come to see themselves in the light of what Sophie terms the big "plan of God," mediated through the new pastor's "kingdom" preaching. Sophie links "kingdom" theology closely with a *missio Dei* theocentric focus, described as God having a big (eschatological) missional plan to reconcile the whole cosmos to himself. The goal is an eternal future, with the realization of the eschatological kingdom of God (Sophie's view). In Sophie's view and that of Peter, people can fit themselves into this larger plan. Sophie captures this view well:

> I would say that his [the pastor's] big strength . . . in the way he preaches . . . a lot about . . . contextualizing appropriately for the mission fields we're on [in the neighborhood and broader city-wide situations of members] . . . we have teaching . . . about our personal involvement in God's plan as opposed to something the pastor does.

Brenda (alongside other leaders) spoke of a teaching series on the Holy Spirit, where the Spirit "being at work as it focuses on wherever you are, and I think that really helped!" It helped because it focused on God being "incarnationally" engaged with her in her ordinary[55] everyday life, beyond the church. This fits well with Niemandt's[56] third critical qualitative measure, which shifts the focus from concentration on church programs to a theocentric view, where members see themselves as participants in God's mission outside the church. This is vital to emphasize, as it is intrinsic to how disciples after Christendom are inspired by the mission of God to be participants in making disciples alongside the Spirit, at work with them. It is interesting that Brenda critiqued the church as still

> in recent years having too much focus . . . on mission being what the church is doing (locally), but actually the church is the people, so it needs to be on the people and what they are doing.

Brenda considered that there needs to be more emphasis on members being further equipped to engage in Christian life and mission, as disciple-makers in their work places and homes, rather than just simply in the local neighborhood closest to the MLC church location.

However, conversely, Peter spoke of emergent positive signs of change that the Holy Spirit series (which lasted for several months) has stimulated among members,

55. Astley, *Ordinary Theology*.
56. Niemandt, "Five Years."

> We've been looking and asking should this crazy contact hour
> we've created [weekly Sunday church corporate worship] be the
> focus or should it be a reflection of what is happening Monday
> to Saturday [in member's lives]?

What Peter meant is that church services need to become a celebration of what members have experienced with God in their daily lives, outside of the church, as they have lived as followers of Christ seeking to follow him in what they do.

Brenda offered an important corrective angle compared to Peter's view, suggesting that this celebration of the life of faith outside the church, and its services (ministries), should not negate the need to properly care for the youth, who need the church to be a place that nurtures their faith. She spoke of one member of the youth leadership team having a picture of a harvest barn (in about 2012), which was to be filled with a rich harvest—representing in the youth team's view—that God was communicating that they needed to focus on discipleship of the church's youth, to prepare them for the life of faith lived beyond the church.

Brenda commented that there has been significant growth in their youth work over the past few years, subsequent to this prophetic picture. Brenda suggested many of the youth at present need support to develop a sustainable, mature faith. In this sense the youth ministry embraces the theocentric view, with an inward and outward focus, although many of the youth clearly still need time to develop a stronger, more outwardly focused sustainable missional faith, where they can come to see themselves as participating in God's mission. Hence it is important for MLC to make sure it both nurtures those whose faith is developing and maturing, as well as to encourage those whose faith has matured much more, to live lives of missional participation with God in their everyday lives.

Lucinda suggested that some middle-aged adult members also find it hard to embrace the new emerging missional focus. It is interesting that these middle-aged members are those with children and young people in their families. There is clearly a need for a mixed economy approach to ministry, requiring an inward nurturing community of faith, as well as a more outwardly focused missional emphasis that celebrates God's work in the everyday life of members. The pastor suggested this was also true for some of the older senior members. James spoke of what might be at the root of this "hard to break mind-set" that resists a missional focus.

He spoke of a fundamental evangelical problem, where the primary goal of its tradition is to get people "saved." In this evangelical view, the church exists to provide services such as knowledge of how to be saved.

The goal, after this initial decision to accept Christ as personal savior, is to remain saved. In James's view, it creates a needy mentality, where members look to the church to meet their "needs," rather than "helping them to mature" to take responsibility for their own spiritual lives. James believes the primary need is now for MLC to engage in "discipleship" of all members and to empower them to grow into "mature" spiritual people, as followers of Christ. He suggested that people need to move from remaining in a more needy, "child-like" spiritual state, where they look to trained leaders to meet their needs, toward them taking responsibility, "maturing" in their faith. It seems that this is part of the "mind-set" that is "hard to break." However, James's criticism needs to be tempered with reference to another significant change in MLC's faith community.

Since the changes that have come through the graduate leaders influence, sixteen new groups have started in people's homes, adding to the four others that were already running before the new pastor came: with 85 percent of church members meeting in them. These groups often meet close to where members live in their own neighborhoods, which fits well with the focus of the life of faith being embraced beyond the church, rather than it only happening in church services. The pastor suggested this has led to a more outward missional theocentric focus, compared to the way MLC was in the past. Peter spoke positively of the freedom each group has to determine its own focus,

> No one is asking what are you doing, you have to tell us, they're free to experiment and be themselves.

This seems to imply a strong qualitative measure similar to what Niemandt suggests to be evidence of a theocentric focus:[57] away from a concentration on what happens in the corporate church, compared to God's work in everyday life. The small life groups may be suggested to be encouraging members to be more mature spiritual persons, dealing with their faith in groups that are mutually missional and pastoral in their orientation, in this reconfiguration of how people relate to each other, contrary to James's assessment (see above).

The pastor is considered, by each of the seven leaders interviewed, as a leader who encourages people to "experiment" and to be allowed to learn from their "mistakes." It is this open and flexible attitude that probably has helped to contribute to the church being on a journey of transformation, toward emerging perceptions of some of its members perceiving themselves to be participants in God's mission. The pastor expressed it in terms of what

---

57. Niemandt, "Trends in Missional Ecclesiology."

good missional leaders might exhibit, as a measure of their leadership potential. He commented,

> Good leaders have followers, not followers who do what they are told but rather who are empowered to use their gifts to help others.

In addition to the pastor's successful team-building strategies, two college graduate leaders (Lucinda and Peter), have developed a "following," or "team," that were working with them at the time of the interviews, and one (Sophie) as yet has not. The other nongraduate leaders have also demonstrated team-building skills, which in part have been facilitated by the pastor.

Lucinda is leading a missional cafe that is serving a deprived community near MLC's meeting place. She spoke of her God-given sense of "vision" and "calling" that has partly led to the café's missional work in the neighborhood. She is developing a small "team" of lay people (from MLC), who are helping her to work with people in this neighborhood. Peter has also been developing a "following" and "team" of about twelve persons, who are working toward an emerging church-planting initiative in the city. Peter spoke of one member who moved into the area, where the new church plant is planned to take place, commenting that she had discerned that God had called her to serve in a school in that community a few years previously.

Sophie has not as such, as yet, been able to develop a "following" and "team" to work with her in one of her missional initiatives, in an enclosed elderly people's village that has been developed in the city. Whatever might be said about these emergent missional initiatives outside the MLC church, they are supported to one degree or another by the congregation of this church, and its designated leadership team. In this sense each missional endeavor is considered to be part of a broader participation in God's mission in the church's neighborhood, or in the broader city (like the life groups), which fits with Niemandt's (2010) third qualitative measure: "a shift from church programmes to living and participating in God's mission" beyond the church.

Critical Conclusions

There seems to be enough evidence to suggest that Niemandt's three qualitative measures of a missional church are evident in the process of the ongoing formation of a fresh recontextualization of MLC's faith tradition: from an ecclesia-centric horizon to more of a theocentric outlook. It seems that some members see themselves as participants to some extent in God's mission and that he is active in their everyday lives as his followers.

To what extent has a *missio Dei* theology been mediated, communicated, and understood at a grassroots level through the instrumentality of graduate leaders from the college to MLC's ordinary members? This provisional empirical research has had limited success (as a small-scale piece of research) in determining a fuller and more comprehensive answer to this question. What does seem clear, is that the thematically coded findings analyzed demonstrate broad agreement that things are changing in MLC—toward what might be thought of as a new living tradition, which is being caught by an increasing number of members—not just leaders.

It seems to be framing and informing the outlooks of some who are perceiving themselves to be participants in God's mission, as his followers and as disciple-makers in their own right. The evidence indicates that graduates, including the pastor, have led some members to see themselves as taking part in an outwardly focused missional ministry, suggesting strongly that mediation[58] is taking place effectively.

Churches like MLC are to be found throughout the UK. The good news is that the missional movement of the Spirit of Jesus can lead God's people to begin to see themselves in new ways, as participants in God's mission, to disciple those they walk alongside on an everyday basis. Each of us may think of ourselves as part of the mobile missional body of Christ, who are called to incarnate as Christ did alongside people in our everyday contexts. We are arguing for the absolute necessity for every believer to become missional disciple-makers. The challenge that every missional leader needs to take up is to equip believers to follow Christ, as he beckons, "Come follow me and I will make you a fisher of men."

58. Ward, *Participation and Mediation*, 106–20.

Chapter 10

Conclusions

The last chapter focused on what may be encouraging signs that congregations can be led by missional leaders who seek to equip members to interpret themselves in fresh ways as disciples who are called to participate in God's mission. Indeed, if anecdotal evidence may be considered relevant, then both writers know of missional communities that are inspired to shape disciples who consciously see themselves as participants in the mission of Christ.

Newbigin commented, "The Church is sent into the world to continue that which he came to do, in the power of the same Spirit, reconciling people to God (John 20:19–23)."[1] God is by nature a relational being. The *missio Dei* is fundamentally founded on a relationship with a relational Triune God. Fundamentally, God through the Spirit of Christ at work in the lives of disciples, may be said to motivate them to participate in the *missio Trinitatis*.

Discipleship is the starting point for mission. As important as the church is as a sacred sphere for the faithful to worship God together, the church is not an end in itself. Put in other terms, the church is not the instigator of mission. It is the relational God who inspires and reveals his mission to his people who have an intimacy of relationship with God.

There is a potential danger in much of the missional church conversation whereby disciple-making becomes just another program the church offers. Newbigin's comment, noted above, sets the goal of mission to be reconciliation of which the church equips disciples to undertake. As we noted in chapter 2, Matthew's vision of discipleship is based on the presence of Jesus until the "end of the age" with his followers (disciples). It is his followers who have a relationship with Christ who are sent on a mission to "make" yet other disciples. Indeed, Matthew's gospel is the only one to mention the

---

1. Newbigin, *Gospel in a Pluralist Society*, 230.

εκκλησια (the church).[2] Yet the church is not posited in Matthew 16 where it appears, as an institution that functions with discipleship as one of its activities. It is rather a community that gathers around the presence and motivating power of Christ who are vivified by his presence. Matthew's gospel makes this plain enough: "Where two or three are gathered in my name there I am there among them."[3] This saying no doubt encouraged members of the churches for whom Matthew's gospel was written, but it is unlikely that the notion of a more structured ecclesiastical entity of church was the experience of the churches Matthew wrote for. Rather a gathering around the presence of the living Christ as the source of their gathered life was to be taken as a normative experience for worship. Presence here must surely be read in what seems to be the larger purpose of Matthew's gospel, which Dan suggested (in chapter 2) to be that the gospel was written as a sort of manual for discipleship for an early Christian missional church context.

Of course, using the language of "missional church" is to import a contemporary nomenclature. The missionary structure of the Gospel of Matthew may, nevertheless, be considered strongly implied, as the gospel ends with the risen Messiah sending his followers to go and make new disciples of all who will follow him throughout the world (Matt 28:16–20). This gospel's mission declaration is made to disciples who seek to keep on transcending their own limited horizons made up of people just like them, to go to those not like them, as Christ's presence beckons and empowers them to participate with his Spirit.[4] Hence it is disciples who form missional communities that continue to shape new followers to do the same, rather than an institution called the church, led by professional leaders and based on long-established creedal structures that institutes the *missio Dei*.

We realize we need to take great care at this point, not wanting to appear to imply that the church has no importance. The church has great importance. What we are challenging readers to consider here is the kind of importance the church has.

Perhaps one way to highlight our thinking here will be to focus on the vital topic of church planting. The college we both teach at, as part of other ministries we engage in, has a strong focus on preparing leaders to plant churches. Indeed, we have planted churches ourselves and have a passion to see God's people gather together. So what is our point here?

It has to do with what we focus on. The human psyche seems to be structured in such a way that what we focus on we magnify. Hence if our

2. Matt 16:18.
3. Matt 18:20 NRSV.
4. Witherington, *Matthew*, 422.

focus is on planting new churches, then the tendency will be to magnify this as the main issue to take up our time and attention. The challenge, as we see it, is that Christ did not call us primarily to plant churches but to make disciples. Christ is present with his people as they gather to engage in the missionary Spirit's work of reconciling people into a relationship with the Triune God. God himself, as a relational being of persons, is the basis to all gathered communities made up of people united by his Triune love.[5] God exists relationally and seeks dynamic relationships with all those made to participate in his image.[6] The church is actually those who live in an ongoing conscious experience of participating in God's relational desire to bring all into the Triune community. God's church may be defined as an open community sent to invite others to become part of God's family and express his life in the world.

At the 2010 centenary of the Edinburgh conference, Vinoth Ramachandra shared his concerns about two missing elements in the proceedings.

First, he noted that the continuing importance of the communication of the gospel had largely been left off the agenda. Second, he noted that there was no lay presence at the conference. It was made up of church leaders, clergy, and scholars. He made the vital plea that the laity be represented as the real priests of God, sent out to the communities where they live and work to engage in God's mission.[7] He made the important observation that the church was not supporting them to be effective disciples, sent out to the places of their influence to bring Christ to those they lived and worked among. He claimed this was a serious failing, as well as being something fundamental to public theology in the secular sphere. His comments resonate strongly with the arguments we make in this book. He commented:

> It seems that we have been blinded by the neat divisions we have drawn between theology, ethics and mission. Those boundaries need to be deconstructed. We have been reminded in recent years that all theology is mission theology, that the church does theology "on the road" and not just in the library or the pulpit. But then theological education has to be re-oriented radically around the lives of "lay" people, not the agendas of clergy and mission societies. Social and political ethics has become the locus of evangelical proclamation.
>
> We need to go further and deconstruct the boundary between clergy and laity. Yes, the church needs leaders. But

5. Torrance, *Worship, Community and the Triune God of Grace.*

6. Hardy, *Pictures of God*, ch. 8.

7. Ramachandra, *Brief Reflection.*

clericalism has crippled the witness of the church. There are many thoughtful people who are profoundly attracted to Jesus but frankly "put off" by the church. They see a lack of integrity: a huge gulf between the message the church proclaims and the way its leaders behave, not least towards one another. How did a socially subversive, egalitarian movement centred in worshipping and following a crucified Jew change so quickly into a hierarchical, patriarchal and anti-Semitic religious institution? Whether we are Pentecostals, Eastern Orthodox or Roman Catholics we need to keep returning to and humbly pondering that old question. The younger churches seem destined to repeat the sins of the older churches. We in Asia and Africa cannot keep blaming Christendom. I am amused by how many of our Southern bishops and clergy who bitterly condemn Western Christendom cling so tenaciously to titles and status honour and forms of address (and dress!) that they have inherited from Christendom.

. . . In my experience, "lay" men and women of different church backgrounds rarely have problems working together in facing common concerns. They have no sacred turf to protect. Remember that John R. Mott, the architect of the 1910 Edinburgh conference was himself a layman. It was his experience of working with the Student Volunteer movement and the YMCA that lay the ecumenical ground work for that conference. If left to church leaders and church-based mission societies, Edinburgh 1910 is unlikely to have happened.

And if, as Dana Roberts reminded us on the first morning of this conference, one of the unintended consequences of Edinburgh 1910 was the dismantling of the boundaries between so-called Christian nations and non-Christian nations, can we pray that one of the consequences of this conference will be the steady erosion of clergy-laity boundaries and the recovery of the priesthood of all believers?[8]

This rather copious quotation is obviously intentional. His comments raise important missional issues that readers from differing church backgrounds may resonate with. This corresponds to some of Andy's current research in missional education and discipleship formation.

Resources need to be invested in how God's people may be shaped and formed to consciously participate in the Triune mission in their localities.

To retain its cutting edge, the Western church needs to reimagine itself as a discipleship agency and resource. This does not devalue the need for trained professional leaders, but they need to be of a type who can not only

8. Ibid., 2–3.

care for the faithful, teach the faithful, and guide them, but they also need to be those who encourage and equip missional disciples, among all believers, to consciously seek to discern and participate in God's ongoing mission.

The church is called to transcend its own limited horizons and to look with hope to the proleptic coming of the eschatological reign of God, of which all of God's people are disciples and members. In other words, the church is not the ultimate goal of Triune mission, but rather all of Christ's people need to join together as the one family of the Father in heaven. Missional disciples after Christendom are called to be shaped as brothers and sisters in the context of the cosmic kingdom of God.[9]

Newbigin reminded the church that each local congregation is at its best a hermeneutic of the gospel.[10] People who observe the life of God's people lived out intentionally together will see what it looks like, and feels like, to be part of God's family of love. Moreover, Newbigin reminded the church that each congregation is to be a kind of foretaste of the kingdom.[11] The church as a relational community needs to live that subversive countercultural life,[12] that models how the reign of God's love can transform the world.

Also, the people of God are sent to offer a positive critique to the world and its ways of life and being, which run counter to the reign of God's love and grace.[13] Not all of culture is neutral. Indeed, some aspects of culture are godless and unholy, and they need challenging.[14]

When Newbigin returned to the UK upon his retirement from mission work in India in the 1970s, he was shocked by the degree of secularization he encountered.[15] It was not the same place he had left some years earlier. He came with the eyes of a missionary and sought to use that lens to begin a practical conversation on how to bring the gospel back to the West. He saw that Christendom had ended and that something new was to come. What that new thing might be he could not discern, except that its ultimate goal would be the full and final establishment of the kingdom of God.[16]

Missional conversations, inspired partly by Newbigin's influence among others, continue. There is not just one conversation. What has often been missed with regards to Newbigin's contributions is that he came with a

9. Akkerman and Maddix, *Missional Discipleship*, 18.

10. Newbigin, *Gospel in a Pluralistic Society*, ch. 18.

11. Newbigin, *Sign of the Kingdom*, 462–63.

12. Ibid.

13. Ibid.

14. Goheen, "Gospel, Culture, and Cultures," 2.

15. Laing and Weston, *Theology in Missionary Perspective*, 3–10.

16. Ibid.

different lens to many of those in the West, who are caught up in its secular as well as an emerging post-secular perspective. Newbigin came with the eyes of a missionary. He interpreted what needed to occur for the gospel of God's reign to be brought to it from the lens of an experienced practitioner expert in mission.[17] Many of us may read his work through the lens of the church, and get hoodwinked as a result into reading his work from a church-centric perspective. Newbigin did not come with a church-centric lens as such, but with a *missio Dei* lens. In his view, it was for the church not to domesticate the Spirit to its agendas, but for it to self-transcend itself and follow the pre-ecclesial work of the sovereign Spirit, as it led the way ahead for the church to follow and participate in broader society alongside God.[18] We need this missional lens to be our primary focus, to help missional disciples to transcend a church-centric view of themselves, and rather, to engage in theocentric action.

This theocentric action means that we need to seek to discern and intentionally and consciously shape all Christ's followers' to become disciple-makers in their everyday life contexts—as they engage in the Triune God's ongoing mission. This is the prophetic challenge that comes as part of Newbigin's missional legacy as much as it is to be part of the way missional disciples after Christendom seek to participate in the *missio Trinitatis*.

Challenges and Recommendations

The challenge of ongoing discipleship faces each new generation. We recognize that in writing this book we have picked up only on some of the issues and much more work of this type is needed.

Missional discipleship needs to transcend what still seems to be an ingrained Christendom view on what is entailed in discipleship formation. It has to move away from just simply being another program that the church offers. It rather needs to work out how to disciple people related to the demands of their contextual setting. This is no easy task in a complex multicultural and pluralistic Western context and it will take well-informed leadership, lay and professional, to engage in contextually relevant ways in their communities as they continue to discern the *missio Dei*. At the heart of this is the need for a new way of missional community that embodies the life of fellowship and relational intimacy of Christ. In the words of Eugene Peterson, it is "a long obedience in the same direction."[19] Change most definitely occurs slowly.

17. Ibid.

18. Newbigin, *Open Secret*, 54–58.

19. Peterson, *Long Obedience in the Same Direction*.

We also believe that the church needs to keep on challenging itself to reimagine mission. It has much more than the personal salvation of individuals to consider, or the discipleship of individuals. It also requires a broad vision of what the in-breaking reign of God is bringing about. It is for missional disciples to participate with the Spirit in ushering in the kingdom in their spheres of influence in their everyday lives. Holistic mission is required, which is well expressed in the Lambeth Declaration's five marks of mission:

- To proclaim the Good News of the Kingdom

- To teach, baptize and nurture new believers

- To respond to human need by loving service

- To transform unjust structures of society, to challenge violence of every kind and pursue peace and reconciliation

- To strive to safeguard the integrity of creation, and sustain and renew the life of the earth.[20]

Moreover, we have noted earlier in the book that Habermas and Drane have argued for an increase in late modern interest in spiritual and religious matters. Habermas has spoken of the evident developments of a postsecular consciousness in the West. Drane has also argued that the church remains low on the priority list of spiritual seekers. Christians need to challenge their faith communities to be much more open to help people explore the spiritual realm. This will challenge the church to be much more experimental in the ways that it worships God and in exploring a fuller range of spiritual disciplines.

Furthermore, we have argued that the laity needs to be equipped and encouraged to develop a consciousness of themselves as missionaries in their own right. Ramachandra's voice, mentioned above, needs to be echoed copiously in our churches. We argued in chapter 9 that missional leaders need to be able to help equip the laity to see themselves as participants in the *missio Dei*. This suggests that they need to develop a consciousness of themselves as those who have been sent out by Christ to engage in all that he is doing.

We also noted Cray's call to civic discipleship in the public square. The language of Christians working in the public sphere for the common good has been highlighted. Civic disciples will need to seek to be both salt and light in the world that Christ has sent them to be his ambassadors within. The nature of salt is that it has a strong flavor indicative of its importance to bring richness and taste that is appreciated. Disciples after Christendom need to have their presence felt by intentional action to engage in the

20. Anglican Communion, "Marks of Mission," http://www.anglicancommunion. org/identity/marks-of-mission.aspx.

common good with those who seek to do the same although not in the name of Christ. Moreover, civic discipleship that is salt-like will also act as a preservative in a culture that can all too easily degenerate, as, for example, young adults seek to live a hedonistic, consumer-driven life. Christians have an important role to play as they live out the fruit of the Spirit, which can produce qualities like, love, joy, peace, patience, kindness, etc. Moreover, Christians need to be a strong influence in politics, education, medicine, social policy, justice, enforcement, research, science, etc.

Another challenge we need to consider is how existing mature older Christian leaders are preparing their successors for leadership. Are older leaders passing on the baton of good Christian missional leadership to younger adults? Are leaders helping to equip, train, prepare, and release younger leaders so that they can learn from their older mentors' wisdom, as they engage in leadership themselves?

One of our colleagues has more than once asked the question, "Do I believe in a bigger church or a better world?" A question we need to ask ourselves is, "What are we after in mission?" Is the goal to just get bigger churches, full of numerous members who the clergy can lead in acts of corporate worship, and minister to in a range of ways? Or is the aim to release lay people to become transformative influences in the world to make it a better place, which can be made good as people are influenced by the Spirit of Christ? It would seem to us that the goal of mission is not primarily church growth, but rather the shaping and transformation of people to become increasingly like Jesus Christ. If this is a goal of mission, then the works of Christ will naturally flow from the beliefs and actions of those who model their lives on his. Moreover, churches will grow and be planted as a natural result of people being discipled.

We also need to remain on the cutting edge of theological education, that is practical in its goals to train leaders, who can help to stimulate imagination and conversations among those they lead, so they can engage in all kinds of missional initiatives. This will require the courses and programs that we design to be innovative and provocative, so that participants are challenged and stimulated to do things in new, fresh ways, in order to address new challenges that keep on popping up in the late modern context of discontinuous change.

There is also another danger that we face, that the rest who are now coming to the West to bring the gospel back to it seek to invent a new Christendom. It could be argued that a kind of new Christendom is coming to birth in some African nations, and it would be all too easy for this to influence the missional aspirations of those who live here to seek to reinvent it here. Our view is that Christendom largely failed to effectively disciple people. We also would argue that the church is in a better place when it is on the liminal edge. The good thing about liminality is that it is causing believers to seek for what is coming next. The kingdom of God is not the coming of a new version of Christendom. Hence, we might ask, what is it?

Leaving the question open is part of the journey for what is to come next. It would seem that it is vital that we need to intentionally shape missional disciples who will seek to participate in the *missio Trinitatis* in their everyday lives. Jesus beckons, "Come follow me and I will make you fishers of men."

The kingdom of God is in the process of coming and the people of God are called to faithfully participate with the Spirit of Jesus in ushering it in. Disciples who hear God's voice are the ones that bring life into the church and its faith community. The church does not own discipleship as one of its many programs, but rather Christ equips those who follow him to call all of the people of God, leaders and laity alike, to be missional disciples in the contexts of their every day lives. In order for the local church to be a hermeneutic of the gospel, and a foretaste of the kingdom of God, it needs to become a sending agent of all of its members, into the world to participate with the Spirit in the *missio Trinitatis*. Jesus shaped disciples who would continue to discern his presence among them. He planted disciples on the firm foundation of this kind of relationship with himself. Missional discipleship focused on the *missio Dei* is the foundation of Christian community, life, and worship, rather than the church becoming an institution which seeks to do many things, of which one might be to shape some of its people to be mature disciples.

Bibliography

Abell, S. *Inside Out: How to Have Authentic Relationships with Everyone in Your Life.* London: Hodder and Stoughton, 2011.

Abramovich, Giselle. "15 Mind-Blowing Stats about Generation Z." CMO.com. June 12, 2015. http://www.cmo.com/features/articles/2015/6/11/15-mind-blowing-stats-about-generation-z.html#gs.rsSmEZQ.

Adams, K., et al., eds. *Dreams and Spirituality: A Handbook for Ministry, Spiritual Direction and Counselling.* London: Canterbury, 2015.

Akkerman, J., and M. Maddix. *Missional Discipleship: Partners in God's Redemptive Mission.* Kansas City: Nazarene, 2013.

Altemeyer, B. "The Decline of Organized Religion in Western Civilization." *International Journal for the Psychology of Religion* 14 (2004) 77–99.

Astin, H. *Body and Cell: Making the Transition to Cell Church; A First-Hand Account.* Crowborough, UK: Monarch, 1998.

Astley, J. *Ordinary Theology: Looking, Listening and Learning in Theology.* Farnham, UK: Ashgate, 2002.

Aune, D. E. "Understanding Jewish and Christian Apocalyptic." *Word and World* 25 (2005) 233–45.

Bacon, W. *Studies in Matthew.* New York: Holt, 1930.

Bailey, K. E. *Jesus through Middle Eastern Eyes: Cultural Studies in the Gospels.* London: SPCK, 2008.

Ballard, P., and J. Pritchard. *Practical Theology in Action: Christian Thinking in the Service of Church and Society.* 2nd ed. London: SPCK, 2006.

Balz, H., and G. Schneider. *Exegetical Dictionary of the New Testament.* Vol. 2. Grand Rapids: Eerdmans, 1991.

Bandura, A. *Social Foundation of Thought and Action.* Englewood Cliffs, NJ: Prentice Hall, 1986.

———. *Social Learning Theory.* Englewood Cliffs, NJ: Prentice Hall, 1977.

Barker, C. *Cultural Studies.* 3rd ed. London: Sage, 2008.

Baron, R. *Opposites Attract: How to Use the Secrets of Personality Type to Create a Love That Lasts.* New York: HarperCollins, 2011.

Barrett, C. K. *Acts: A Shorter Commentary.* London: T. & T. Clark, 2002.

————. *The Gospel according to St. John: An Introduction with Commentary and Notes on the Greek Text*. 2nd ed. Philadelphia: Westminster, 1978.

Barrett, L. Y. *Treasure in Clay Jars: Patterns in Missional Faithfulness*. Grand Rapids: Eerdmans, 2004.

Barth, M. *Ephesians 4–6*. Anchor Bible Commentary. New York: Doubleday, 1974.

Bartholomew, C. G., and M. W. Goheen. *The Drama of Scripture: Finding Our Place in the Biblical Story*. 2nd ed. London: SPCK, 2014.

Bauckham, R. *Jesus and the Eyewitnesses: The Gospels as Eyewitness Testimony*. Grand Rapids: Eerdmans, 2006.

Bauder, W., et al. "Disciple." In *New International Dictionary of New Testament Theology*, 1:491–92. Grand Rapids: Zondervan, 1986.

Bauman, Z. *Liquid Modernity*. Cambridge: Polity, 2000.

Belleville, L. "'Imitate Me, Just as I Imitate Christ': Discipleship in the Corinthian Correspondence." In *Patterns of Discipleship in the New Testament*, edited by R. N. Longenecker, 12–42. Grand Rapids: Eerdmans, 1996.

Bender, H. S. "Footwashing." In *The Mennonite Encyclopedia*, edited by H. S. Bender and C. H. Smith, 347–51. Scottdale, PA: Mennonite, 1955.

Ben-Gurion, D. "The Bible: Israel's Spiritual and National Roots." *Jewish Bible Quarterly* 24 (1996) 213–20.

Berger, P. L., ed. *Between Relativism and Fundamentalism*. Grand Rapids: Eerdmans, 2010.

————. *The Desecularization of the World: Resurgent Religion and World Politics*. Grand Rapids: Eerdmans, 1999.

Betz, H. D. *The Sermon on the Mount*. Edited by A. Y. Collins. Hermeneia. Minneapolis: Fortress, 1995.

Bevans, S. B. *Models of Contextual Theology*. Maryknoll: Orbis, 2012.

Bevans, S. B., and R. P. Schroeder. *Prophetic Dialogue: Reflections on Christian Mission Today*. Maryknoll: Orbis, 2011.

Biesecker-Mast, G. J. "Spiritual Knowledge, Carnal Obedience, and Anabaptist Discipleship." *Mennonite Quarterly Review* 71 (1977) 201–26.

Blevins, D. G., and M. A. Maddix. *Discovering Discipleship: Dynamics of Christian Education*. Kansas City: Nazarene, 2013.

Blomberg, C. L. *The Historical Reliability of John's Gospel*. Leicester, UK: InterVarsity, 2001.

Bock, D. L. *A Theology of Luke and Acts*. Edited by A. J. Köstenberger. Grand Rapids: Zondervan, 2012.

Bonhoeffer, D. *The Cost of Discipleship*. Translated by R. H. Fuller. London: SCM, 1937.

————. *Life Together*. Translated by J. W. Doberstein. London: SCM, 1954.

Bosch, D. J. *Transforming Mission*. Maryknoll: Orbis, 1991.

Bowers, L. B. *Invitational Ministry: Move Your Church from Membership to Discipleship*. St. Louis: Chalice, 2013.

Bradley, I. *The Celtic Way*. London: Darton, Longman & Todd, 1993.

Branson, M. L. "A Missional Church Process: Post-Intervention Research." *Journal of Religious Leadership* 13 (2014) 99–132.

Bricheno, P., and M. Thornton. "Role Model, Hero, or Champion? Children's Views concerning Role Model." *Educational Research* 47 (2007) 383–96.

Brisson, E. C. "Matthew 25:14–30." *Interpretation* 56 (2002) 307–10.

Brown, P. *The Rise of Western Christendom*. Rev. ed. Oxford: Wiley-Blackwell, 2013.

Brown, R. E. *The Gospel according to John I–XII*. Anchor Bible 29. Garden City: Doubleday, 1966.

———. *An Introduction to the New Testament*. London: Doubleday, 1997.

———. "Johannine Ecclesiology: The Community's Origins." *Interpretation* 31 (1977) 379–93.

Bruce, F. F. *1 & 2 Thessalonians*. Word Biblical Commentary. Waco: Word, 1982.

Brueggemann, W. *The Land: Place as Gift, Promise, and Challenge in Biblical Faith*. London: SPCK, 1978.

Bryman, A. *Social Research Methods*. 3rd ed. Oxford: Oxford University Press, 2008.

Byrne, B. *The Hospitality of God: A Reading of Luke's Gospel*. Collegeville: Liturgical, 2000.

Cary, J. W. *Free Churches and the Body of Christ: Authority, Unity, and Truthfulness*. Eugene, OR: Cascade, 2012.

Castelli, E. *Imitating Paul: A Discourse of Power*. Louisville: John Knox, 1991.

Castells, M. *Networks of Outrage and Hope: Social Movements in the Internet Age*. 2nd ed. Cambridge: Polity, 2015.

———. *The Power of Identity*. Vol. 2. Chichester, UK: Wiley-Blackwell, 2010.

Chadwick, H. *The Church in Ancient Society*. Oxford History of the Christian Church. Oxford: Clarendon, 2001.

Chan, Y. S. L. *The Ten Commandments and the Beatitudes: Biblical Studies and Ethics for Real Life*. Lanham, MD: Rowman & Littlefield, 2012.

Charlesworth, J. H., ed. *Jews and Christians: Exploring the Past, Present, and Future*. New York: Crossroad, 1990.

Chenoweth, B. "Identifying the Talents: Contextual Clues for the Interpretation of the Parable of the Talents (Matthew 25:14–30)." *Tyndale Bulletin* 56 (2005) 61–72.

Chilcote, P. W. *Making Disciples in a World Parish: Global Perspectives on Mission and Evangelism*. Eugene, OR: Pickwick, 2011.

Christal, J. D. "Disciples and Discipleship in the Gospel of Mark: A Study of Mark 10:23–31 in Relation to the Concept of Discipleship in the Markan Narrative." STL diss., Boston College School of Theology and Ministry, 2011.

Chung, M. "Paul's Understanding of Spiritual Formation: Christian Formation and Impartation." PhD diss., University of Nottingham, 2009.

Clarke, A. D. "'Be Imitators of Me': Paul's Model of Leadership." *Tyndale Bulletin* 49 (1998) 329–60.

Clements, R. E. "Relation of Children to the People of God in the Old Testament." *Baptist Quarterly* 21 (1966) 195–205.

Cohn, R. L. "Negotiating (with) the Natives: Ancestors and Identity in Genesis." *Harvard Theological Review* 96 (2003) 147–66.

Combi, C. *Generation Z: Their Voices, Their Lives*. London: Hutchinson, 2015.

Conzelmann, H. *The Theology of St. Luke*. London: SCM, 1982.

Cooke, R. *New Testament*. SCM Core Text London: SCM, 2009.

Cray, G. *Disciples & Citizens: A Vision for Distinctive Living*. Nottingham, UK: InterVarsity, 2007.

Croft, S. *Transforming Communities*. London: Darton, Longman & Todd, 2007.

Cullmann, O. *The Johannine Circle*. Translated by J. Bowden. Philadelphia: Westminster, 1976.

Currie, M. *About Time: Narrative, Fiction and the Philosophy of Time*. Edinburgh: Edinburgh University Press, 2007.

De Boer, W. *The Imitation of Paul: An Exegetical Study*. Kampen, Netherlands: Kok, 1962.

Deterding, P. E. "Eschatological and Eucharistic Motifs in Luke 12:35–40." *Concordia Journal* 5 (1979) 35–94.

Dodd, B. *Paul's Paradigmatic "I": Personal Example as Literary Strategy*. JSNT Supplement Series 177. Sheffield, UK: Sheffield Academic, 1999.

Dodd, C. H. *The Interpretation of the Fourth Gospel*. Cambridge: Cambridge University Press, 1998.

Dominy, B. B. "Spirit, Church, and Mission: Theological Implication of Pentecost." *Southwestern Journal of Theology* 35 (1993) 34–39.

Donahue, J. R. *The Theology and Setting of Discipleship in the Gospel of Mark*. Milwaukee: Marquette University Press, 1983.

Donaldson, T. L. "Guiding Readers—Making Disciples: Discipleship in Matthew's Narrative Strategy." In *Patterns of Discipleship in the New Testament*, edited by R. N. Longenecker, 30–49. Grand Rapids: Eerdmans, 1996.

Drane, J. *Do Christians Know How to Be Spiritual? The Rise of New Spirituality, and the Mission of the Church*. London: Darton, Longman & Todd, 2005.

———. *Evangelism for a New Age: Creating Churches for the Next Century*. London: Pickering, 1994.

———. *Introducing the New Testament*. 3rd ed. Oxford: Lion, 2010.

Dunn, J. D. G. *Baptism in the Holy Spirit*. Studies in Biblical Theology, 2nd series. London: SCM, 1974.

———. *Jesus' Call to Discipleship*. Cambridge: Cambridge University Press, 1992.

———. *The Parting of the Ways*. 2nd ed. London: SCM, 2006.

———. *Unity and Diversity in the New Testament: An Inquiry into the Character of Earliest Christianity*. 3rd ed. London: SCM, 2006.

Dunn, M. *The Emergence of Monasticism*. London: Blackwell, 2003.

Du Plessis, I. J. "Discipleship according to Luke." *Religion and Theology* 2 (1995) 58–71.

Dyas, D. "'Pilgrims Were They All?' Aspects of Pilgrimage and Their Influence on Old and Middle English Literature." PhD diss., University of Nottingham, 1998.

Edwards, R. *Discovering John*. London: SPCK, 2003.

Ehrensperger, K. *Paul and the Dynamics of Power*. Library of New Testament Studies 325. London: T. & T. Clark, 2007.

Engelsviken, T. "Missio Dei: The Understanding and Misunderstanding of a Theological Concept in European Churches and Missiology." *International Review of Mission* 92 (2003) 481–97.

Estep, W. R. *The Anabaptist Story: Introduction to Sixteenth-Century Anabaptism*. 3rd ed. Grand Rapids: Eerdmans, 1996.

Evans, C. A., and S. E. Porter, eds. *Dictionary of New Testament Background*. Downers Grove: InterVarsity, 2000.

Feddes, D. J. *Missional Apologetics: Cultural Diagnosis and Gospel Plausibility in C. S. Lewis and Lesslie Newbigin*. Monee, IL: Christian Leaders, 2012.

Fee, G. *The First Epistle to the Corinthians*. New International Commentary on the New Testament. Grand Rapids: Eerdmans 1986.

———. *Paul, the Spirit, and the People of God*. Grand Rapids: Baker Academic, 1990.

———. *Paul's Letter to the Philippians*. New International Commentary on the New Testament. Grand Rapids: Eerdmans, 1995.

Ferguson, E. *The Early Church at Work and Worship*. Vol. 2, *Catechesis, Baptism, Eschatology and Martyrdom*. Cambridge: Clarke, 2014.

Fitzmeyer, J. A. *The Gospel according to Luke (I–IX)*. New York: Doubleday, 1981.

———. *The Gospel according to Luke X–XXIV*. New York: Doubleday, 1985.

Flett, J. G. *The Witness of God: The Trinity, Missio Dei, Karl Barth, and the Nature of Christian Community*. Grand Rapids: Eerdmans, 2010.

Folkemer, L. D. "A Study of the Catechumenate." *Church History* 15 (1946) 286–307.

Foss, S. K. *Rhetorical Criticism: Exploration and Practice*. 3rd ed. Long Grove, IL: Waveland, 2004.

Foust, T. F., et al., eds. *A Scandalous Prophet: The Way of Mission after Newbigin*. Grand Rapids: Eerdmans, 2001.

Fowl, S. E. "Imitation of Paul / of Christ." In *Dictionary of Paul and His Letters*, edited by G. F. Hawthorne et al., 428–31. Leicester, UK: InterVarsity, 1993.

France, R. T. *Divine Government: God's Kingship in the Gospel of Mark*. Vancouver: Regent College Publishing, 1990.

———. *The Gospel according to Matthew*. New International Commentary on the New Testament. Grand Rapids: Eerdmans, 2007.

———. *The Gospel of Mark: A Commentary on the Greek Text*. Carlisle, UK: Paternoster, 2002.

———. *Matthew*. Tyndale New Testament Commentaries. Grand Rapids: Eerdmans, 1985.

———. *Matthew: Evangelist and Teacher*. Exeter, UK: Paternoster, 1989.

Frederick, H. R., et al. "The Effect of the Accountability Variables of Responsibility, Openness, and Answerability on Authentic Leadership." *Journal of Research on Christian Education* 25 (2016) 302–16.

Frend, W. H. C. *The Early Church: From the Beginning to 461*. Rev. ed. London: SCM, 1991.

Fulkerson, M. M., and S. Briggs, eds. *The Oxford Handbook of Feminist Theology*. Oxford: Oxford University Press, 2011.

Gardner, J. *Mend the Gap: Can the Church Reconnect the Generations?* Nottingham, UK: InterVarsity, 2008.

Gibbs, E., and R. K. Bolger. *Emerging Churches: Creating Christian Community in Postmodern Cultures*. London: SPCK, 2006.

Goheen, M. "Gospel, Culture, and Cultures: Lesslie Newbigin's Missionary Contribution Cultures and Christianity A.D. 2000." International Symposium of the Association for Reformational Philosophy, Hoeven, Netherlands, August 21–25, 2000.

Gompertz, W. *Think like an Artist*. London: Penguin, 2015.

Gorman, M. J. *Becoming the Gospel: Paul, Participation and Mission*. Grand Rapids: Eerdmans, 2015.

———. *Cruciformity: Paul's Narrative Spirituality of the Cross*. Grand Rapids: Eerdmans, 2001.

———. "The Search to Belong: Rethinking Intimacy, Community, and Small Groups." *Christian Education Journal* 2 (2005) 479–83.

Graber-Miller, K. "Mennonite Footwashing: Identity Reflections and Altered Meanings." *Worship* 66 (1992) 148–70.

Graham, E. L., et al. *Theological Reflections: Methods*. Canterbury, UK: SCM, 2005.

Gray, D. P. "Incarnation: God's Giving and Man's Receiving." *Horizons* 1 (1974) 1–13.

Green, J. B. "Good News to Whom? Jesus and the 'Poor' in the Gospel of Luke." In *Jesus of Nazareth Lord and Christ: Essays on the Historical Jesus and New Testament Christology*, edited by J. B. Green et al., 59–74. Grand Rapids: Eerdmans, 1994.

Gregersen, N. H., ed. *Incarnation: On the Scope and Depth of Christology*. Minneapolis: Fortress, 2015.

Grenz, S. J. *A Primer on Postmodernism*. Grand Rapids: Eerdmans, 1996.

Grindheim, S. "Ignorance Is Bliss: Attitudinal Aspects of the Judgment according to Works in Matthew 25:31–46." *Novum Testamentum* 50 (2008) 313–31.

Guelich, R. *The Sermon on the Mount: A Foundation for Understanding*. Dallas: Word, 1982.

Guldalian, S. "The Millennials: Reflections on Reaching a Lost Generation for Christ." *Missio Apostolica* 21 (2013) 41–47.

Guthrie, D. *New Testament Introduction*. Downers Grove: InterVarsity, 1970.

Haapiainen, T.-M. "The Development and Outlines of Missio Dei in G. F. Vicedom's Theology." *Svensk Missionstidskrift* 100 (2012) 45–64.

Habermas J., ed. *Europe: The Faltering Project*. Cambridge: Polity, 2009.

———. "Notes on a Post-Secular Society." Originally given as a lecture, March 15, 2007, Nexus Institute of the University of Tilberg, Netherlands; appeared in *Blätter für deutsche und internationale Politik*, April 2008. Available at http://www.signandsight.com/features/1714.html.

———. "Secularism's Crisis of Faith: Notes on Post-Secular Society." *New Perspectives Quarterly* 25 (2008) 16–29.

Hagner, D. A. *Matthew 1–13*. Word Biblical Commentary. Dallas: Word, 1993.

Hall, B. T. *The Hidden Dimension*. London: Anchor, 1966.

Happé, P. *English Mystery Plays: An Introduction*. London: Penguin, 1975.

Hardinge, L. *The Celtic Church in Britain*. London: SPCK, 1972.

Hardy, A. *Pictures of God: Shaping Missional Church Life*. Watford, UK: Instant Apostle, 2015.

Hardy, A., et al. *Power and the Powers: The Use and Abuse of Power in Its Missional Context*. Eugene, OR: Cascade, 2015.

Hardy, A., and D. Yarnell. *Forming Multicultural Partnerships: Church Planting in a Divided Society*. Watford, UK: Instant Apostle, 2015.

Harrison, J. R. "The Imitation of the 'Great Man' in Antiquity: Paul's Inversion of a Cultural Icon." In *Christian Origins and Greco-Roman Culture*, edited by S. E. Porter and A. W. Pitts, 213–54. Leiden: Brill, 2013.

Hartin, P. J. *Exploring the Spirituality of the Gospels*. Collegeville: Liturgical, 2010.

Harvey, L. *A Brief Theology of Sport*. London: SCM, 2014.

Hastings, R. *Missional God, Missional Church: Hope for Re-Evangelizing the West*. Downers Grove: InterVarsity, 2012.

Hawthorne, G. F. "The Imitation of Christ: Discipleship in Philippians." In *Patterns of Discipleship in the New Testament*, edited by R. N. Longenecker, 143–62. Grand Rapids: Eerdmans, 1996.

Hays, C. M. "Rich and Poor." In *Dictionary of Jesus and the Gospels*, edited by J. B. Green et al., 800–810. 2nd ed. Nottingham, UK: IVP Academic, 2013.

Hecht, R. D., and V. F. Biondo III, eds. *Religion and Culture: Contemporary Practices and Perspectives*. Minneapolis: Fortress, 2008.

Henderson, D. M. *A Model for Making Disciples: John Wesley's Class Meetings*. Nappanee, IN: Asbury, 1997.

Henderson, S. W. *Christology and Discipleship in the Gospel of Mark.* Society for New Testament Studies Monograph Series 135. Cambridge: Cambridge University Press, 2006.

Hengel, M. *The Charismatic Leader and His Followers.* Translated by J. C. G. Greig. London: T. & T. Clark, 1981.

———. *Judaism and Hellenism.* Vol. 1. Eugene, OR: Wipf and Stock, 2013.

Heuertz, C. L., and C. D. Pohl. Christine. *Friendship at the Margins: Discovering Mutuality in Service and Mission.* Downers Grove: InterVarsity, 2010.

Hiebert, P. G. *The Gospel in Human Contexts: Anthropological Explorations for Contemporary Missions.* Grand Rapids: Baker Academic, 2009.

Hill, C. *The English Bible and the Seventeenth-Century Revolution.* London: Penguin, 1994.

Hippolytus. *The Apostolic Tradition of Hippolytus.* Translated with introduction and notes by B. S. Easton. Cambridge: Cambridge University Press, 1936.

Hirsch, A. *The Forgotten Ways.* Grand Rapids: Brazos, 2006.

Hirsch, A., and D. Hirsch. *Untamed: Reactivating a Missional Form of Discipleship.* Grand Rapids: Baker, 2010.

Holistic Mission Occasional Paper no. 33. Produced by the Issue Group on this topic at the 2004 Forum for World Evangelization, hosted by the Lausanne Committee for World Evangelization, Pattaya, Thailand, September 29 to October 5, 2004.

Hollinghurst, S. *Mission-Shaped Evangelism.* Norwich, UK: Canterbury, 2010.

Holmes, P. R. *Church as a Safe Place.* Milton Keynes, UK: Authentic, 2008.

Holmes, P. R., and S. B. Williams. *Becoming More Like Christ: A Contemporary Biblical Journey.* London: Paternoster, 2007.

Holpuch, A. "Ongoing Child Sex Abuse in the Catholic Church Casts Shadows on Pope's US Visit." *Guardian,* September 10, 2015. https://www.theguardian.com/us-news/2015/sep/10/pope-francis-us-visit-catholic-sex-abuse.

Hooker, M. D. *The Gospel according to St Mark.* Black's New Testament Commentaries. London: Continuum, 2006.

———. "A Partner in the Gospel: Paul's Understanding of Ministry." In *Theology and Ethics in Paul and His Interpreters,* edited by E. H. Lovering Jr. and J. Sumney, 83–100. Nashville: Abingdon, 1996.

Hooker, M. D., and F. Young. *Holiness and Mission: Learning from the Early Church about Mission in the City.* London: SCM, 2010.

Horman, R. *The Art of the Sublime: Principles of Christian Art and Architecture.* London: Routledge, 2006.

Horsley, R. A. *1 Corinthians.* Abingdon New Testament Commentaries. Nashville: Abingdon, 1998.

Hunsberger, G. R. *Bearing the Witness of the Spirit: Lesslie Newbigin's Theology of Cultural Plurality.* Grand Rapids: Eerdmans, 1998.

Hunsicker, D. "John Wesley: Father of Today's Small Group Concept?" *Wesleyan Theological Journal* 31 (1986) 192–211.

Hunter, J. D. "What Is Modernity? Historical Roots and Contemporary Features." In *Faith and Modernity,* edited by P. Sampson et al., 21–27. Oxford: Regnum, 1994.

Hurtado, L. "Following Jesus in the Gospel of Mark—and Beyond." In *Patterns of Discipleship in the New Testament,* edited by R. N. Longenecker, 17–25. Grand Rapids: Eerdmans, 1996.

———. *Lord Jesus Christ: Devotion to Jesus in Earliest Christianity*. Grand Rapids: Eerdmans, 2005.

Inge, J. *A Christian Theology of Place*. Explorations in Practical, Pastoral and Empirical Theology. London: Routledge, 2003.

Ireland, Mark, and Mike Booker. *Making New Disciples: Exploring the Paradoxes of Evangelism*. London: SPCK, 2015.

Jenkins, Philip. *The Next Christendom: The Coming of Global Christianity*. 3rd ed. Oxford: Oxford University Press, 2011.

Jersak, B. *Can You Hear Me? Tuning In to the God Who Speaks*. Oxford: Monarch, 2008.

Johnson, D. W. *Reaching Out: Interpersonal Effectiveness and Self-Actualization*. 3rd ed. New Jersey: Prentice Hall, 1986.

Johnson, D. W., and F. P. Johnson. *Joining Together: Group Theory and Group Skills*. New Jersey: Prentice Hall, 1982.

Jones, C., et al. *The Study of Liturgy*. London: SPCK, 1978.

Jones, L. G., and C. Musekura. *Forgiving as We've Been Forgiven: Community Practices for Making Peace*. Downers Grove: InterVarsity, 2010.

Karkainen, V.-M. *The Trinity: Global Perspectives*. Louisville: Westminster John Knox, 2007.

———. *Trinity and Religious Pluralism: The Doctrine of the Trinity in Christian Theology of Religions*. London: Routledge, 2004.

Keating, B. "The Idiom of 'Prolepsis.'" *Kingdom Ready* (blog; no longer active). November 24, 2013. http://lhim.org/blog/2013/11/24/the-idiom-of-prolepsis.

Kerr, D. A. "'Come Holy Spirit—Renew the Whole Creation': The Canberra Assembly and Issues of Mission." *International Bulletin of Missionary Research* 15 (1991) 98–104.

Kerr, D. A., and K. R. Ross, eds. *Edinburgh 2010: Mission Then and Now*. Conference papers. http://www.ocms.ac.uk/regnum/downloads/Mission%20Then%20and%20Now-final-WM.pdf.

Kim, K. *Joining in with the Spirit: Connecting World Church and Local Mission*. London: Epworth, 2009.

Kim, Y. S. *A Theological Introduction to Paul's Letters: Exploring a Threefold Theology of Paul*. Eugene, OR: Cascade, 2011.

Kingsbury, J. D. *Conflict in Mark: Jesus, Authority, Disciples*. Minneapolis: Fortress, 1989.

Kittel, G., ed. *Theological Dictionary of the New Testament*. Translated by G. W. Bromiley. Grand Rapids: Eerdmans, 1983.

Koester, H. *Introduction to the New Testament: History and Literature of Early Christianity*. 2nd ed. Vol. 2. New York: de Gruyter, 2000.

Koulopoulos, T., and D. Keldsen. *The Gen Z Effect*. Brookline, MA: Bibliomotion.inc., 2014.

Kreider, A. "Baptism, Catechism, and the Eclipse of Jesus' Teaching in Early Christianity." *Tyndale Bulletin* 47 (1996) 315–48.

———, ed. *The Origins of Christendom in the West*. Edinburgh: T. & T. Clark, 2001

———. *The Patient Ferment of the Early Church*. Grand Rapids: Baker, 2016.

———. "*Ressourcement* and Mission." *Anglican Theological Review* 96 (2014) 239–61.

———. *Worship and Evangelism in Pre-Christendom*. Joint Liturgical Studies 32. Cambridge: Grove, 1995.

Kreider, A., and E. Kreider. *Worship and Mission after Christendom*. Milton Keynes, UK: Paternoster, 2009.

Kurian, G. T., and M. A. Lamport, eds. *Encyclopedia of Christian Education*. Vol. 3. London: Rowman & Littlefield, 2015.

Ladd, G. E. *A Theology of the New Testament*. Rev. ed. Grand Rapids: Eerdmans, 1993.

Laing, M. T. B., and P. Weston, eds. *Theology in Missionary Perspective: Lesslie Newbigin's Legacy*. Eugene, OR: Pickwick, 2012.

Lane, B. L. "Landscape and Spirituality: A Tension between Place and Placelessness in Christian Thought." *The Way Supplement* 73 (1992) 4–13.

Lane, W. L. *The New International Commentary on the New Testament: The Gospel of Mark*. Grand Rapids: Eerdmans, 1974.

Larkin, W. J. "Approaches to and Images of Biblical Authority for the Postmodern Mind." *Bulletin for Biblical Research* 8 (1998) 129–38.

Ledwith, M. *Community Development: A Critical Approach*. 2nd ed. Bristol: Policy, 2005.

Lewis, R. *Mentoring Matters: Building Strong Christian Leaders, Avoiding Burnout, Reaching the Finishing Line*. Grand Rapids: Lion Hudson, 2009.

Lincoln, A. T. *Ephesians*. Word Biblical Commentary. Waco: Word, 1990.

Lishman, J., ed. *Handbook for Practice Learning in Social Work and Social Care: Knowledge and Theory*. 2nd ed. London: Kingsley, 2007.

Longenecker, R. N. *Biblical Exegesis in the Apostolic Period*. Grand Rapids: Eerdmans, 1999.

———, ed. *Patterns of Discipleship in the New Testament*. Grand Rapids: Eerdmans, 1996.

———. *Studies in Hermeneutics, Christology and Discipleship*. Sheffield, UK: Sheffield Phoenix, 2004.

———. "Taking Up the Cross Daily: Luke-Acts." In *Patterns of Discipleship in the New Testament*, 50–76. Grand Rapids: Eerdmans, 1996.

Luz, U. *Matthew 1–7: A Commentary*. Edited by H. Koester. Translated by J. E. Crouch. Rev. ed. Hermeneia. Minneapolis: Fortress, 2007.

MacCulloch, D. *A History of Christianity*. London: Penguin, 2009.

MacGinty, G. "The Influence of the Desert Fathers on Early Irish Monasticism." *Monastic Studies* 14 (1983) 85–91.

Maddix, M. A., and J. R. Akkerman. *Missional Discipleship: Partners in God's Redemptive Mission*. Kansas City: Beacon Hill, 2013.

Maddow, R. L. "'Visit the Poor': Wesley's Precedent for Wholistic Mission." *Transformation* 18 (2001) 37–50.

Marriner, K. T. *Following the Lamb: The Theme of Discipleship in the Book of Revelation*. Eugene, OR: Wipf & Stock, 2016.

Marshall, I. H. *The Gospel of Luke—A Commentary on the Greek Text*. New International Greek Testament Commentary. Grand Rapids: Eerdmans, 1978.

Massimo, R. "Longing for a Postsecular Condition: Italy and the Postsecular." From the workshop Politics, Culture and Religion in the Postsecular Society, at the Institute for East-Central Europe and the Balkans (University of Bologna), in Faenza, Italy, May 12–13, 2011.

Matson, D. L. "Divine Forgiveness in Paul? Justification by Faith and the Logic of Pauline Soteriology." *Stone-Campbell Journal* 19 (2016) 59–83.

Mattili, A. J. "Johannine Communities Behind the Fourth Gospel: George Richter's Analysis." *Theological Studies* 38 (1977) 294–315.

Mazur, J. E. *Learning and Behavior.* 7th ed. Harlow: Pearson, 2014.

McClendon, J. W. *Biography as Theology: How Life Stories Can Remake Today's Theology.* Nashville: Abingdon, 1974.

McGrath, A. E. *Christian History: An Introduction.* Oxford: Wiley-Blackwell, 2013.

———. *Historical Theology: An Introduction of the History of Christian Thought.* 2nd ed. Chichester, UK: Wiley-Blackwell, 2013.

———. *The Twilight of Atheism: The Rise and Fall of Disbelief in the Modern World.* London: Rider, 2004.

McKnight, S. *Kingdom Conspiracy: Returning to the Radical Mission of the Local Church.* Grand Rapids: Brazos, 2014.

McReynolds, K. "The Gospel of Luke: A Framework for a Theology of Disability." *Christian Education Journal* 13 (2016) 169–78.

Mellow, H., and T. Yates, eds. *Mission and Spirituality: Creative Ways of Being Church.* Sheffield ,UK: Cliff College Publishing, 2002.

Mendieta, E. "A Postsecular World Society? On the Philosophical Significance of Postsecular Consciousness and the Multicultural World Society." Interview with Jurgen Habermas. Translated by Matthias Fritsch. The Immanent Frame, Social Science Research Council, February 3, 2010. Available at http://blogs.ssrc.org/tif/2010/02/03/a-postsecular-world-society.

Mobsby, I. *God Unknown: The Trinity in Contemporary Spirituality and Mission.* Norwich, UK: Canterbury, 2012.

Mohrlang, R. *Matthew and Paul: A Comparison of Ethical Perspectives.* Society for New Testaments Studies Monograph Series 48. Cambridge: Cambridge University Press, 1982.

Moloney, F. J. *Mark: Storyteller, Interpreter, Evangelist.* Peabody: Hendrickson, 2004.

Moltmann, J. *The Crucified God.* London: SCM, 2001.

Moltmann, J., et al. *A Passion for God's Reign.* Edited by M. Volf. Grand Rapids: Eerdmans, 1998.

Morris, L. *The Gospel according to John.* New International Commentary on the New Testament. Grand Rapids: Eerdmans, 1977.

Moule, C. F. D. *The Birth of the New Testament.* 3rd ed. London: Black, 1981.

Moynagh, M. *Church for Every Context: An Introduction to Theology and Practice.* With P. Harrold. London: SCM, 2012.

Murray, S. *The Church After Christendom.* Milton Keynes, UK: Paternoster, 2004.

———. *The Naked Anabaptist.* Milton Keynes, UK: Paternoster, 2011.

———. *Post-Christendom: Church and Mission in a Strange New World.* Milton Keynes: Paternoster, 2004.

Murray Williaims, S., and S. Murray Williams. *The Multi-voiced Church.* Milton Keynes: Paternoster, 2012.

Murray-Beasley, G. R. *Jesus and the Kingdom of God.* Grand Rapids: Eerdmans, 1986.

Nepper-Christensen. "μαθητης, ου, ο, μαθητευω." In *Exegetical Dictionary of the New Testament,* edited by H. R. Balz and G. Schneider, 2:373–74. Grand Rapids: Eerdmans, 1991.

Newbigin, L. *Foolishness to the Greeks.* London: SPCK, 1986.

———. *The Gospel and Pluralist Society.* London: SPCK, 1989.

―――. *The Light Has Come: An Exposition of the Fourth Gospel.* Grand Rapids: Eerdmans, 1982.

―――. *The Open Secret: An Introduction to the Theology of Mission.* London: SPCK, 1995.

―――. *Proper Confidence: Faith, Doubt and Certainty in Christian Discipleship.* London: SPCK, 1995.

―――. "Sign of the Kingdom." *Scottish Journal of Theology* 35 (1982) 462–63.

Niemandt, C. J. P. "Five Years of Missional Church: Reflections on Missional Ecclesiology." *Missionalia* 38 (2010) 397–412.

―――. "Trends in Missional Ecclesiology." *HTS Teologiese Studies / Theological Studies* 68 (2012) 1–9.

North, J. L. "Ambassadors for Christ: An Exploration of Ambassadorial Language in the New Testament." *Journal of Theological Studies* 49 (1998) 278–81.

Nouwen, H. *The Wounded Healer: Ministry in Contemporary Society.* London: Darton, Longman & Todd, 2013.

Nydam, R. J. "The Relational Theology of Generation Y." *Calvin Theological Journal* 41 (2006) 321–30.

Oakes, P. *Philippians: From People to Letter.* Society for New Testament Studies Monograph Series 110. Cambridge: Cambridge University Press, 2001.

O'Brien, P. T. *The Letters to the Ephesians.* Pillar New Testament Commentary. Grand Rapids: Eerdmans, 1999.

O'Loughlin, T. *Washing Feet: Imitating the Example of Jesus in the Liturgy Today.* Collegeville: Liturgical, 2015.

Palacios, J. M. *The Catholic Social Imagination: Activism and the Just Society in Mexico and the United States.* Chicago: University of Chicago Press, 2007.

Palfrey, J., and U. Gasser. *Understanding the First Generation of Digital Natives.* New York: Basic, 2010.

Parler, B. L. *Things Hold Together: John Howard Yoder's Trinitarian Theology of Culture.* Harrisonburg, VA: Herald, 2012.

Peers, L. P. "The Problem Trap: A Narrative Therapy Approach to Escaping Our Limiting Stories." *Congregations* 34 (2008) 19–22.

Peterson, E. *A Long Obedience in the Same Direction: Discipleship in an Instant Society.* Downers Grove: InterVarsity, 1980.

Phillips, T. E. Review of *The Followers of Jesus as the 'Servant': Luke's Model from Isaiah for the Disciples in Luke-Acts,* by Holly Beers. *Religious Studies Review* 41 (2015) 196.

Pilavachi, M., and A. Croft. *Everyday Supernatural: Living a Spirit-Led Life without Being Weird.* Colorado Springs: Cook, 2016.

Pilgrim, Walter E. *Good News to the Poor: Wealth and Poverty in Luke-Acts.* Minneapolis: Augsburg, 1981.

Pippert, W. G. "Faith Should Rewrite Your Job Description: Zaccheus's Encounter with Jesus Caused Him to Do His Job Differently." *Christianity Today,* September 1982.

Rainie, L., and B. Wellman. *Networked: The New Social Operating System.* Cambridge: MIT Press, 2012.

Raitt, J. "St. Thomas Aquinas on Free Will and Predestination." *Duke Divinity School Review* 43 (1978)188–95.

Ramachandra, V. *A Brief Reflection on Edinburgh* 2010. http://www.edinburgh2010. org/en/resources/papersdocumentsc3da.pdf?no_cache=1&cid=34626&did=223 98&sechash=a5f01cda.

Renfro, A. "Generation Z: The Biggest Cheaters since Homer." *Getting Smart* website, April 12, 2012. http://www.gettingsmart.com/2012/04/generation-z-the-biggest-cheaters-since-homer.

———. "Z Future Is Here!" *Getting Smart* website, November 10, 2011. http:// gettingsmart.com/2011/11/z-future-is-here.

Robinson, J. A. T. *But That I Can't Believe*. London: Collins, 1967.

———. *Honest to God*. London: SCM, 1963.

Robinson, M. *Rediscovering the Celts*. London: HarperCollins, 2000.

———. *Winning Hearts, Changing Minds*. Oxford: Monarch, 2001.

Rogers, A. P. *Congregational Hermeneutics: How Do We Read?* Farnham: Ashgate, 2015.

Rogers, G. *Holistic Ministry and Cross-Cultural Mission in Luke-Acts*. N.p.: Ministry and Mission Resources, 2003.

Rogerson, J. W., and J. M. Lieu, eds. *The Oxford Handbook of Biblical Studies*. Oxford: Oxford University Press, 2008.

Roldan-Roman, I. "Reclaiming the Reign of God for the Poor: Matthew 25:31–46." *Review & Expositor* 109 (2012) 465–71.

Ross, C., and S. B. Bevans. *Mission on the Road to Emmaus: Constants, Context, and Prophetic Dialogue*. Maryknoll: Orbis, 2015.

Ross, S. R. "Albert Bandura." In *The Praeger Handbook of Education and Psychology*, edited by J. L. Kincheloe and R. A. Horn Jr., 1:49–56. London: Praeger, 2007.

Rowe, C. K. *Early Narrative Christology: The Lord in the Gospel of Luke*. Berlin: de Gruyter, 2006.

Roxburgh, A. J. *Missional: Joining God in the Neighborhood*. Grand Rapids: Baker, 2011.

Ryle, J. C. *John*. Classic New Testament Commentary. London: Collins, 1990.

Sagovsky, N., and P. McGrail, ed. *Together for the Common Good: Towards a National Conversation*. Norwich, UK: SCM, 2015.

Saleska, J. "Trinity Sunday: Matthew 28:16–20." *Concordia Theological Quarterly* 47 (1983) 331–32.

Sampson, P., et al. *Faith and Modernity*. Oxford: Regnum, 1994.

Samra, J. G. "A Biblical View of Discipleship." *Bibliotheca Sacra* 160 (2003) 219–34.

Savage, S., et al. *Making Sense of Generation Y: The World View of 15-to 25-Year-Olds*. London: Church, 2011.

Savitt, K. "Gen Z: The Age of the Curator." Youtube video, 10:32. Posted November 18, 2010. https://www.youtube.com/watch?v=ZfqF1r7LBCA&feature=youtu.be.

Schlag, K. H. "Imitation and Social Learning." https://homepage.univie.ac.at/karl. schlag/research/imitation/imitation_sociallearning.pdf.

Schleiermacher, F. *On Religion: Speeches to Its Cultured Despisers*. Translated with introduction by J. Oman. London, 1893.

Scholer, D. M., ed. *Social Distinctives of the Christians in the First Century: Pivotal Essays by E. A. Judge*. Grand Rapids: Baker Academic, 2008.

Schweitzer, D. "The Passionate God." *Touchstone* 21 (2003) 34–45.

Schweitzer, F. *The Postmodern Life Cycle: Challenges for Church and Theology*. St. Louis: Chalice, 2004.

Seccombe, D. P. *Possessions and the Poor in Luke-Acts*. Linz: Studien zum Neuen Testamentund Seiner Umwelt, 1982.

Seemiller, C., and M. Grace. *Generation Z Goes to College*. San Francisco: Jossey-Bass, 2016.

Sharp, C., et al. *Playing for Success: An Evaluation of Its Long Term Impact*. Research report. Nottingham, UK: Department for Education and Skills, 2007.

Sheldon, C. M. *In His Steps*. 1897. Available online at: https://www.ccel.org/ccel/sheldon/ihsteps.html.

Sheldrake, P. *Spaces for the Sacred*. London: SCM, 2001.

Sim, S., ed. *The Routledge Companion to Postmodernism*. London: Routledge, 2001.

Simpkins, A. "Generation Y and the Gospel: A Research Study into Young People and the Christian Faith." MA diss., Springdale College (Birmingham), 2011.

Simpson, R. *Soul Friendship: Celtic Insights into Spiritual Mentoring*. London: Hodder and Stoughton, 1999.

Sittser, G. L. "The Catechumenate and the Rise of Christianity." *Journal of Spiritual Formation & Soul Care* 6 (2013) 179–203.

Smith, D. M. *New Testament Theology: The Theology of the Gospel of John*. Cambridge: Cambridge University Press, 2002.

Sneed, M. "Israelite Concern for the Alien, Orphan, and Widow: Altruism or Ideology?" *Zeitschrift Für Die Alttestamentliche Wissenschaft* 111 (1999) 498–507.

Snyder, H. A. *The Radical Wesley & Patterns for Church Renewal*. Eugene, OR: Wipf & Stock, 1996.

Sobrino, J. *Christology at the Crossroads: A Latin American Approach*. Translated by J. Drury. New ed. London: SCM, 2012.

Spencer, F. S. *Journeying through Acts: A Literary-Cultural Reading*. Peabody: Hendrickson, 2004.

Spurgeon, C. H. "Paid in Full: The Sacrifice of Calvary Was Not a Part Payment; It Was a Complete and Perfect Payment." *Christianity Today* 42 (1998) 1–6.

Standish, N. G. "Whatever Happened to Humility? Rediscovering a Misunderstood Leadership Strength." *Congregations* 33 (2007) 23–26.

Stark, R. *The Rise of Christianity*. Princeton: Princeton University Press, 1996.

Stoddard, C., and N. Cuthbert. *Church on the Edge: Principles and Real Life Stories of 21st Century Mission*. Milton Keynes, UK: Authentic, 2006.

Stone, B. "The Children of Cyberspace: Old Fogies by Their 20s." *New York Times*, January 9, 2010. http://www.nytimes.com/2010/01/10/weekinreview/10stone.html?_r=1.

Stott, J. R. W. *Ephesians: God's New Society*. Bible Speaks Today. Leicester, UK: InterVarsity, 1979.

———. *The Radical Disciple*. Nottingham, UK: InterVarsity, 2010.

Stuvland, A. "The Emerging Church and Global Civil Society: Postmodern Christianity as a Source for Global Values." *Journal of Church and State* 52 (2010) 203–31.

Sweetland, D. M. "Following Jesus: Discipleship in Luke-Acts." In *New Views on Lukeand Acts*, edited by E. Richard, 15–66. Collegeville: Liturgical, 1990.

Talbert, C. H. *Reading the Sermon on the Mount: Character Formation and Decision Making in Matthew 5–7*. Columbia: University of South Carolina Press, 2004.

Thielman, F. *Ephesians*. Baker Exegetical Commentary on the New Testament. Grand Rapids: Baker, 2010.

Thomas, à Kempis. *The Imitation of Christ*. 1418–1427. English translation of the original Latin text. Up-to-date online version available at: https://www.ccel.org/ccel/kempis/imitation.html.

Thomas, G. *How to Do Your Research Project: A Guide for Students in Education and Applied Social Sciences*. 2nd ed. London: Sage, 2013.

Thomas, J. C. "Footwashing in John 13 and the Johannine Community." PhD diss., University of Sheffield, 1990.

Thompson, J., et al. *Theological Reflection*. London: SCM, 2008.

Thomsen, M. W. "Expanding the Scope of God's Grace: Christian Perspectives and Values for Interfaith Relations." *Currents in Theology and Mission* 40 (2013) 85–94.

Torrance, J. B. *Worship, Community and the Triune God of Grace*. Carlisle, UK: Paternoster, 1996.

Tupper, E. F. "The Self-Limitation of God." *Perspectives in Religious Studies* 34 (2007) 161–91.

Turner, M. *The Holy Spirit and Spiritual Gifts*. Peabody: Hendrickson, 1996.

———. "The Work of the Holy Spirit in Luke-Acts." *Word & World* 23 (2003) 146–53.

Vaage, L. E. "An Other Home: Discipleship in Mark as Domestic Asceticism." *Catholic Biblical Quarterly* 71 (2009) 741–61.

Vallée, Gérard. *The Shaping of Christianity*. New York: Paulist, 1999.

Van Gelder, C. *The Missional Church in Context: Helping Congregations Develop Contextual Ministry*. Grand Rapids: Eerdmans, 2007.

Van Gelder, C., and D. J. Zscheile. *The Missional Church in Perspective: Mapping Trends and Shaping the Conversation*. Grand Rapids: Baker Academic, 2011.

Via, D. O., Jr. "Ethical Responsibility and Human Wholeness in Matthew 25:31–46." *Harvard Theological Review* 80 (1987) 79–100.

Wagner, T. "7 Skills Students Need for Their Futute." Youtube video, 29:11. Posted October 1, 2009. https://www.youtube.com/watch?v=NS2PqTTxFFc&feature=you tu.be, 11:49, 04/08/16.

Walls, J. L., ed. *The Oxford Handbook of Eschatology*. Oxford: Oxford University Press, 2010.

Walvoord, J. F. "Christ's Olivet Discourse on the End of the Age: The Parable of the Ten Virgins." *Bibliotheca Sacra* 129 (1972) 99–105.

Wanamaker, C. A. *The Epistle to the Thessalonians: A Commentary on the Greek Text*. Carlisle, UK: Paternoster, 1990.

Ward, G. *The Politics of Discipleship: Becoming Postmaterial Citizens*. London: SCM, 2009.

Ward, P. *Participation and Mediation: A Practical Theology for the Liquid Church*. Canterbury, UK: SCM, 2008.

Watson, S., and A. Moran, eds. *Trust, Risk and Uncertainty*. Basingstoke, UK: Palgrave Macmillan, 2005.

Watters, E. *Urban Tribes: Are Friends the New Family?* London: Bloomsbury, 2004.

Wenger, E. *Communities of Practice: Learning, Meaning, and Identity*. Cambridge: Cambridge University Press, 2016.

Werner, D. "John Wesley's Question: 'How Is Your Doing?'" *Asbury Journal* 65 (2010) 68–93.

Whitmarsh, T. *Greek Literature and the Roman Empire: The Politics of Imitation*. Oxford: Oxford University Press, 2001.

Wiebe, B. "Messianic Ethics: Response to the Kingdom of God." *Interpretation* 45 (1991) 29–42.

Wild, R. A. "'Be Imitators of God': Discipleship in the Letter to the Ephesians." In *Discipleship in the New Testament*, edited by F. F. Segovia, 127–43. Philadelphia: Fortress, 1985.

Wilkins, M. J. *The Concept of Disciple in Matthew's Gospel as Reflected in the Term Μαθητς.* Supplements to Novum Testamentum 59. Leiden: Brill, 1988.

———. *Discipleship in the Ancient World and Matthew's Gospel.* 2nd ed. Eugene, OR: Wipf & Stock, 1995.

Willard, D. *The Great Omission: Reclaiming Jesus's Essential Teachings on Discipleship.* Oxford: Monarch, 2006.

Williams, J. F. "Discipleship and Minor Characters in Mark's Gospel." *Bibliotheca Sacra* 53 (1996) 333–43.

Winch, G. *Emotional First Aid: Practical Strategies for Treating Failure, Rejection, Guilt, and Other Everyday Psychological Injuries.* New York: Hudson, 2013.

Wink, W. *The Powers That Be: Theology for a New Millennium.* New York: Galilee Doubleday, 1998.

Witherington, B., III. *1 and 2 Thessalonians: A Social-Rhetorical Commentary.* Grand Rapids: Eerdmans, 2006.

———. *Jesus the Seer: The Progress of Prophecy.* Minneapolis: Fortress, 2014.

———. *Matthew.* Macon: Smyth & Helwys, 2006.

Worthington, E. L. *A Just Forgiveness: Responsible Healing without Excusing Injustice.* Downers Grove: InterVarsity, 2009.

Wright, C. J. H. *The Mission of God's People: A Biblical Theology of the Church's Mission.* Grand Rapids: Zondervan, 2010.

Wright, N. T. *How God Became King.* London: SPCK, 2012.

———. *The New Testament and the People of God.* London: SPCK, 1993.

———. *The Resurrection of the Son of God.* London: SPCK, 2003.

Yoder, J. H. *The Politics of Jesus.* 2nd ed. Grand Rapids: Eerdmans, 1994.

Zempel, H. *Community Is Messy: The Perils and Promise of Small Group Ministry.* Downers Grove: InterVarsity, 2012.

Zizioulas, J. D. *The Eucharistic Communion and the World.* London: T. & T. Clark, 2011.